From Mukogodo to
Maasai: Ethnicity and
Cultural Change in Kenya

Westview Case Studies in Anthropology

Series Editor

EDWARD F. FISCHER
Vanderbilt University

Advisory Board

Tecpán Guatemala: A Modern Maya Town in Global and Local Context, Edward F. Fischer (Vanderbilt University) and Carol Hendrickson (Marlboro College)

Daughters of Tunis: Women, Family, and Networks in a Muslim City, Paula Holmes-Eber (University of Washington)

Fulbe Voices: Marriage, Islam, and Medicine in Northern Cameroon, Helen A. Regis (Louisiana State University)

Magical Writing in Salasaca: Literacy and Power in Highland Ecuador, Peter Wogan (Willamette University)

The Lao: Gender, Power, and Livelihood, Carol Ireson-Doolittle (Willamette University) and Geraldine Moreno-Black (University of Oregon)

Namoluk Beyond the Reef: The Transformation of a Micronesian Community, Mac Marshall (University of Iowa)

Black Skins, French Voices: Caribbean Ethnicity and Activism in Urban France, David Beriss (University of New Orleans)

From Mukogodo to Maasai: Ethnicity and Cultural Change in Kenya, Lee Cronk (Rutgers University)

Forthcoming

The Tanners of Taiwan: Life Strategies and National Culture, Scott Simon (University of Ottawa)

The Iraqw of Tanzania: Negotiating Rural Development, Katherine A. Snyder (Queens College, City University of New York)

Urban China: Private Lives and Public Culture, William Jankowiak (University of Nevada, Las Vegas)

Muslim Youth: Tensions and Transitions in Tajikistan, Colette Harris (Virginia Tech University)

From Mukogodo to Maasai

Ethnicity and Cultural Change in Kenya

LEE CRONK

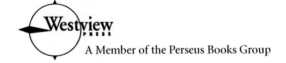

A Member of the Perseus Books Group

Westview Press books are available at special discounts for bulk purchases in the United States by corporations, institutions, and other organizations. For more information, please contact the Special Markets Department at the Perseus Books Group, 11 Cambridge Center, Cambridge, MA 02142, or call (800) 255–1514 or (617) 252–5298, or e-mail special.markets@perseusbooks.com.

Published in the United States of America by Westview Press, 5500 Central Avenue, Boulder, Colorado 80301–2877 and in the United Kingdom by Westview Press, 12 Hid's Copse Road, Cumnor Hill, Oxford OX2 9JJ.

Find us on the World Wide Web at www.westviewpress.com

Library of Congress Cataloging-in-Publication Data

Cronk, Lee.
   From Mukogodo to Maasai : ethnicity and cultural change in Kenya / by Lee Cronk.
      p.   cm. — (Westview case studies in anthropology)
   Includes bibliographical references.
   ISBN 0-8133-4094-2 (pbk. : alk. paper)
   1. Yaaku (African people)—Ethnic identity.   2. Yaaku (African people)—Cultural assimilation.   3. Yaaku (African people)—Social conditions.   4. Masai (African people)—Ethnic identity.   5. Masai (African people)—Colonization.   6. Masai (African people)—Social life and customs.   I. Title.   II. Series.
DT433.545.Y32C76 2004
305.8'096762—dc22

                                                                          2004013609

Contents

List of Figures

List of Tables

Series Editor Preface

The one great rule of culture is that it is always changing. Anthropologists have long been attuned to cultural change, although the way we conceptualize change has itself changed dramatically over the years. Indeed, culture is today seen more as an ongoing process than as a list of stable traits or characteristics. Arjun Appadurai has provocatively suggested that we abandon the term *culture* as a noun (and thus any connotation that it is a static thing), using only its adjectival form (as in speaking of "cultural traits," "cultural beliefs," and so on).

If quotidian change in the form of cultural sedimentation and erosion is the norm, there are also moments of more torrential transformation. Such is the case that Lee Cronk documents in this study of the Mukogodo of Kenya.

Until the mid–1920s, the Mukogodo were gatherers and hunters, falling somewhere between bands and tribes in the classic anthropological typology of bands, tribes, chiefdoms, and states. They spoke a Yaaku language and lived a seminomadic existence, making their homes in caves and under rockshelters. For subsistence, the Mukogodo gathered wild foods, hunted hyrax and other game, and kept bees. They described their diet as one of "honey and meat" and they lived a materially adequate if not abundant existence.

The Mukogodo, however, were looked down upon by their pastoralist Maasai neighbors, who saw them as dirty, poor, and uncultured. Under British colonial policies the Mukogodo found themselves in increasingly close contact with the Maasai and quickly adopted key elements of their higher-status culture. In the late 1920s and early 1930s, the Mukogodo made a remarkably swift transition in virtually all aspects of their lives and cultural patterns. Over the course of a decade, they switched from hunting and gathering to herding cattle; they settled down in Maasai-style huts and villages; they even dropped their native tongue to become Maa-speaking. In effect they became Maasai. Yet, the Maasai do not accept them as Maasai. To them, the Mukogodo are still *il-torrobo*, a pejorative term with connotations of poverty, pollution, and powerlessness.

Cronk's previous work builds on the insights of behavioral ecology in analyzing Mukogodo social and cultural patterns. In the present work we clearly see the fruit of these labors. Cronk shows, for example, how the colonial-era inflation in bridewealth (toward favoring cattle) led women to marry pastoralists, thus encouraging men to adopt pastoralism to avoid bachelorhood. His attention to data also leads to some surprising conclusions, such as a de facto favoritism toward daughters (even if this does not translate into gender discourse).

Yet, what really sets *From Mukogodo to Maasai* apart is the balance of contemporary notions of cultural change and hybridity with the data from behavioral ecology. Cronk brings together the sensibilities of two distinct traditions in cultural anthropology, one more symbolic and cultural, the other more material and social. And in doing so he paints a rich portrait of the many facets of ethnic change among the Mukogodo.

While theoretical fashions wane and wax within the discipline of anthropology, fine ethnographic description never goes out of style. Cronk's ethnographically grounded and well-written account exemplifies the enduring potential of the genre. He deftly employs the Mukogodo data to illustrate a number of significant patterns in African ethnography. He describes their patrilineal descent through a segmentary lineage system—and shows how flexible such systems can be in practice. He describes the rituals of male and female circumcision—while noting that some upwardly mobile Mukogodo now take their sons to the hospital for the procedure. He describes not only the dramatic switch to becoming Maa-speaking pastoralists but the waves of change that have accompanied development projects, tourism, and increasing contact with the wider world.

In this regard, Cronk's work makes an important contribution to the Westview Case Studies in Anthropology series and to the discipline as a whole. This series presents works that recognize the peoples we study as active agents enmeshed in global as well as local systems of politics, economics, and cultural flows. In presenting rich humanistic and social-scientific data borne of the dialectic engagement of fieldwork, this volume, along with the other books in the series, moves toward realizing the full pedagogical potential of anthropology: imparting to the reader an empathetic understanding of alternative ways of viewing and acting in the world as well as a solid basis for critical thought regarding the historically contingent nature of our own cultural knowledge.

EDWARD F. FISCHER
NASHVILLE, TENNESSEE

Preface

This book is about several different journeys. First, it is about a series of actual journeys, ranging from a few months to a year and a half, that I have taken to Kenya to spend time with the Mukogodo people. Second, it is about a journey that the Mukogodo people have taken over the past century from one way of life to a radically different one, giving them a new way of making a living, a new language, and a new set of beliefs. Third, it is about a journey that I have taken, as a scholar but also simply as a person, over the twenty or so years since I first heard about the Mukogodo. Learning about them has become a major part of my life, and I have enjoyed this journey a great deal. As you will see in the pages that follow, all these literal and metaphorical journeys have had their share of problems and setbacks. Ultimately, however, they have all been rewarding, and even though there are surely many obstacles ahead for all of them, I have high hopes for the future. And perhaps these journeys will eventually inspire one more: your own anthropological fieldwork.

This book is an ethnography. If you are a student, this may be the first ethnography you have ever read. Ethnography is a genre of nonfiction. Two other nonfiction genres are biography and journalism. In recent years, ethnographers have often blended these genres by incorporating biographies of the people they study and long, unedited quotes from informants in the style of journalism. This book does neither of those things. Though many Mukogodo individuals are described, this book does not include any biographies, and my writing style is not journalistic. Rather, it is an *ethnography*—a description of an ethnic group—with a large dose of *ethnology*—the analysis of ethnographic data with an eye toward broader comparisons and generalities.

As you can tell from the title, this book is about "Mukogodo" and "Maasai." The Maasai are quite famous, so you may have heard of them already. Perhaps the word *Maasai* is what attracted you to this book in the first place. But this book is, first and foremost, about the people who call themselves Mukogodo. Although they now also would like to be called Maasai, their story is quite different from that of most people who use that label. This book focuses on the distinctiveness of Mukogodo history and culture, not on the characteristics they share with Maasai and others who speak the Maa language, such as the Samburu. Good publications already exist on those peoples, many of which you will find listed at the ends of the chapters that follow and in the bibliography.

Two languages are important to this book: Yaaku, the language that the Mukogodo used to speak, and Maa, the language they now speak. The authorities on Yaaku are Bernd Heine and his colleagues Matthias Brenzinger and Ingo Heine. An authority on Maa is Frans Mol. Because neither Yaaku nor Maa is normally written, there are no standardized spellings for words in them. In this book, I use the spellings that are used by authorities on these languages when those spellings produce pronunciations that closely match what one hears in the Mukogodo area. When the pronunciation of a word I hear during my fieldwork differs significantly from the one given by the authorities, I spell the word the way I hear my Mukogodo informants pronounce it.

Anthropologists have an obligation to protect the people they study. In some cases, they accomplish this by giving a false name to the entire community they have studied. In other cases, they give pseudonyms instead of informants' real names. It would not be feasible for me to give all ethnic groups mentioned in this study false names. However, when something I say might be embarrassing or cause other problems for a particular individual, I have either avoided using a name at all or given a false one. For the same reason, I am sometimes vague about the ethnic identities of individuals mentioned. When mentioning people in ways that will do them no harm, I use their real names and do not hide their ethnic identities.

Names in Maa typically consist of at least three elements: a first name, a word or syllable in the middle that means "of," and a lineage or family name. For males, the word "of" is *ole*, and for females it is *ene*. My name, for example, would be Lee Ole Cronk. However, most Mukogodo drop the first vowels from *ole* and *ene* and slide them into the family name, and so that is how I write most Mukogodo names. Thus, my name would be Lee LeCronk. I make exceptions for certain Mukogodo individuals who make a point of spelling their names with the full *Ole* or *Ene*.

Because this book is written mainly for students, I have not provided the detailed references of a typical scholarly work. Instead, the bibliography lists my major sources, and each chapter concludes with a list of recommended readings. Almost all of my research findings originally appeared in peer-reviewed scholarly journals and edited volumes. Readers who are interested in detailed references and other technical information should consult those publications.

The chapters of this book are arranged so as to lead the reader on a journey both through Mukogodo history and through the events that led to the book's creation, which I like to call the ethnographic text formation process. Chapter 1 begins those journeys by focusing on my fieldwork experiences and methods of data collection. Chapter 2 is a capsule description of Mukogodo society before the early twentieth century, when they spoke Yaaku, lived in rockshelters, and subsisted primarily on honey and wild meat. Chapter 3 describes how and why the Mukogodo shifted in the course of just a few years to a new way of life, one based on livestock and the language and culture of their new Maa-speaking neighbors. Chapter 4 draws a picture of what life has been like for the Mukogodo since that transition, focusing on their place at the bottom of a regional socioeconomic hierarchy. Chapter 5 presents my findings on daughter favoritism among the Mukogodo, placing their parenting behavior and attitudes in both evolutionary and cross-cultural contexts. Chapter 6 focuses on recent events in the Mukogodo area and the ongoing efforts of the people there to improve their status and to be accepted as true Maasai. Finally, a brief postscript gives the reader suggestions for what he or she can do to help the Mukogodo.

Whatever shortcomings this book might have are entirely my responsibility, but I must share credit for its good points with many different people and organizations. Because many of them have already been thanked in my previous publications on the Mukogodo, I will focus here on those who helped with this book in particular and those who may not yet have been adequately thanked.

I may never have become interested in people like the Mukogodo had I not been introduced to Kenya through a field school run by two geographers, Gary Gaile and Alan Ferguson. That experience changed and enriched my life. I am indebted to the members of my graduate committee, Robert Abugov, Napoleon Chagnon, Malcolm Dow, William Irons, and Brian Shea, for their encouragement and guidance. For financial support, I am grateful to the National Science Foundation, the Population Council, the Fulbright Program, the Institute for Humane Studies, Texas A&M University, Rutgers University, and the Rutgers Center for Human Evolutionary Studies. The Kenyan government has provided me permits to conduct research in that country, and the National Museums of Kenya, the Institute for African Studies, and the University of Nairobi have provided institutional affiliations and logistical support during my visits. Matthias Brenzinger has generously allowed me to include in this book a story from one of his visits to Mukogodo. Michael Alvard, D. Bruce Dickson, William Irons, Jeniffer Koinante, Beth L. Leech, Judy Leech, Scola Ene Matunge, Peter Ole Matunge, Kay Moffett, and Paul Spencer were provided with copies of a draft manuscript and provided many useful insights and comments. My editor at Westview, Karl Yambert, and series editor Edward F. Fischer have been encouraging and helpful since I first approached them with the idea for this book, and they have worked hard to see it through to the end.

My greatest debt, however, is obvious. This book would not have been possible if not for the generosity, hospitality, tolerance, and cooperation of so many people in the Mukogodo area. While it may be chutzpah, hubris, or folly that leads someone raised in an American suburb to think that he can write a meaningful book about a group so different from his own, that is what I have tried to do. I hope that my Mukogodo friends are pleased.

I

Koisa's People

"Where's Koisa?"

"Write to your father in America," the man instructed. "Tell him to tell Koisa to come home." Simple enough, it would seem. But, unfortunately, he asked the impossible.

The speaker was Parmentoi LeSakui, a Mukogodo man in his late fifties or early sixties. Like most Mukogodo of his generation, he could not be sure of his exact age because birthdates were not recorded until recently. Physically, he was a fairly typical Mukogodo man: tall and thin, dressed as always in a favorite hat, cloak, and loincloth. One distinguishing feature was his big toe, which jutted out from inside his tire sandals at a right angle due to an injury he received as a young man. Though he could be cantankerous, LeSakui was extraordinarily helpful and generous.

Along with his best friend Parmashu, LeSakui had been acting as guide for me and my wife, Beth Leech, during our first two weeks of fieldwork among the Mukogodo of Kenya during late 1985. Although Mukogodo men of their generation could rarely read, Mukogodo children had been attending schools for a few decades by the time we arrived. A few of the kids living in the area where we began our work had been looking through some of my books and papers and sounding out words when they stumbled across the name Koisa LeLengei. Hearing that name, all of the adults around began to pay close attention.

Koisa had been one of LeSakui and Parmashu's best friends, though at that point they had not seen him for more than fifteen years. Back in 1969, a German linguist named Bernd Heine had visited the Mukogodo area in order to study their old language, known as Yaaku. Even by that time the language was mostly unspoken, having been replaced by Maa, the language of a variety of peoples living in the Rift Valley area of Kenya and Tanzania, but a few older men and women, including Koisa, could still speak it. Heine, who was teaching at the University of Nairobi, asked Koisa to come with him to Nairobi so that he could learn more about the language before it disappeared entirely. Like many Mukogodo men of his generation, Koisa had no wife or family to support, and he agreed to come along.

Koisa disappeared about two weeks after arriving in Nairobi, and he has not been seen since. Readers who are familiar with Nairobi can probably imagine what might have happened. Like many big cities, Nairobi can be a dangerous place. Heine speculated that Koisa had become a victim of one of Nairobi's criminal gangs, and he dedicated his study of the Yaaku language to Koisa's memory.

But Mukogodo of Koisa's generation are not familiar with Nairobi and its perils, and the idea that he might have died was not something that they found easy to accept. More often, they would insist that he had gone off to *Ulaya*, the land of the white people, in order to teach them the Yaaku language. Older Mukogodo often assume that Ulaya must be a small place with few people because there seem to them to be so few white people in the world, so the idea that Koisa might have been able to teach Yaaku to a large proportion of the world's white people seems to them quite logical and reasonable. Very often during our time with the Mukogodo, older people would greet us in the Yaaku way—"Aichee!"—in order to hear us respond in the way we had learned from Heine's articles: "Eiuwo!" But then they would be disappointed to learn that not only could we say no more than that in the old language, but we also had no idea where Koisa was and had never seen him. Occasionally, we would get requests like LeSakui's for us or our kin to find him and send him home. Rarely, we would be confronted with anger and disbelief that someone that they held so dear could have been torn away from them the way Koisa was.

Younger Mukogodo usually had a different reaction. They knew the story of Koisa well enough, but many younger Mukogodo men and a few women have spent time in Nairobi, usually working as nightwatchmen, and they know its dangers well. To them, the idea that Koisa became a crime victim is not so hard to accept.

The contrasting reactions among Mukogodo about Koisa's disappearance show, in abbreviated form, the essence of this book: change. Mukogodo of Koisa's generation and before were born in rockshelters, grew up speaking Yaaku, and ate honey and wild game. Younger people were born in small houses, grew up speaking Maa, and drink milk and eat meat from goats, sheep, and cattle. In the past few decades, Mukogodo have also begun attending schools, getting jobs in and outside the Mukogodo area, and even traveling to Ulaya itself. Change has been the norm for most of humanity for the past century or more, and nowhere has it been faster or more dramatic than among the Mukogodo.

FALLING OFF A LOG

Becoming interested in the Mukogodo had been as easy as falling off a log. In fact, that's exactly how it happened. It was the summer of 1981, and I was one of twenty Northwestern University students being shown around East Africa by Gary Gaile and Alan Ferguson, who at that time worked in Northwestern's Geography Department. The most fascinating part of our six-week trip was spent among the Samburu, a Maa-speaking pastoralist group in northern Kenya. An American named Michael Rainey had set up a field school there, giving American students the chance to live among Samburu herders for a few days.

Part of our time with the Samburu was spent with a group of *murran* (singular: *murrani*). *Murran* is usually translated as "warriors," and it is true that one of the roles of a *murrani* is to defend his family's livestock. But the name actually means something more like "circumcised guys," reflecting the fact that one becomes a *murrani* while a teenager after going through an initiation procedure that includes circumcision. These days most *murran* spend more time primping, hanging out with friends, and flirting with girls than in military engagements.

One favorite *murrani* pastime is to take a sheep or two into the forested hills that dot the East African countryside, camp in a cave, and gorge themselves on mutton. We had the privilege of sharing this experience for a couple of nights with a group of Samburu *murran*, including everything from singing around the campfire to lapping up blood from the neck of the slaughtered animals. During the days, we would take hikes in the forest, which is how I fell over the log.

Let me say in my defense that it was a huge log, it was very slippery, and it was right across our path. But what was it doing there? I could see that it had been deliberately chopped down. After I had picked myself up, I asked our Samburu guides through a translator why the tree had been cut down. "Il-torrobo," they replied, using the Maa term for people who live in and around the forested hills that dot the East African countryside and who once lived primarily by hunting, gathering, and beekeeping. The Samburu *murran* thought it likely that these mysterious, poorly studied people had cut the tree down in order to get honey, one of their favorite foods. To my young imagination, shaped by the fantasy novels of J. R. R. Tolkien and his imitators, this was like walking through Mirkwood and finding evidence that elves or hobbits lived nearby and yet kept coyly out of sight, as if trying to pique my curiosity about them even further.

PREPARING FOR THE FIELD

In retrospect, the idea that the Torrobo (as they are known to scholars) of the Karissia Hills had chopped down that tree to get to a beehive seems farfetched. I now know that honey hunters do not routinely cut down large trees, preferring instead to climb them to get at a hive. But the memory stuck, and a few years later when it was time for me to pick a group to study so that I could obtain my Ph.D. in anthropology, I turned to the literature on the Torrobo.

That literature is mostly about a group more properly called Okiek. The Okiek live in and around forests in central Kenya and speak a language called Kalenjin, varieties of which are also spoken by groups of herders and farmers in western

Kenya. What makes the Okiek and other groups "Torrobo" is the fact that they have at some times in their history lived near Maa speakers, hunting and keeping bees. As you will learn in more detail in a later chapter, *il-torrobo* is a term Maa speakers use to refer to hunters, and it is better thought of as a status designation than as an ethnic label. Nevertheless, there was a small but interesting literature on various Torrobo groups, and I read everything I could find.

I needed to find a group where I could test my advisor William Irons's ideas about adaptation and cultural change. I knew that many Torrobo groups had been changing in recent decades, hunting less and herding and farming more and sometimes going through drastic cultural changes along the way. One particularly intriguing group was the Mukogodo, or, as I called them after having read Heine's articles on their old language, Yaaku. I wrote to a variety of experts in the field and was greatly encouraged by their replies. Christopher Ehret, a historian at UCLA well known for his pathbreaking use of Yaaku and other languages to reconstruct East African history, was particularly heartening: "I can think of no better group for you to study, given your interests, than the Mukogodo." Armed with Irons's hypothesis and Ehret's endorsement, I obtained funding for my fieldwork from the Population Council, National Science Foundation, and Institute for Humane Studies. Knowing that I would need someone who could talk to women about sensitive reproductive topics, I asked my girlfriend (now my wife), Beth Leech, to be my research assistant. As a journalist, Beth had conducted many interviews. Like me, she had been a student on that fateful 1981 trip to Kenya, and while in college she had studied anthropology, African history, and Swahili. Beth turned out to be a perfect fieldworker: patient, curious, observant, tolerant of adversity, and possessing a knack for languages.

Although Swahili is the common language for communication between ethnic groups in East Africa, Beth and I knew that not everyone in the Mukogodo area would be able to speak it. The Mukogodo used to speak their own unique language, called Yaaku, but for the past few decades their language has been Maa, the same language spoken by larger groups like the Samburu and Maasai. We set out to find a Maa speaker in the Chicago area, where we were living at the time, who would be willing to give us some lessons in the language. I prepared posters saying "Maa speaker wanted" and distributed them to all locations in the Chicago area where a Maa speaker—or at least someone who spoke more of it than we could at the time—might be passing by: universities, African studies centers, and places with lots of missionaries, like the Moody Bible Institute. We did not really expect anything to come of those posters, but a Kenyan student at Moody did spot one and took it home to her husband, a Maasai named James Ole Takona who was earning his doctorate in education at Loyola University. James agreed to tutor us every week for a few months before we left for Kenya, so by the time we left we had a good grasp of Maa grammar and the ability to say a few important phrases.

FREQUENTLY ASKED QUESTIONS

We traveled from Chicago to Kenya in the fall of 1985 by a somewhat circuitous route that took us to New York, London, France, and Moscow before we finally landed in Nairobi. On the way, Americans and others asked us many questions about our fieldwork, and I noted the most common ones in my journal. The questions ranged from insightful to silly, but since many readers might be asking the same questions, perhaps it's worth answering them again here:

Do they know you're coming?   Probably not! Before leaving home, I sent letters to all government officials and others in the Mukogodo area whose mailing addresses I could find, informing them about our plans to work in the area and asking them to let people know we were coming. After we arrived, it became clear that few of these letters had arrived, and those that had made it there had not had any effect.

What will you eat?   Some anthropologists eat what the people they study eat and little else, but when you are studying an impoverished group like the Mukogodo, that is often not feasible. Many families simply do not have enough food on hand to feed extra people. We also wanted to avoid having too much influence on how Mukogodo individuals behaved, and even if we had paid for food we would have changed the amount of time they had to spend acquiring it. So we made plans to buy and prepare our own food. We had enough experience in Kenya to know that our food would need to be nonperishable, easy to cook, and portable, like rice and beans. And, despite their poverty, Mukogodo are quite generous with the food they have, and we drank a great deal of milk, tea, and a curds-and-whey preparation called *kule naaoto*, and ate many meals of maize meal. Meat was a very rare treat because animals are usually slaughtered only on special occasions, such as a marriage or the birth of a child, and every once in a while we would get a taste of honey or a cup of honey wine.

How will you bathe?   This is a detail we had not worked out before we left, but soon after arriving we learned to keep clean with just a bucket of warm water, some soap, and a wash cloth.

How often will you get to town, and what size town is near there?   We really had no idea how to answer this question because we had not yet been to the Mukogodo area. We anticipated spending most of our time backpacking and making it to a town only rarely. As it turned out, we spent only about a third of our time backpacking, and we were able to drive to the bustling market town of Nanyuki about once a month to buy supplies. Don Dol, the dusty headquarters of Mukogodo Division, was much closer but had little to offer.

Will you have a gun?   No. A gun is rarely a good idea in an anthropological field setting. Kenya has strict laws governing gun possession, and we had no use for one and no interest in acquiring one.

How dangerous are the animals?   Not as dangerous as the traffic in Nairobi! While there certainly are dangerous animals in Africa, they are only rarely a problem for people. Two of the most dangerous species, hippos and crocodiles, do not even live in the Mukogodo area.

You must be having more supplies shipped over (asked after seeing our bags). No! When Beth and I arrived in Kenya, we each had a backpack and a daypack and nothing more. The other supplies we needed were easy to buy in Nairobi and Nanyuki.

IN THE FIELD, AT LONG LAST

There is a saying in Maa: *Te nilo enkop nanya nkik, nenya sii iyie.* Translation: *If you go to a land where people eat shit, eat it yourself.* Anyone who could actually follow this advice would make a good anthropological fieldworker, because the watchword of the discipline is *immersion.* Different fieldworkers have different goals and different styles, and they immerse themselves in the society and culture to different degrees. Some barely get their feet wet, so to speak, spending only a short time in the field, using translators to speak with informants and assistants to gather data and living apart from the people they are studying. Others dive in head first, spending years in the field, learning the local language, converting to the local religion, becoming adopted by a family, going through appropriate rituals, and generally living as much as possible like the people they are studying. Beth and I operated somewhere in between those two extremes, metaphorically wading in up to our chests or so in the Mukogodo way of life.

We arrived in Kenya in October 1985. Our first few weeks were spent buying a vehicle and supplies and obtaining a research permit from the Kenyan government. The permit process was lengthy, which gave us plenty of time to travel around Kenya and ask those who might know about the Mukogodo area. What we learned was not encouraging. No one we spoke with—government officials, journalists, fellow researchers—had ever heard of the "Yaaku," as we were calling them at the time. Few had even heard of the "Mukogodo," which, as we soon learned, is a much more common name than Yaaku. But, with nothing to lose but time, once we had a permit we headed off for the field, hoping that somehow we would find these elusive people.

As it turned out, they were not elusive at all. In fact, they were positively eager to be "discovered." Not knowing where exactly we would find people who identified themselves as "Yaaku," we took a tip from Bernd Heine's article on their language that they can be found near a mountain called Ol Doinyo Lossos. We drove toward the mountain, taking the most direct route shown on the map and stopping at a police post called Loregai on the way. The chief of the police was quite amused by our arrival. It was clear that he expected us to have a look around for a day or two and then leave, and he generously offered to introduce us to some friends of his who might be able to help us find these "Yaaku" we sought.

The policeman, Beth, and I squeezed into our tiny Suzuki jeep and drove into the Mukogodo forest a few miles until we reached a huge glade called the Anandanguru Plain. There he introduced us to some acquaintances of his, including a man he referred to as "the chief of the Mumonyot," the name of another Maa-speaking people in the general area. We chatted as best we could in a mixture of bad Swahili and even worse Maa and accepted shots of throat-searing moonshine whisky called *chang'aa*, still warm from the still. When the police chief said goodbye, Beth and I set up camp, explaining as best we could to the handful of people who had assembled to watch that we were looking not for them but rather for some people called "Yaaku."

"That's us!" they cried. It turned out that everyone around us was "Yaaku." The "chief of the Mumonyot" turned out to be Parmentoi LeSakui, a full-blown Mukogodo with no claim to the position of Mumonyot chief. His best friend, a man from the Parmashu family, was also there. Though they were nearly constant companions, Parmashu was quite different from LeSakui. Quiet and self-effacing, he had a peculiar gait thanks to an incident when he was a *murrani*. While hunting an elephant with friends, the animal had picked him up with its trunk and thrown him, and he landed on both his knees. Despite whatever profits he made from the ivory trade, Parmashu, like many Mukogodo men, could not afford to marry until late in life, so he had only one wife and several young children. He was known as a good carver, and during our travels in the forest he would keep an eye out for high-quality timber for things like bows, stools, and game boards. Leboo LeMoile, a slightly younger man with a passion for shooting rats with his bow and arrow and a good sense of humor, was there as well. LeMoile was a forest guard, hired by the Kenyan government agency that had jurisdiction over most of the Mukogodo area to keep an eye out for illegal logging and forest fires. They were positively delighted to be referred to as "Yaaku," a quaint, old-fashioned name that they themselves had nearly forgotten but that they much preferred to the way outsiders usually referred to them: "Torrobo." The policeman's confusion about the identity of the people in the area undoubtedly reflected not only a lack of interest on his part but also a common Mukogodo tactic of being cagey and evasive with outsiders, particularly those perceived as actual or potential enemies.

What a relief it was to know that we had found the people we had set out to find and to be so warmly and quickly accepted by them. It was the rainy season, so LeSakui, Parmashu, and LeMoile helped us find a relatively dry place to pitch our tent. We ended up camping inside a small abandoned building. Although it was rapidly falling apart, it kept the rain off and was preferable to camping out in the open. With a few whacks from a machete to widen the door, we were even able to park our Suzuki inside.

STEP ONE: THE CENSUS

We explained as best we could that we needed to conduct a census of the Mukogodo. LeSakui and Parmashu took us under their wing, guiding us from one Mukogodo settlement to another so that we could record who lived there, their relationships to one another, their genders, and their ages. When we had exhausted the area around Anandanguru, we moved to the area near the town of Don Dol. We were greeted just as warmly in the Don Dol area as we had been at Anandanguru. Kosima Ole Leitiko, who was roughly our own age, took over the role of guide, and within a few weeks we had completed the census, developed an understanding of the Mukogodo way of life, and rapidly improved our ability to speak Maa.

Many experts on ethnographic fieldwork will tell you that a census is not necessarily the best way to begin because the questions one must ask in order to do a good census are often considered rather personal: How old are you? How many children do you have? Such questions can often elicit more hostility than rapport from the people you are hoping to study. We decided to go against that advice for a couple of reasons. Most important, we simply needed a good census in order to be able to begin our work because the focus of our research plans was on Mukogodo demography—residential patterns, marriage patterns, numbers of children, and so on. We also needed to know things as basic as where exactly the Mukogodo all were, which was a bit of a challenge. Unlike some of the people anthropologists study, the Mukogodo do not all live in one or a few villages, and they don't necessarily stay in one place for very long. Rather, they live in settlements that range in size from about twenty to about fifty people scattered throughout the Mukogodo forest and surrounding areas. Though some such settlements last for years, more often they last for just a few weeks or months before the residents decide to move elsewhere in search of food and water for their livestock. Doing the census first gave us a chance to learn the lay of the land, the trails, and the names of the various hills and valleys where people were most likely to be found.

Most people not only found our questions to be easy enough to answer, they actually seemed to take great delight in the attention they were receiving, and we made many good contacts and future friends during those first few weeks of census collecting. Of course, to get information one must be willing to give it, and people were full of questions about us and our home. Mostly the questions were fairly routine. "Do you have cattle?" was the most common. But Beth and I remember one encounter with an inquisitive Mukogodo man quite vividly. His name was Taraya LePardero, and we found him to be extraordinarily clever and witty. At first, we were a bit put off by him because he drilled us with questions so rapidly that he taxed both our patience and our ability to speak Maa. He wanted to know, for instance, why Beth had dark brown hair while mine was light brown. Good question! Unfortunately, all we could say was that Beth's ancestors and mine had come from different parts of Europe, and so they had different colors of hair. Unlike most Mukogodo, he had heard of America, and he was aware of some of the facts of the world at the time, such as that Ronald Reagan was president of the United States and Margaret Thatcher was prime minister of the United Kingdom. But he wanted to know one other thing we found difficult to answer: "Who is smarter, British or Americans?" Well, we said, it's hard to say, because they are both clever in different ways. . . He cut us off with another question: "Which one went to the moon?" "Americans," we replied. "All right, then Americans are more clever," he announced. We could hardly argue with that logic, and subsequently Taraya became one of our best friends. While I was visiting him several months later, Taraya asked his young son "Le ng'ai lashumbai?" ("Whose white person is this?") I was delighted when his son answered, somewhat sheepishly, "Maa . . . lino." ("Listen . . . yours.")

It's fair to say that not much happens in Mukogodo Location most of the time, so our visits to settlements to conduct the census were exciting occasions. Small children were often frightened by us, either because they had never seen white people before or because the only ones they had encountered were doctors and nurses anxious to give them painful vaccinations. Older children were fascinated by our difference, often marveling at such things as our hair. "The hair is nice," one little girl repeated over and over again, stroking my arm one day. "Like a lion!" Other children were fascinated by the way they could see my veins through my pale skin, our moles, and the way we tanned and burned, it never having occurred to them that the sun could burn skin.

Adults also found us amusing. One woman, Ngoto Lemedero NeLioini, had a favorite joke she liked to play on Beth. "Where's your husband?" she would ask, and Beth would point at me. "Where's the other one?" she would then ask, and when Beth would say, "I don't have another one," she would cackle and howl. Apparently she had heard that there were people somewhere in the world who allowed women to have more than one husband, just as Mukogodo men can have more than one wife, and she found this idea absolutely hilarious. Despite the fact that Beth did not have any husbands other than me, Ngoto Lemedero never got tired of this joke. Others found us perplexing and entertaining in other ways. The biggest puzzle we presented to our Mukogodo hosts was our childlessness. Since we clearly were not still children, why did we have no children? We did our best to explain that we did plan to have children, but not until we were out of school and had jobs. This did not, however, satisfy everyone. One day while Beth was sitting around with a few Mukogodo women, the women began discussing among themselves why Beth had not had any children. Someone suggested that perhaps she was just too "small," meaning too young, to have children. To settle the matter, an old woman suddenly reached over, squeezed one of Beth's breasts, and announced, "Eh, ke gini"—"Yes, she's small." Five years later we finally did have our first child, and on my next visit to Mukogodo I was greeted everywhere I went by women's delighted cries of "Ketoishe!"—"She gave birth!"

Conducting the census also gave us a chance to work on our Maa. Because our conversations were limited to just a few narrow topics, any mistakes we might make were relatively easy to catch and correct. For instance, at one settlement we asked a routine question about who the head of a particular household was, and we got back a one word response: "Kelotu." So we dutifully started writing this down in our census book as the man's name: Kelotu. Our Mukogodo hosts started laughing as we did this, and we quickly remembered from our Maa lessons that *kelotu* simply means "he's coming." In other words, they were asking us to hang on a minute while he came to answer our questions in person. Another important phrase we learned in those days was "Eshomo entim": "He/she/it went to the forest." The first time we were told this, we figured that the man in question must be off on a long trek through the forest, probably in search of honey. But he actually reappeared quickly, with neither a honey bucket nor anything else to show for his trouble. It turned out that "he's in the forest" is just a euphemism, analogous to our own euphemistic phrase "he's in the bathroom." A few weeks later, after we had begun gathering other sorts of data, Beth was told that a man "Eshomo Lala." Knowing that the Swahili for "sleep" is *lala,* she thought that they were speaking a sort of baby talk to her, telling her that the man was taking a nap. But he continued to "take a nap" for the whole rest of the day, and eventually she figured out that "Lala" was the name of a place and that he had actually moved away weeks earlier.

Our Mukogodo friends were very patient with our mistakes and very appreciative of our efforts to learn Maa, and within a few weeks after our arrival we had switched from speaking mostly Swahili to speaking almost entirely Maa, albeit a simplified version of a very rich and complex language. At some point, we began telling people that we simply did not speak Swahili, but that we did speak Maa. This struck many people as bizarre because most Mukogodo assume that Swahili is the lingua franca not just of East Africa but of the entire world. Some never got used the idea that we could speak Maa, and we had many conversations in which a Mukogodo or other Maa speaker spoke Swahili to us and we replied in Maa. But most people got used to speaking Maa with us and even seemed to enjoy being able to use their mother tongue rather than their second language to communicate with us. One day I had to chuckle when a woman we had met soon after our arrival told her brother, who was home visiting from his job in Nairobi, "Don't speak Swahili to him—he hates it!" Non-Mukogodo people in the area were also surprised by our preference for Maa over Swahili. While in Don Dol one day, Beth overheard one woman explaining to another in Swahili that Beth could speak Maa better than Swahili. Surprised and also a little skeptical about Beth's ability to speak Maa, the second woman decided to test her with a question in Maa: "Anu ilo nkop inchi?" ("When are you returning to your country?") Beth responded in perfectly idiomatic and typically inscrutable Maa, "Kenya!" ("At some vague time in the future!") Convinced, the woman declared in Swahili, "Najua sana!" ("She knows it very well!")

Conducting the census and keeping records of the whereabouts of everyone in Mukogodo Location during 1986 also gave us a body of detailed information possessed by no one else, not even any Mukogodo. This was brought home to me while conducting an interview with a man about the arrangements he had made with other men to share livestock. He could not remember the name of one of his livestock-sharing partners, so he turned to his wife for help. "Why ask me?" She asked. "Ask him"—meaning me—"He knows everyone!" My detailed knowledge of the Mukogodo individuals and their family relationships was also often a source of entertainment. When I returned to the Mukogodo area in 2001 after an absence of eight years, Leboo LeMoile, the forest guard we had met on our first day there, was delighted to find that I could still remember the names of his many children. So he decided to test me: "What was the name of my first wife?" I hesitated to answer because I knew that she had died, and it is not Mukogodo custom to discuss the dead. But he insisted, so I complied: "Soita." He grinned, laughed out loud, and gave a typical Mukogodo expression of amazement: "Taaba!"

STEP TWO:
SETTLING IN AT KURI-KURI

Before we had left America, our expectation was that we would end up spending most of our time backpacking and living either in tents or rockshelters. That turned out to be unnecessary, at least most of the time. As luck would have it, there was an empty house next to one of the local schools, Kuri-Kuri Primary. It had been built for the teachers, but because there was no water supply at the school they preferred to live a few kilometers away in the town of Don Dol and walk to work. Unlike the teachers we could afford to own a vehicle, so we could fetch water at a pump a few miles away and bring it back to the house. In exchange for some rent to the school, we made that little house at Kuri-Kuri our home for 1986. Conveniently, it was right next door to the settlement of our friend Kosima Ole Leitiko and near several other families we were getting to know, so we could both immerse ourselves and have our own private space at the same time.

One way to describe the house at Kuri-Kuri is that it would not pass "the lawnmower test." What I mean is that a typical American will pour a concrete slab for the floor of a structure even if all it is going to do is hold his lawnmower. Our little house had just a dirt floor, walls made from the bits of bark-covered wood called *offcuts* trimmed from the logs at the sawmill, a corrugated metal roof, and a few windows with shutters but no glass. We set up a makeshift kitchen in one corner, with a fire on the floor and a water bag on the wall, a small table in another corner, and a couple of cots off to the side. The result was a living arrangement that was comfortable enough for us and light enough that we could read and write. This is not typical of Mukogodo houses, which usually have no windows and are quite dark and smoky inside. But it was still close enough to the way that the Mukogodo live that they felt comfortable visiting. We made it clear to one and all that our door was always open and that they were always welcome to come by for tea, coffee, and cookies. Needless to say, we got a lot of visitors, and I got some of my very best information from people as they sat, sipped, and munched. People also asked us many, many questions about America, particularly about the landscape and wildlife, so we decorated the walls with photographs cut from magazines of American animals and scenes that helped us explain ourselves to them.

Although the house at Kuri-Kuri was our home, we spent only about two-thirds of our time there. The rest of the time we were on car-camping and backpacking trips to portions of the Mukogodo area that we could not reach from our house. These trips lasted anywhere from a couple of days to more than a week, and they were invaluable for the insights we gained into how Mukogodo live when they are far from the roads, stores, and churches of the Don Dol area. Fortunately, the Mukogodo Hills are a delightful place for hiking and camping, with gorgeous vistas over the Siekuu Valley, cool cedar forests, hidden springs, and lots of wildlife. Some African wildlife can be dangerous, of course. Although buffaloes were our greatest fear, we actually had problems only with an elephant that we surprised in the bush, an aggressive cobra, and few bee stings.

In addition to such physical challenges, all fieldworkers must also deal with psychological challenges, including loneliness, homesickness, and ethnocentrism and culture shock. Because we had each other, loneliness was less of a problem for me and Beth than it is for many anthropologists in the field. Homesickness was also a minor problem because, particularly for me, the field was where I had been hoping to be for so long, and my life as a poor graduate student back in America was not something I was anxious to return to very quickly. Ethnocentrism is something that even anthropologists, trained to be cultural relativists, must be on guard for, because it is ubiquitous. Even our Mukogodo hosts could be quite ethnocentric, assuming that their way was, if not the only way, the one and only right way. One older Mukogodo woman epitomized this phenomenon. She had been very successful in the Mukogodo way of life, with twelve adult children, including many grown sons whose homes she could now move among. On one occasion, she sat Beth down and gave her a little lecture. Clearly, she thought, we did not know how to live. There we were, with a vehicle, but with no children or livestock. So she gave this advice, spoken slowly as if to a child and accompanied with hand gestures to make sure the point got across, "First, you sell your vehicle. Then you buy some cows. Then you milk the cows and drink the milk." Simple as that! On another occasion, she asked me what age set I was in. Age sets are a common social institution among East African pastoralists in which men of a particular age group are identified by a common name and go through life's stages together. I explained that we did not have age sets where I came from, but that if I were Mukogodo I would be in the Kiroro age set. She scoffed at that: "Yes, you do have age sets where you come from. Age sets are part of God."

That sort of simplistic ethnocentrism is easy enough for trained anthropological fieldworkers to guard against, but culture shock—a visceral reaction against cultural differences—is not necessarily something that can be controlled through sheer intellect. But in our case it would be wrong to say that we experienced culture *shock*. Culture *grate* would be a better term. After all, we had already spent time with people very much like the Mukogodo and we had read everything we could about the Mukogodo and people like them. We had a good idea of what to expect. But some cultural differences don't hit you in the face. Rather, they get under your skin and make you itch and itch, wearing you down over time. This was certainly the case with Mukogodo gift-giving practices. In America, Beth and I were taught to say please and thank you, not to ask people for their personal possessions, and not to look a gift horse in the mouth. In much of the rest of the world, asking other people to give you their possessions is normal, and it is customary to criticize gifts received. There is a logic behind this, that of reciprocity. Whereas the tradition in which Beth and I were raised was to give gifts with no strings attached and no expectation of a return, the norm for many people, including the Mukogodo, is reciprocity. Gifts are given with some expectation that a return will be made in the future. Thus, gifts are useful as ways of establishing and maintaining relationships, including friendships. Because gifts received are understood to entail obligations for repayment, it is quite normal to request things. And because it is to the receiver's advantage to reduce the size of the expected return gift, it makes sense to criticize the gift, arguing that it is not as wonderful as the giver might imagine.

This very different ethic of gift giving is something that we knew about before leaving, thanks to the work of scholars like Marcel Mauss, Marshall Sahlins, and Richard Lee. But it never seemed real to us until Mukogodo people started asking us for things: "Give me your shirt." "Give me a dress." "Give me your knife." "Give me your radio." "Give me your watch." "Give me a jerry can." "Give me some wire." And, from the children, "Give me sweets!" Because there is no word for *please* in Maa, with the politeness being implied by the tone of voice, these requests sound downright rude when translated into English, but they are not. They are simply the normal way of interacting with people in a setting like Mukogodo. And although Maa does have a word for *thank you*, it is often accompanied by criticisms of the gift. Jerry cans might have holes, or they might smell bad. Clothing might not be the right size or color. Such complaints make sense as part of a negotiation over the expected repayment. But it is one thing to understand this intellectually and quite another to understand it at a gut level. At that level, we found the constant requests grating, to say the least. Because the requests were so constant that it would have been impossible to comply with them, we decided on a different strategy. Whenever someone would ask for something, we would make a note of the request and jot it down on a list so that we would know who had requested which of our belongings when we left. And, when we left, we did our best to pass our belongings—pots, pans, jerry cans, cots, etc.— out among the people who had helped us the most and who had requested them.

STEP THREE:
THE ROUTINE OF DATA COLLECTION

Anthropologists are not the only people whose work involves crossing cultural boundaries. Missionaries and development workers are called upon to do so as well, and in today's multicultural society almost everyone in a service job must interact routinely with people of very different cultural backgrounds. But anthropologists are different because for them it is the crossing of the cultural boundary itself that is the whole point. Because of that emphasis, we collect data systematically as well as anecdotally. Methods of data collection are as diverse as the discipline of anthropology itself, but the two basic techniques are straightforward: interviews and behavioral observations. Both can be done in a variety of styles, ranging from casual and informal to formal and highly structured. In our case, we developed a battery of methods that were suitable both for a variety of circumstances during our time in the field and for collecting the different sorts of data we needed in order to answer the questions we had in mind. Here is a list of the main categories of data we collected in 1986:

Census   We conducted a census of all of the people living in Mukogodo Location, including people with Mukogodo ancestry and people living in the area from other ethnic groups, as well as Mukogodo people living in neighboring locations. As you will see in later chapters, the question of who is and who is not Mukogodo is not one with a single, easy answer. However, we needed somehow to define our study group. For the purposes of this research project, we decided to count as Mukogodo people who belonged to families that had once spoken the Yaaku language, lived in rock-shelters, and made a living from wild game and honey. This excluded a few families, mostly from the neighboring Samburu and Mumonyot, who have moved into the area over the past few decades and intermarried and co-resided with Mukogodo so much that they are now often considered to be Mukogodo by locals. The reason for this definition of Mukogodo was that our project focused primarily on the Mukogodo transition from hunting and gathering to pastoralism, so we needed a definition that took that transition into account. Using this strict definition of Mukogodo, we learned that there were between 800 and 900 Mukogodo living in and around Mukogodo Location in 1986. If we had used a looser definition, as do most Mukogodo themselves, that number would have been slightly over 1,000. During the course of the year, we attempted to interview all adult Mukogodo individually, and we also met most of the children in the process.

The census included questions about the genders and ages of all individuals and was organized by settlement (*enkang'*; plural, *inkang'itie*) and household. As settlements moved and as settlement composition shifted throughout 1986, we did our best to keep track of individuals and households. We also included questions about everyone's parentage to make it easier to identify relationships and to help with the collection of genealogies. Age estimates are tricky in a place like Mukogodo because only recently have people begun to record exact birth dates. There are a variety of techniques available to deal with this problem. For instance, the Mukogodo age-set system alone allowed us to estimate men's ages to within five to seven years. Ages can also be determined with reference to events of known date, such as the date of Kenyan independence and by comparing relative ages. The result is a body of demographic data that is accurate enough for many purposes, including those we had in mind when we designed the project. On the other hand, it is not fine-grained enough for studies that require precise information about ages, such as analyses of birth spacing patterns.

Genealogies   As among many people around the world, the principle of descent is important to Mukogodo social organization. The Mukogodo identify four clans, which in turn are broken down into thirteen patrilineages. I conducted interviews with elders of eleven of those patrilineages in order to reconstruct their family histories. In most cases I was able to reconstruct them back to the middle of the nineteenth century, and sometimes slightly earlier. Two of the thirteen lineages are now extinct, meaning that they went through a generation in which none of their male members left any legitimate heirs, so for them I had to use elders from related lineages and a few surviving women who were born to those lineages as my genealogical informants. Genealogical information is an invaluable window not only on to social relations but also history, and these data were crucial in my reconstruction of Mukogodo history over the previous century.

Bridewealth   A common practice in Africa and elsewhere is that a man must pay his wife's family for the privilege of marrying her. This is known as bridewealth. When the Mukogodo were living as hunters and gatherers, they paid beehives as bridewealth. A man would fashion five or six hives, essentially hollowed logs about a meter long and a third of a meter in diameter, and give them to his father-in-law. When they obtained livestock, bridewealth shifted accordingly, and it became customary to pay at least one sheep and one cow, and usually quite a bit more. The sheep is normally given to the mother-in-law, and from that time on the husband calls her "sheep receiver" and she calls him "sheep giver" (the word in both cases is actually the same: *Pakerr*). The father of the bride receives the cow, along with however many other head of livestock and other goods have been negotiated, and from that time on the husband and father-in-law call each other "cow giver" and "cow receiver," respectively (again, the word in both cases is the same: *Pakiteng'*). In order to be able to analyze variations in bridewealth payments, especially as they related to the shift from hunting and gathering to pastoralism, I collected estimates of bridewealths for 400 marriages involving

Mukogodo going back into the nineteenth century. Most of these estimates were obtained from my genealogical informants, and when I obtained more than one estimate for a given bridewealth I averaged them for purposes of analysis. I was also able to obtain some information about bridewealths for current marriages from the parties involved. However, this proved more difficult than obtaining such information from relatively disinterested parties because bridewealth levels are a sensitive topic.

Reproductive histories   Because we were concerned with demographic issues, it was essential that we obtain reproductive histories for as many Mukogodo women as possible. Accordingly, Beth interviewed nearly all Mukogodo women who had experienced at least one menstrual period. The interviews, which were conducted in private, were designed to obtain as complete a record as possible of each woman's reproductive life from the date of her first menses through all of her pregnancies and through menopause. She also included a series of questions about women's reproductive goals. These data proved crucial to our analysis of Mukogodo child care patterns, which is presented in Chapter 5.

Behavioral observations   All anthropologists make observations of people's be-havior, but mostly these are recorded as discursive notes and referred to as "partic-ipant observation." For some purposes, it is better to collect data about behavior in more systematic and quantifiable ways so that observations can be compared more reliably, both within one group of people and among different groups. One tech-nique for this, called behavioral scans, has been developed by anthropologists fol-lowing the lead of animal behaviorists, psychologists, and even industrial engineers who conduct time-and-motion studies. The basic idea is to focus on particular kinds of behaviors and to gather data about them in consistent ways. The work that results is tedious and time consuming, but the data can be very valuable. There are two broad categories of behavioral scan techniques. One is called a focal follow. As the name implies, it involves following an individual around and recording his or her behavior at some fixed frequency, such as every minute or every five min-utes, for some length of time, such as an hour or a day. Another technique is to do an instantaneous scan, which is an attempt to take a sort of snapshot, with a pad and paper or, these days, a handheld computer, of the activities of a whole group of people at a single point in time. In 1986 we were interested not in the behaviors of particular individuals but rather in finding out how Mukogodo households and settlements allocated time among different subsistence tasks, and so we chose to use the instantaneous scan method. Those data are discussed in Chapter 4. When I returned in 1993, I had different research goals, and so used the focal follow tech-nique instead. Those data are discussed in Chapter 5.

Diet survey   During each behavioral scan day, we asked everyone in the settle-ment what they had eaten the day before. This method, referred to as a 24-hour recall interview, is a standard fieldwork technique for understanding diet. When the person in question was a small child, we asked his or her mother or other caregiver what he or she had eaten the day before. The original goal of this survey was to understand the range of variation across Mukogodo in terms of their reliance on wild versus domesticated foods. As it turned out, the reliance on wild foods was almost nonexistent apart from small amounts of honey, so instead what we have is a picture of variation in terms of reliance on foods produced by the household itself, chiefly milk plus small amounts of meat, honey, and maize and beans grown by a few families in small plots, versus foods that are either purchased or donated as famine relief, chiefly dry maize, maize meal, beans, cooking oil, and powdered milk.

Livestock census   In order to understand variations in wealth and herd management across all Mukogodo, I interviewed more than 120 Mukogodo men about their livestock. Most men own at least a few small stock (sheep and goats) these days, though some have no stock at all and a few have large herds of both small stock and cattle and a few donkeys.

Notes on history, society, and culture   In addition to the data we collected using formal interview and observational methods, we also collected a great deal of information through more informal interviews and conversations. Most of my information about Mukogodo history, for example, came from informal chats with older men and women while we drank coffee or tea and ate cookies together. Similarly, Beth obtained a great many insights about women's lives during informal chats with friends. Inevitably, we came to rely upon a few people more than others because they were willing to talk and interested in helping us understand Mukogodo. These are the sorts of people anthropologists refer to as "key informants" or, more accurately and politely, "key consultants." One of my key consultants, for instance, was Stephen Lereman LeLeitiko, a man in his fifties who had an amazing mind and an encyclopedic knowledge of Mukogodo history. Even people from other ethnic groups in the area, such as the Mumonyot, would direct me to him when I asked questions about their history. One of Beth's best friends and key consultants on women's affairs was a relative of Stephen Lereman's, Mary NeLeitiko. Mary was a bright and witty young woman who delighted in helping Beth perfect her Maa and understand the lives of Mukogodo women.

We developed a particularly close relationship with one remarkable old man named Kutiniyai LeKitiman, the last true cave dweller in Mukogodo. When we arrived in Mukogodo in late 1985, LeKitiman and his brother had just moved from their rockshelter home because his brother was ill and needed medical attention. His brother soon died, and then LeKitiman himself became quite ill. Like many Mukogodo men of his generation, he had no wife or other family, and he set up housekeeping with another old man just down the hill from our house at

Kuri-Kuri. Unlike virtually all other Mukogodo, LeKitiman still felt more comfortable speaking Yaaku than Maa; he spoke Maa with an accent and some hesitance, and our common struggle with the language brought us closer. For a time during 1986, he visited us daily, both so that we could feed him and so that we could occasionally drive him to the dispensary at the local Catholic mission for treatment for whatever it was that was ailing him, which was never definitively diagnosed. During one of his healthy spells that year, he and I even headed off to visit his cave, which was several days' walk from our house. Unfortunately, it was my turn to get sick, and although we did sleep in some rockshelters along the way, I never got to see his cave home. My understanding is that after we left his health improved again and he headed back to the wilderness to forage for himself once again. He finally passed away a couple of years later, truly bringing to an end an era of Mukogodo history.

Official records   In addition to data collected in the field, Beth and I also obtained invaluable information from a variety of written sources in the Mukogodo area and elsewhere. In Don Dol, we obtained records from the local Roman Catholic mission on visits to their dispensary and mobile clinic and from the local office of the Kenyan government's livestock development program. In Nairobi, we obtained temperature and rainfall records for the Mukogodo area from the Kenya Meteorological Department and examined documents from the colonial era on the Mukogodo area in the Kenya National Archives.

REVISITING THE MUKOGODO AREA

Since Beth and I finished our fieldwork in 1987, I have made three trips back to the Mukogodo area. The first, in 1992, was with my archaeologist colleague from Texas A&M University, Dr. Bruce Dickson. We were accompanied by a Texas A&M undergraduate student named Martin Allen, and we were joined by Kennedy Mutundu, a graduate student in anthropology at Washington University in St. Louis. Our goal was to survey the Mukogodo rockshelters for future excavation. In 1993 I returned to Kenya to follow upon my study of Mukogodo parental behavior. The results of this study are described in Chapter 5. That same year I also helped Dickson and his crew with their excavations of one of the rockshelters we had surveyed in 1992. Dickson eventually excavated two Mukogodo rockshelters, Shurmai and Kakwa Lelash, and surveyed the surrounding area. This work has resulted in several publications and Ph.D. dissertations, including Kennedy Mutundu's at Washington University in St. Louis and those of G-Young Gang and Fred Pearl at Texas A&M University. I returned to the Mukogodo area in 2001, mainly to collect data on ethnicity. Those data are described in Chapter 6. The summer of 2001 also provided an opportunity for me to revisit the Kenya National Archives and to explore another set of colonial archives held in London at the British Public Records Office.

MY THEORETICAL INSPIRATION:
HUMAN BEHAVIORAL ECOLOGY

Anthropology may have the broadest subject matter of any discipline: the entire human experience. Any field with a subject matter that broad is necessarily going to be extraordinarily diverse in terms of what interests its practitioners, and anthropology is indeed diverse. Anthropologists work in a huge variety of scholarly traditions, from the most intuitive and humanistic to the most quantitative and scientific. Some derive their inspiration from literary criticism, others from economics, and still others from linguistics. This diversity gives anthropology a great deal of internal tension, but also a lot of energy and dynamism.

My own position in all of this is toward the scientific end of things. This means that I try to phrase my research questions as hypotheses that can be tested using data that I can gather in the field. I do occasionally engage in interpretations, using my ability to empathize with the people I study to understand their point of view, but that is not my primary concern, and I do not think that it is what I am particularly good at. The reason I approach things in this way is that I am chiefly interested in the evolution of human behavior. My inspiration comes from evolutionary biology and the study of animal behavior. This is an approach, often called *human behavioral ecology*, that has grown up over the past few decades as biologists, anthropologists, psychologists, and others have begun to use evolutionary biological theory to better understand the minds and behaviors of humans and other animals. The basic idea is simple: Does an organism's behavior match what we would expect based on our understanding of how evolution works?

The driving force in evolution, the thing that gives it a direction, is natural selection. This simply means that organisms of any species vary from individual to individual, and some variations leave more offspring than others. This is known as differential reproduction. Because natural selection is driven by differential reproduction, those of us who study the evolution of behavior tend to pay a great deal of attention to behaviors that impinge on reproduction, such as mating and parenting. We are also interested in other sorts of behavior, such as cooperation, conflict, resource acquisition, and even art and religion.

This may seem quite straightforward, and usually it is. However, when human behavioral ecology was developing in the 1970s, anthropologists, particularly cultural anthropologists, had a quick and mostly negative reaction to it: What about culture? Even a quick glance around the world is enough to convince anyone that culture—which I define as *socially transmitted information*—is an extraordinarily powerful force in shaping human behavior: people are biologically everywhere the same, but they have very diverse beliefs and behaviors. When people began to suggest that biology might also play a role in shaping behavior, those who study culture were understandably unnerved and, for the most part, unimpressed.

Earlier in this chapter I mentioned my graduate advisor, William Irons. In the 1970s, he was part of the new movement that became human behavioral ecology.

However, he was also trained as a cultural anthropologist, and he understood that this new approach had to find some way of accommodating culture. He suggested that culture is indeed a powerful force in shaping human behavior, but that it is most likely to do so in ways that are biologically adaptive. To test this, Irons and others have examined dozens of societies around the world to see whether what they value culturally leads to biological adaptation. Because natural selection is driven by differential reproduction, the specific prediction is that success in achieving cultural values should correlate with reproductive success. And indeed it does, routinely, all around the world. I will present one test of this hypothesis using my data from Mukogodo in Chapter 4.

Irons also recognized that culture does not always stay the same. That is, in fact, the great thing about culture: it allows us to change our behavior rapidly, without having to wait for our genes to change. This gives us a big advantage over organisms with little or no culture. Irons included an additional hypothesis concerning cultural change: When cultures change, they should do so in a way that tracks environmental change and so keeps behavior biologically adaptive. This is the specific idea I set out to test among the Mukogodo. I wanted to see whether their shift from hunting and gathering to pastoralism made adaptive sense at the level of individual reproduction. As you will see in Chapter 3, I found that it did, though the reason is rather surprising, even to me.

When I went to the field, I was well versed not only in Irons's ideas about the adaptiveness of culture but also in evolutionary theory and animal behavior studies more generally, and I was keen to find ways to test the many hypotheses I had learned about in my classes. Some of those ideas concerned reasons why parents might sometimes favor sons over daughters or daughters over sons. It turned out that the Mukogodo presented an opportunity to explore that issue as well, as I'll discuss in Chapter 5. These studies have become part of a body of research on dozens of peoples around the world over the past thirty years that confirm human behavioral ecology's validity and promise as an approach to anthropological research.

Keep in mind that my approach to the Mukogodo is just one of the many ways that anthropologists work. Another anthropologist might go there and look at completely different issues, choosing to focus on, say, their folktales rather than their reproductive patterns. Indeed, the German linguist Bernd Heine, whom we met at the beginning of this chapter, has continued to conduct studies not only of Yaaku but also the Mukogodo variant of Maa, along with studies of their botanical knowledge and beekeeping practices, together with his colleagues Matthias Brenzinger and Ingo Heine. In addition, Swiss anthropologist Urs Herren, who arrived in Mukogodo Division just as Beth and I were leaving in 1987, has conducted a study of the pastoralist economy of the non-Mukogodo peoples living in Mukogodo Division. Perhaps this book will inspire others to do new sorts of research in the Mukogodo area. Even better, perhaps Mukogodo themselves will soon be contributing to the literature on the area.

ETHNOGRAPHIC
TEXT FORMATION PROCESSES

At the same time that human behavioral ecology was developing, cultural anthropologists were radically rethinking the core of the discipline: ethnography. Ethnography means, quite simply, writing about ethnic groups, and books called ethnographies have been the main form of scholarship in cultural anthropology for decades. More broadly, ethnographic texts can take a variety of forms, not just books but also articles, films, recordings, and still photos. For most of the twentieth century, ethnographies were written in an authoritative style sometimes referred to as "ethnographic realism." This style produced ethnographies that sounded authoritative, with lots of declarative statements about what the people being studied believe and do. Messy details, such as how the fieldwork was actually done and disagreements among informants, were mostly ignored in the quest for a clear, well-organized account of a society and its culture.

But eventually anthropologists began to realize that society and culture themselves are not always so clear or so well organized. They then became concerned with how to document cultures and societies in ways that both reflect them better and that are more open about how ethnographic texts are created. This insight, known as the postmodern or textualist critique of ethnography, was fully articulated by people like George Marcus, Dick Cushman, Michael M. J. Fischer, and James Clifford in the 1980s. It is a powerful argument that should be taken seriously by everyone who conducts ethnographic fieldwork, attempts to write ethnography, reads ethnography, or uses information contained in ethnographies. The upshot of the critique is that it is best to face up to the complexities of culture and of efforts to understand and record it, and that includes being open with one's readers about how ethnographic texts are created. This critique has inspired a profound rethinking of the entire process of doing ethnography, ranging from how the characteristics of the fieldworker influence the final result, to how fieldnotes are taken, to how the final ethnography is written.

Those who originated the textualist critique, along with many other anthropologists, argue that it spells doom for efforts to build an anthropological science of human behavior. My opinion is that they are dead wrong about this. Far from preventing cultural anthropologists from doing science, an appreciation of the textualist critique is actually essential to accomplishing that goal. This is a point I like to explain to my students with an analogy from archaeology. Archaeologists know that if they want to understand the things they find in the ground, they must understand how their sites came to be. They need to understand, for instance, how human behavior creates various sorts of distributions of artifacts—trash piles, living sites, ritual sites, and so on. And they must understand how natural processes—erosion, burrowing animals, seismic activity, decay of organic materials—rearrange those sites. Without such an understanding, archaeologists would have a terrible time trying to use their excavations to reconstruct human prehistory. Similarly, if we want to understand contemporary behavior documented in ethnographic texts, then we need to know how those texts are created. Just as archaeologists must understand *archaeological site formation processes*, cultural anthropologists and anyone else who reads and uses ethnography must understand *ethnographic text formation processes*.

The problem is that even today many ethnographic texts are not written in a way that allows the reader to understand how they were created. They appear simply to have sprung up from nothing, like mushrooms after a rain. My hope is that this chapter has helped you to understand how this particular ethnographic text was created: who I am, what methods I used, how I chose my subject matter, and so on. The textualist critique will also inform the rest of this book. Although it would be tedious indeed for me to trace back every single bit of information to its source, I will do my best to keep you apprized of the status of my claims about the Mukogodo, whether they are my own speculation, musings or memories from a single informant, or the result of the analysis of large data sets compiled from many different informants. In this way, you will have the information you need to be a savvy reader of this particular ethnographic text.

RECOMMENDED READING

For other interesting accounts of anthropological fieldwork, try *I've Been Gone Far Too Long: Field Study Fiascoes and Expedition Disasters* (Monique Borgerhoff Mulder and Wendy Logsdon, editors, RDR Books, 1996) and *Dancing Skeletons: Life and Death in West Africa* (Katherine Dettwyler, Waveland Press, 1994). For insights into human behavioral ecology, I recommend my book *That Complex Whole: Culture and the Evolution of Human Behavior* (Westview Press, 1999) and *Adaptation and Human Behavior: An Anthropological Perspective* (Lee Cronk, Napoleon Chagnon, and William Irons, editors, Aldine de Gruyter, 2000). For more about the Maa language, there are no better sources than Frans Mol's three books: *Maa: A Dictionary of the Maasai Language and Folklore* (Marketing and Publishing Ltd., 1979), *Lessons in Maa: A Grammar of Maasai Language* (Maasai Centre, 1995), and *Maasai Language and Culture Dictionary* (Maasai Centre, 1996).

2

"People Who Live in Rocks"

THE ROCKS THEMSELVES

When I went hiking with my cave-dwelling friend LeKitiman, I did not pack a tent. There was no need to, because he knew all the best places to stay. Which is to say, he knew every rockshelter, large and small, in the Mukogodo hills. One theory about the word *Mukogodo* is that it originally meant "people who live in rocks," and that certainly described LeKitiman. And getting to know the Mukogodo people, not just LeKitiman, means getting to know the hills themselves. Every hillside, cliff, and valley has a name, and those names—Kanduko, Pesho, Toirai, and many others—serve as addresses for the people living there. These places are all linked by a network of trails that run like highways up and down the ancient hills and through the heavily eroded valleys.

Sitting just north of Mount Kenya in the northeast corner of a region called the Laikipia Plateau, the hills are some of the oldest rocks in the world, dating to the time before about half a billion years ago known as the Precambrian (see Figure 2.1). The hills form a series of roughly parallel ridges running southeast to northwest. The easternmost ridge rises dramatically from the surrounding plain and is marked by a series of striking peaks: Lolkurugi, whose name means Crow Mountain; Ol Doinyo Lossos, with its distinctive pyramidal shape; Ol Doinyo Loo Lbang'i, or Hemp Mountain; the thickly forested Kiapei; the cliff-faced Ol Doinyo Parsenik; and, finally, at the southern end of the range, Ol Doinyo Sang'a. To the west is another prominent ridge marked by Ol Doinyo Lengileng'e with its knoblike peak in the north and Wandiki, which, at more than 7,000 feet (about 2,100 meters), is the highest peak in the range, just east of our house at Kuri-Kuri. Between those two ridges lies the Siekuu River, which, like all streams in the area, flows only after a heavy rain. Figure 2.2 shows Beth collecting water in a rainy season pool in the bed of the Siekuu River. At the southern end of the Siekuu Valley

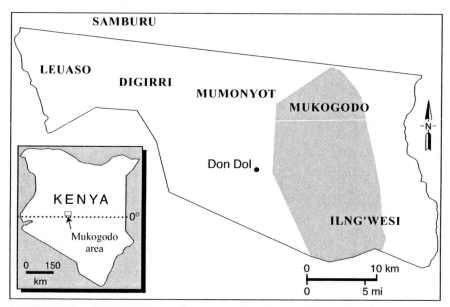

*Figure 2.1   Map of the Mukogodo area, showing approximate locations of some of the ethnic groups men-
tioned in the text. The border shown is that of the area now known as Mukogodo Division, which during the
colonial period was called the Dorobo Reserve. The shaded area shows the approximate location of the
Mukogodo forest and hills.* MIKE SIEGEL, RUTGERS CARTOGRAPHY LAB.

where the ridges meet sits the large, grassy glade called Anandanguru, where we
made our first Mukogodo friends.

West of Wandiki and Kuri-Kuri, the ridges continue, gradually losing altitude
until they reach the Euaso Nyiro, or Brown River, the only permanently flowing
water in the area. The Euaso Nyiro forms the western boundary of Mukogodo
Division. On the south, the ancient rocks of Mukogodo gradually give way to the
more recently formed slopes of Mount Kenya, a huge extinct volcano and Africa's
second highest peak. To the east and north, the hills drop off quickly to the low-
land, which Maa speakers call *purkel*, a flat area of sandy alluvial deposits and
rocky outcroppings. The lowlands are crossed by more dry river beds such as the
Kipsing to the north and the Enkare Ntare, which means "Water of the Small
Stock," to the east.

LORIEN AND OTHER FANTASTIC PLACES

My first encounter with a Kenyan forest in 1981 had brought to mind the woods
described in the fantasy novels of J. R. R. Tolkien, and those same vivid images return every time I hike in Mukogodo. For me, the highlight of those walks is the
cool, shady stands of *morijoi* trees (*Acokanthera schimperi*). Dark, gnarled, and

Figure 2.2   Beth collecting water from a rainy season pool in the Siekuu Valley. LEE CRONK

twisted, the *morijoi* even possess a sort of magic: they are the source of the poison once used by Mukogodo hunters. To further delight a Tolkien fan there is even a place named Lorien, though I cannot report having seen any elves there.

The Mukogodo forest is quite unlike what most people imagine when they think of an African forest. Rather than being hot, humid, and rainy, the Mukogodo forest is dry and, thanks to the altitude, surprisingly cool. The dominant species are cedar (*Junipera procera*), wild olive (*Olea africana*), and, reflecting the fact that the area is prone to drought, cactuslike candelabra trees (*Euphorbia* spp.). Particularly in areas with dense stands of cedar and olive trees, the effect is more like what one expects to find in the Mediterranean or California regions rather than tropical Africa. Below the forests are grasslands, such as those in the huge glade called the Anandanguru Plain as well as the area stretching out west from our base at Kuri-Kuri. At the lowest altitudes, chiefly in the Siekuu Valley and in the *purkel*, the dominant species are thorny acacia trees (*Acacia* spp.).

This quick description of the vegetation of the area is clearly that of a non-Mukogodo. Mukogodo themselves are passionate botanists, possessing an intimate knowledge of the plants in their area and their many uses, particularly as medicines. Indeed, the Maa word for medicine is the same as that for plant: *ol-cani*. Some anthropologists say that fieldworkers should allow the people they study to dictate the focus of their research. If I had followed that advice, I would probably have done ethnobotany because of the tremendous interest so many Mukogodo have in plants. Just within the first few weeks of my arrival I had documented the names, uses, and descriptions of more than 150 different species of plant, despite the fact that this was not important to my research plans. After only ten days in Mukogodo, I jotted in my journal that "I am getting so tired of writing down tree names."

Fortunately, there are other scholars who do have a great interest in ethnobotany. A group of German linguists has documented Mukogodo botanical knowledge (Brenzinger et al. 1994), and it is truly encyclopedic. In addition to the many medicinal plants, some plants can be used as food for people, some provide for forage for animals, some provide construction materials, others are used as fuel, and so on. Perhaps the favorite tree of most Mukogodo is the *lorien*, or wild olive tree. Although they do not harvest its fruits, the wood is prized for fires because it burns slowly and with little smoke. Olive wood is especially prized for the flavor it gives milk when they use it to char and sterilize the insides of their milk gourds, and it is common for people visiting an area where there is no *lorien* to bring a few sticks as a housewarming gift. Beth and I came to like both the tree and the word *lorien* so much that we decided that it might make for a nice name for our first child, though we Americanized it to Lauren. The most polite way to refer to a Maa speaker is not by his or her name but rather with reference to their children, and so Beth and I are now known by many Mukogodo as Ngoto and Menye Lorien: "The Mother and Father of Lorien."

The distribution of wild animal species is also determined largely by altitude. The lowlands to the east and north of the forest contain a great deal of large game, including zebra, giraffe, and a wide range of antelopes, including the cowlike eland, the graceful gerenuk, and the tiny dik-dik. Carnivores, including lions, are also there. In the forest live other antelopes, such as bushbuck, along with many buffalo. Rhinos used to live in the forest, but more than thirty years ago conservationists removed the few that remained there to protect them from poachers. The largest predator in the forest is the leopard. Some large animals, including elephants and impala, live at all altitudes in the Mukogodo area. A wide variety of smaller animals also live in the area, including snakes, birds, and the rodentlike hyrax. The main primate species, other than humans, are olive baboons and vervet monkeys. A large number of nocturnal species also live there but are rarely observed, including aardvarks and honey badgers.

Most of the wild animals in the area stay away from humans, and, now that Mukogodo no longer hunt for food, humans mostly do the same for the animals. But some confrontations inevitably occur. Buffalo, when surprised, can be very dangerous. One pregnant woman was killed not long before we arrived in 1985, and about a year after that event her husband's leg was broken by a buffalo in almost the same spot. Elephants can be very aggressive as well, and a Mukogodo man was killed when he surprised one on a trail in early 1987. Elephants are also crop raiders. Although most Mukogodo do not raise many crops, some families plant small stands of maize and beans in years when rainfall is good. Almost no fence is strong enough to keep out a hungry elephant, and they often destroy entire gardens. One woman living at Anandanguru told us a terrifying story about huddling in the dark with her children while an elephant, having just dined on her maize field, scratched its backside on her house. Leopards hunt livestock, and it is suspected that one old Mukogodo man might have been killed by one in the early 1990s, though no one knows for sure because his body was never recovered. Other animals are just pests, such as the baboons that raid crops and occasionally eat lambs and kids (i.e., baby goats) and the honey badgers that destroy beehives.

A COOL, DRY PLACE

The Mukogodo area, like the rest of the Laikipia Plateau, has a climate that is wonderful for visitors but that can be problematic for people who live there. Due to the altitude, it is much cooler than one would expect from a place so close to the equator. At our house at Kuri-Kuri, the high temperature was usually around 85 degrees Fahrenheit (29 degrees Celsius), but at night the temperature can drop to around 55 degrees Fahrenheit (13 degrees Celsius). Humidity is very low. Temperature is strongly affected by altitude, and so in the lowlands surrounding the forest it is typically about 10 to 20 degrees Fahrenheit (about 6 to 11 degrees Celsius) warmer than at Kuri-Kuri. Temperatures do not vary much through the year, though I have been told by some Mukogodo that August is slightly cooler than the rest of the year.

Rainy and cloudy days are also quite cool. Rain is perhaps the single greatest preoccupation of Mukogodo and other East African herders. Rain's importance is reflected in the fact that the Maa word for God, *Enkai*, is also the word for the sky, the source of rain. A typical question to ask while greeting someone in Maa is the location and amount of recent rains, and people frequently asked me and Beth whether it had rained recently back home in America. Kenya has two rainy seasons, one that usually peaks in April and another in November or December, that are produced by the same Indian Ocean weather patterns responsible for the monsoons in South Asia. Most of Kenya receives more rain during the "long rains" of March and April, but in Mukogodo the heaviest precipitation usually arrives during the so-called "short rains" of November and December. During and immediately after a good rainy season, vegetation thrives, turning the landscape green and providing plenty of grass for livestock, and the hills' many natural rock catchments fill with water. During the dry seasons as well as during the area's frequent droughts, vegetation turns brown and dies back and most water sources dry up. The average annual rainfall between 1964 and 1984 in Don Dol was 538 millimeters (21 inches). That is roughly comparable to the average annual precipitation in San Angelo, Texas, which is also a plateau region with many livestock. But rainfall in Mukogodo is highly variable. Long droughts are common, such as in 1980, when 223 millimeters (less than 9 inches) fell. That is comparable to the average annual precipitation in Albuquerque, New Mexico, and other parts of America's southwestern deserts. Exceptionally rainy years also occasionally occur. The rainiest on record was 1968, when more than a meter of rain (39 inches) fell. That is comparable to the average annual precipitation in Albany, New York.

Rainfall also varies a lot with altitude, with more rain usually falling in the grassy and forested highlands than in the semiarid lowlands. However, the only official rain gauge outside Don Dol, at Anandanguru, is not well maintained. I know this because I happened to come across it while taking refuge from the rain in the house of one of the Anandanguru forest guards. Sitting on a bed, which is the only place to sit in most Mukogodo houses, I felt something hit my boot, and I pulled a graduated glass cylinder—the Anandanguru rain gauge—out from under the bed. I asked the forest guard's wife what it was, and she said, "The thing of the white people." Needless to say, no rain was being measured that day! Despite the spotty records at Anandanguru, enough data are available that we can be confident that rainfall there is usually slightly higher than at Don Dol, in keeping with its slightly higher altitude.

THE ORIGINS OF "THE PEOPLE WHO LIVE IN ROCKS"

Throughout the 1990s, a team of archaeologists led by D. Bruce Dickson of Texas A&M University surveyed and excavated the rockshelters in the Mukogodo hills in an effort to reconstruct the prehistory of the region. Figure 2.3 shows one of their digs in progress. Although when the project began in 1992 our original goal was to examine the caves for evidence of recent occupation by Mukogodo hunter-gatherers, test pits dug in one rockshelter, Shurmai, in 1993 revealed that some of the caves had been occupied for much, much longer. The deepest strata at Shurmai included stone tools manufactured between 40,000 and 50,000 years ago. Other parts of Shurmai as well as another rockshelter called Kakwa Lelash contained stone tools and fossilized and unfossilized animal bone from later occupations, but there is a long gap between those early occupations and any materials that we can confidently associate with the Mukogodo or their direct ancestors.

Another window onto Mukogodo origins is DNA. In 1993 I collected cheek swabs from Mukogodo so that anthropological geneticists Terry Melton and Mark Stoneking of Pennsylvania State University could analyze the DNA in their mitochondria. Mitochondrial DNA (mtDNA) is different from nuclear DNA because it does not undergo recombination and because it is inherited only through women, not through men. In order to get a sample that would reveal as much as possible about Mukogodo origins and relationships to other groups in the region, I used my genealogical data to construct matrilineal descent charts for the entire Mukogodo population. I then sought out individuals whose oldest known female

Figure 2.3   Excavation in the Shurmai rockshelter. D. BRUCE DICKSON

ancestors were identified by my genealogical informants as ethnically Mukogodo. This eliminated a lot of people from the project because so many non-Mukogodo women have married into the group over the past century. I also collected cheek swabs from some individuals known to have non-Mukogodo female ancestors for comparative purposes. The results revealed that my genealogies are very accurate: in only one case did an individual's mtDNA not match that of those who were supposed to be in the same matriline. In some cases, mtDNA from different matrilines matched, suggesting that if we could obtain genealogies that went back farther in time, we would probably find that people in those matrilines share a common ancestress. Interestingly, Mukogodo mtDNA is similar to that of other African foragers such as the Mbuti of Zaire and the Hadza of Tanzania, possibly suggesting some deep connection among these peoples.

Languages provide another way to explore history. Africa is home to four major language families—Khoisan, Afro-Asiatic, Nilo-Saharan, and Congo-Kordofanian (or Niger-Kordofanian)—and all four play a part in the Mukogodo story. Khoisan languages are now spoken only in southwestern Africa and possibly by two groups a few hundred kilometers south of Mukogodo in Tanzania, the Hadza and Sandawe. Although the inclusion of Sandawe and Hadza in the Khoisan family is not accepted by all linguists, they share some distinctive features with Khoisan languages, most notably the use of a variety of click sounds, which are indicated in writing with punctuation marks such as !, =, and /. It is thought that all of those languages may be representatives of a time several thousand years ago when Khoisan-speaking hunters and gatherers lived across most of sub-Saharan Africa. A tiny remnant of that period might be found in the old Mukogodo language, Yaaku. Linguistic historian Christopher Ehret at the University of California at Los Angeles has identified a similarity between the Sandawe word for bee (*l'eka*) and the Yaaku word for honey (*sika*). As slim as that connection is, it is suggestive that today's Mukogodo may have their cultural roots in the very distant past when East Africa was a land of only hunter-gatherers.

Yaaku itself is not Khoisan but rather Afro-Asiatic, which means that it is very distantly related to such languages as Hebrew and Arabic. Yaaku is part of the Eastern Cushitic branch of the Afro-Asiatic family, which also includes Somali and Rendille. Christopher Ehret has used Yaaku and other languages to reconstruct much of East African history, and it appears that Yaaku is a remnant of a time when speakers of it and related languages lived not only in the Mukogodo area but also across much of the rest of what is now Kenya and Ethiopia. Based on reconstructions of their vocabulary, we think that the Yaakuans were herders and that they were the predominant ethnic group in East Africa between about 3,000 and 1,000 years ago. Archaeologists have found sites elsewhere in Kenya that may have been created by Yaakuan-speaking pastoralists more than 2,000 years ago. Those sites include an arrangement of stones that suggest that the Yaakuans had sophisticated astronomical and calendrical knowledge, and analyses of ancient rock art suggest that they may have left a lasting cultural mark on East African pastoralists through their animal brands.

Although ancient speakers of Yaakuan languages may have mostly been herders, those who were to become Mukogodo were probably primarily hunters. This is suggested by the origins of the word *yaaku* itself. Around a thousand years ago, almost all Yaakuan speakers were displaced or absorbed by herders speaking Southern Nilotic languages, part of the Nilo-Saharan family. Today, Southern Nilotic languages are spoken by people who live far to the south and west of the Mukogodo area, like the Kalenjin of Kenya and the Datog of Tanzania. The word *yaaku* appears to have begun as a Southern Nilotic word for "hunters," suggesting that a reliance on hunting among the ancestors of the Mukogodo goes back at least as far as the advent of the Southern Nilotes. The Yaaku language itself was well suited to the life of a hunting and beekeeping group. For example, Yaaku includes five words for different types of beehive, one of which means "a beehive with three openings and long endings." Maa, in contrast, has just one word for beehive, which is also used for any other sort of container, from a 35mm film canister to a paint bucket.

The fourth African language family, Congo-Kordofanian, is represented in most of East, Central, and Southern Africa by the subgroup of closely related languages called Bantu. The closest Bantu speakers to Mukogodo are Meru, who live southeast of the Mukogodo Hills on the northeastern slopes of Mount Kenya. Historian Jeffrey A. Fadiman has used Meru oral histories to reconstruct much of their history, and they include the earliest mentions of a group called something like "Mukogodo": *Mokuru, Mukoko, Mugukuru, Mu-uthiu, Mukuru, Mugukuru,* and *Aruguru.* Fadiman's modern Meru informants say that these names all refer to the people now known as Mukogodo. This fits well with an assertion made by a British colonial surveyor as well as some of my Mukogodo informants that the name *Mukogodo* means "people who live in rocks" because one word for rock in Meru and closely related languages spoken nearby is *ngogoto*. This certainly is more plausible than suggestions made by other of my informants, such as the idea that the word *Mukogodo* comes from a plant called *mookoni* that they used to eat or from a Maa phrase meaning "the decorated ox" *(ol-mong'o koodo).* Fadiman's Meru informants reported that the people they remember as Mukogodo lived during the early 1700s as hunters and gatherers in alliance with a group of Eastern Cushitic pastoralists, trading forest products for milk and warning each other of attacks.

WHAT MUKOGODO SAY
ABOUT THEIR EARLY HISTORY

Many Mukogodo are avid historians, and the stories they tell suggest that the people who now consider themselves Mukogodo have deep roots in the area combined with several grafts, some ancient and some more recent. One thing that all my informants agree upon is that the people of the Lentolla lineage, whose territory included the large mountains called Ol Doinyo Lossos and Lolkurugi, are the quintessential Mukogodo, the earliest known inhabitants of the forest. The last Mukogodo cave dweller, the one named LeKitiman whom I introduced in Chapter 1, was a member of that lineage, and he was emphatic that his family had no other point of origin than those two mountains. The fact that the traditional Lentolla territory was also by far the largest of any Mukogodo family also suggests that it may have been the first to establish itself.

Another portion of the Mukogodo, the Sialo clan, seem to have quite a different history, and perhaps became a part of the Yaakuan-speaking hunter-gatherers that we refer to as "Mukogodo" only in the eighteenth or nineteenth centuries. The Sialo territories are located in the southeastern portion of the Mukogodo Hills. That area is the closest to Meru, so it is possible that the Meru oral traditions recorded by Fadiman refer primarily to Sialo Mukogodo rather than to all Mukogodo. This fits well with a specific story about Mukogodo in the nineteenth century that is best remembered by my Sialo informants but either not known or actively denied by informants from other clans. The story is that until the middle or late nineteenth century, they lived in the lowlands east of the Mukogodo Hills around a small hill now called Ol Doinyo Sarge, or Blood Mountain. There they hunted, kept bees, gathered plants, and herded a few goats, in alliance with wealthier, more powerful pastoralists called Kirrimani. Some informants told me that their ancestors were the Kirrimani themselves, while others said that they were distinct groups. In the late nineteenth century, the Kirrimani were defeated by other pastoralists, probably Maa speakers, and moved to what is now northern Kenya, where they merged with the Rendille. The hunters and beekeepers remained behind, perhaps to become the Sialo clan of the Mukogodo. The Rendille version of history complements the Mukogodo view. In the Rendille language, "Kirrimma" is a nickname applied to a group of families from the Saalle clan that were outcast due to their wealth and arrogance. Though not conclusive, the similarity between the clan names Sialo and Saalle is intriguing.

The idea that the Sialo are a relatively recent addition to Mukogodo is supported by the fact that their territories are relatively small and are clustered side-by-side on the slopes of the hills facing Ol Doinyo Sarge. Furthermore, the Sialo have different customs, particularly food taboos, than other Mukogodo. Most Mukogodo would never eat elephant meat, arguing that because elephants have mammary glands that are arranged like a woman's breasts rather than like an udder, eating elephants is tantamount to eating people. The Sialo, however, had no such prohibition. Fadiman's Meru informants tell about a Mukogodo group that once was tolerated in Meru territory because they hunted the elephants that raided Meru crops, and perhaps there is a connection between that story and the Sialo willingness to eat elephant meat. Similarly, most Mukogodo will not eat pigs or their wild relatives, which are considered disgusting, or chickens or their eggs because they forage for their food in manure. My Sialo informants, on the other hand, expressed no such revulsion. When I asked one older Sialo man whether he used to eat wild birds, he replied, "Yes, they taste just like chicken." When I asked members of other clans the same question, they replied, "No, they are just like chicken!" Sialo informants also reported that they ate the piglike warthog as well as ostrich eggs, while members of other clans reported that they did not eat such foods. Finally, some Mukogodo think that the Sialo tend to look a bit different from most other Mukogodo, referring to some of them as "the brown people" because of their tendency to have light brown rather than dark brown skin.

A common strategy in East Africa when droughts strike or when disease destroys crops and herds has been to resort to hunting and gathering, and the Mukogodo and their ancestors have probably been absorbing such economic refugees for many centuries. Two Mukogodo families got their start in this way in the nineteenth century when impoverished Maasai men adopted the Mukogodo way of life, including hunting, beekeeping, and speaking Yaaku. The first to arrive was a man named Kimbai. He founded the lineage called Leitiko, which means zebra in Maa. Based on a reconstruction of his genealogy that I prepared with the help of his direct descendant and my single best genealogical informant, Stephen Lereman LeLeitiko, I estimate that Kimbai arrived in about 1840. He was adopted as part of the Orondi clan, who taught him Yaaku and how to hunt and keep bees, and the Leitiko lineage established a large territory in the forest for hunting and beekeeping.

The second Maasai immigrant was Mairoi Ole Matunge. Mairoi had been a Laikipiak, a section of the Maasai that was defeated in a war with other Maasai in the 1870s. He probably arrived in Mukogodo, impoverished from the war, around 1880. My Mukogodo informants remembered him—or, more likely, stories of him—as having been a remarkable man. He is especially fondly recalled by members of the Matunge lineage he founded. They say that when Mairoi arrived, two Mukogodo men, Lojulo LePokisa and Lorukomotonyi LePardero, recognized him as a fellow *oltung'ani ogol*. This phrase translates literally as "hard person," and it means not so much that he was a "tough guy" as that he was active and hardworking. They adopted him into the Orondi clan and set him up with a small territory. He became very successful as a Mukogodo, eventually marrying four times and having at least twelve children, according to a genealogy I worked on with his descendant Saroni LeMatunge. He is remembered for having organized livestock raids against the Meru. He is also remembered for arranging peace with them, but not until after disaster struck: in retaliation for one of his raids, a group of Meru attacked the Mukogodo living closest to them, members of the Sialo clan, and nearly exterminated an entire Mukogodo lineage. By the time Europeans first came across the Mukogodo in the 1890s, Mairoi was prominent enough that he was referred to by the Europeans as "chief," though the Mukogodo themselves recognized no such status, and the first known photographs of a Mukogodo are probably of Mairoi. One of those photographs is reproduced here as Figure 2.4. A document from the colonial era that I found in the Public Records Office in London indicates that Mairoi died in 1919.

When during all of these events did the group of cave-dwelling, Yaaku-speaking hunters and beekeepers that we call Mukogodo really gel? Based on the stories of Kimbai LeLeitiko and Mairoi Ole Matunge, I estimate that this occurred some time in the middle of the nineteenth century, probably between 1840 and 1880. My reasoning is based on a peculiarity of the Mukogodo system of territories owned by lineages. The Leitiko lineage founded by Kimbai established a territory roughly the same size as those of other Mukogodo lineages, suggesting that the territorial system was still taking shape when he arrived. That territorial system is a good indicator of a shared identity because it suggests some agreement about broad legal issues such as rights to land and the resources it holds, such as game, flowering plants, beehives, water sources, and rockshelters. The Matunge territory, in contrast, is rather small, suggesting that the territorial boundaries, perhaps along with other aspects of a shared Mukogodo culture and ethnic identity, became well established following the arrival of Kimbai but before the arrival of Mairoi.

MAKING A LIVING IN THE FOREST

Residential patterns

I often refer to the Mukogodo as having lived in "caves" because that is the simplest translation for the Maa word *enkapune* (plural: *inkapuniak*) that they themselves

Figure 2.4   Mairoi Ole Matunge. From Ethnology of A-Kamba and Other East African Tribes *by C.W. Hobley.* USED BY PERMISSION OF CAMBRIDGE UNIVERSITY PRESS.

use for their former homes. Actually, their "caves" are mostly just small rock over-hangs, big enough to keep the rain off a large family but not much more than that. There are many such rockshelters tucked all over the Mukogodo Hills. The first to be excavated by Bruce Dickson's team, one called Shurmai in the side of a hill called Shurdiga, is relatively spacious, with a good view of the valley below and a rain-water catchment nearby. Older Mukogodo who lived in the caves as children re-member them with fondness, and even today groups of *murran* will occasionally visit them for meat-roasting parties. I myself would prefer to spend a night in a Mukogodo rockshelter than in one of their houses, mostly because the ventilation is so much better. When the Mukogodo were living in the caves, each family would control several of them located at different locations and altitudes within their ter-ritory, and they would move from one to another as the seasons changed and foods became available in different areas. When hunting in an area with no good rock-shelters, they would also occasionally build small shelters out of brush.

It is not clear whether the territorial rights applied to things other than rock-shelters and beehive placement. Most of my informants reported that in the rock-shelter days not only beehive placement but also hunting, gathering, and water rights were also limited to the members of the lineage that owned a particular ter-ritory. One of my best historical informants, on the other hand, disagreed, arguing that people could hunt anywhere they chose. David Rosen, an American anthro-pology student who spent a few weeks in Mukogodo in 1968, reports that the ter-ritories were for beehive placement and water sources, but not hunting or gather-ing, which were open to everyone. D. G. Worthy, a British colonial official stationed in Don Dol during the late 1950s, was told that each lineage had exclusive rights to all resources in its territory except water, which was open to all. It may be the case that all of these accounts contain elements of the truth, and even those informants who argued that territorial rights were limited remembered that a general respect for territory was considered important. One man remembered that it was considered bad form to travel uninvited in another lineage's territory because seeing another family's flowers, which are crucial for honey production, might breed envy. Good etiquette, if not Mukogodo customary law, also held that it was best to hunt on someone else's territory only if invited to do so, and such invitations are remembered as having been quite common. Also, all projectiles, such as arrows, were marked to indicate the owner of the point, so that if a territorial violation inadvertently occurred when a wounded animal crossed into a neighbor's territory, it would still be clear who had shot the animal in the first place.

Honey

Not all hunter-gatherers delineate territories. The fact that the Mukogodo did have them reflects the importance of beekeeping to their way of life. Unlike game animals, beehives stay put and so can be economical to defend. Beekeeping was so important to Mukogodo that the German linguist Matthias Brenzinger and his colleagues Bernd and Ingo Heine have conducted a detailed study of it. A typical Mukogodo hive is about a meter long and about a third of a meter wide. It is made of a hollowed log, with lids in the ends and a small opening so that bees can come and go. Often, they are made from the crotch of a tree so that they are shaped like a "Y." A finished hive would be placed in the branches of a tree. Figure 2.5 shows our friend Kosima Ole Leitiko checking a hive hanging from a low branch. Like Western beekeepers, Mukogodo men used smoke to make the bees docile so that the honeycomb could be extracted, though they wore no special protective clothing. In addition to the honey, they also harvested some of the combs containing bee larvae. Bee larvae are less sweet than combs containing only honey, but they are still flavorful and contain a lot of vitamin A, and some people actually prefer them to honey.

The combination of comb, honey, and larvae would be stuffed into a bucket and taken home. In the old days, the buckets, called *chang'orr*, were carved from wood and fitted with leather caps, but these days everyone uses old paint or cooking oil cans. Because the art of *chang'orr*-making has virtually disappeared and the few *chang'orrs* remaining in Mukogodo houses are rapidly deteriorating, I have made a point of trying to buy as many of them as I can every time I visit so that they are preserved for the future. Unfortunately, I still have only a handful of them, ranging from a large one that could hold several liters to a tiny one, probably once owned by a child, that could hold only a small cupful. One of honey's wonderful properties is that, rather than rotting, it simply crystallizes and can be stored for long periods of time. When they were living in rockshelters, Mukogodo families would load many *chang'orrs* with honey and stash them in secret caves

Figure 2.5   Kosima Ole Leitiko checking one of his log hives. BETH LEECH

for future use. When we conducted the archaeological survey in 1992, Bruce Dickson and I were hoping to find some of these old *chang'orrs*, like chests of buried treasure stashed away in the caves, but unfortunately by the time we arrived they had all either decayed or been recovered.

These days, most honey is consumed soon after it is harvested, but some is used to make honey wine. The basic recipe for honey wine is simple: put honey, water, and the pith of an aloe plant called *suguroi* in a large gourd and leave it for a few days. Although the honey is essential because of the sugar it provides, the real key to this recipe is the suguroi plant. The plant itself is a succulent that resembles sisal. Its pith looks like a long yellow sponge and, when freshly cut, smells something like pineapple. Suguroi piths need to be dried before use, and it is common to see them spread out on rooftops to dry in the sun. These days it is sometimes easier to buy refined sugar than to obtain honey, so people occasionally make "honey wine" without any honey at all. The result is noticeably less flavorful than real honey wine, but it still tastes good and has about as much alcohol as beer. Whether it is made with honey or sugar, it tastes a little like hard cider.

Many Mukogodo men always seem to have some honey wine on hand, and an occasional cup of it is one of the real treats of a day of fieldwork there. It is also important to have a lot of honey wine on hand for major ceremonies and celebrations, when a great deal of it is consumed.

Although man-made hives were undoubtedly the most important source of honey, Mukogodo men also seek out naturally occurring hives in hollow trees and clefts in the rock. They are aided tremendously by a bird called a *honey guide*. One of the great delights of a hike with Mukogodo men through their forests is an encounter with one of these amazing birds. In Maa, they are called *njoshoroi*, but scientists gave them what is perhaps their most descriptive name: *Indicator indicator*. During a hike in an African forest, you will often hear a distinctive chattering call from the brush alongside the trail. Once you have heard that call, you will always be able to recognize it. If you follow the bird, it will lead you to a beehive that it has already located. The bird's judgment is not always good, and sometimes it leads you to a man-made hive that belongs to someone else or to a naturally occurring hive that is in an inaccessible location, but its trick really does work. Biologists speculate that the honey guide evolved this behavior as a form of symbiosis with the honey badger, a partnership that uses the bird's superior information about the location of hives and the badger's superior equipment for breaking into them—its claws—for the benefit of both species. At some point humans entered the picture as substitutes for the badgers, and now not only Mukogodo but people all over Africa use the honey guide to help them find wild hives.

The importance of honey for Mukogodo as foragers was reflected in the seriousness with which they treated honey theft. This is the theme of a cautionary tale that several of my informants shared with me. The story is that some time long ago, perhaps around the turn of the twentieth century, a boy from one lineage was caught stealing honey from a neighboring lineage's hive. Violence ensued, and in the confusion an arrow put out the eye of the honey thief's mother. The question of whether that story is true in its details is beside the point because it serves to remind future generations of the seriousness of honey theft. Honey theft is still taken very seriously today, although honey is no longer a major source of calories. During 1986, a group of three young men were caught stealing honey from an older man's hive. The man was incensed, but, like most disputes in the Mukogodo area, the case was settled peacefully through a long, careful discussion rather than through violence. At the end of the day it was agreed that the young men would each pay him several head of cattle. Although it was unlikely that any of them would ever actually pay since none had any stock at all at that time, the victim was satisfied that they had publicly acknowledged their responsibility for the theft.

Hunting, trapping, and gathering
Figure 2.6 shows a group of Mukogodo hunters equipped with bows and arrows for hunting large game. Even though Mukogodo hunters did pursue a wide variety

of species, the main source of meat in their diet was surprisingly unspectacular by the standards of African fauna: the hyrax. Hyrax resemble large burrowing rodents like groundhogs and other marmots, though biologists report that they are actually more closely related to elephants than to rodents. The variety favored by Mukogodo hunters was the rock hyrax, which lives in the many nooks and crannies in the rock formations that occur across eastern and southern Africa. Hunting hyrax was a simple affair. LeKitiman, the last Mukogodo cave dweller, described it this way: sharpen a stick, ram it into a hole where hyrax are known to live, and pull out a skewered hyrax. Hyrax too deep in their holes to be skewered could be smoked out. Whether skewered or smoked out, cooking a hyrax was simple: Toss it on the fire, bury it with coals so that it bakes, and then eat it. Excavations of the Mukogodo rockshelters confirm the importance of hyrax to their diet: more than two-thirds of identifiable bones and bone fragments in the upper layers of the rockshelters were from hyrax. Other important food species were mainly antelopes, ranging in size from the tiny dik-diks that are so common in the lowlands on up to huge elands. The largest game routinely eaten were buffalo, which are said to taste like beef, and giraffe, which Mukogodo say taste like goat. Rhinoceros were also hunted, but mainly for the horns, which could be exchanged with non-Mukogodo for livestock, crops, and manufactured goods like beads and iron. Rhinoceros meat was not prohibited, but some informants report that they were not deliberately hunted for meat because their flesh has a strong smell. Perhaps for that reason, some say that rhinoceros meat has great healing powers. Elephants were also hunted, but again mainly for the ivory trade rather than for meat, which was prohibited to most Mukogodo. The exception to this rule, as described above, was the Sialo clan, who had no taboo against eating elephant.

Other than sharpened sticks for skewering hyraxes, the main tool of a Mukogodo hunter was his bow and arrow. Bows were simply curved pieces of wood, and arrows were carried in wooden quivers with leather lids and shoulder straps. Arrow shafts were made from the reedy stalks of a plant called *labaai* (*Psiadia punctulata*) and fitted with iron points. The Mukogodo had no blacksmiths of their own, but because iron has been smelted in East Africa for many centuries, they were able to trade for it. I have seen two main varieties of iron point. One has a large, heavy head and no barbs, and is used to kill smaller game simply by its impact. The other variety has a somewhat smaller head with sharp barbs behind it. This type is slathered with poison made from the *morijoi* tree. The barbed points were designed to lodge themselves under the skin of the prey so that the poison could take effect. Nowadays there is also a third type of arrow that is used for obtaining blood from a cow's neck without killing it. It has a small rounded point and no fletching since it has only to fly a few inches.

Before iron became available, the Mukogodo or their ancestors presumably used obsidian and other types of stone for their projectile points. Although nowadays no Mukogodo have any knowledge of the art of knapping projectile points from stone, it is still easy to find bits of obsidian not only in the rockshelters but

Figure 2.6 Mukogodo hunters. From Peoples and Cultures of Kenya *by Andrew Fedders and Cynthia Salvadori.* USED BY PERMISSION OF CYNTHIA SALVADORI.

also all over the landscape, despite the fact that the closest obsidian source is many kilometers away. These days many children wear necklaces containing small pieces of obsidian, which is thought by some Mukogodo to keep away disease.

The other main hunting weapon was the *punat*, a sort of harpoon with a long, heavy shaft and a large detachable head used for very large game, such as elephants. The British explorer Joseph Thomson (1885: 448–49) gives a vivid description of the use of a *punat*, which he probably observed among another group of Kenyan hunter-gatherers he refers to as "Andorobbo":

> In hunting the elephant the Andorobbo use a peculiar harpoon. In shape it is like the rammer of a cannon, the heavy head being intended to give additional weight in dealing a blow. In the thickened part is placed a weapon like a short but thick arrow, fifteen inches long, the head of the arrow being smeared over with the deadly poison of the murju. The whole spear is little short of eight feet. With

this the elephant is attacked at close quarters, the arrow part being driven into the great brute, and being loosely fixed in the handle, it remains when the latter is withdrawn. Another arrow is then affixed, and the same operation performed. It is said that an elephant will live a very short time after being thus stabbed, and entire herds are killed without one escaping, so dexterous and daring are these hunters.

Although Thomson made this observation more than a century before I started working with the Mukogodo, this is almost identical to the *punat*s I have seen and the descriptions I have heard of their use. I have a *punat* in my office that I asked a Mukogodo man to make for me, and it has exactly the cannon rammer shape Thomson describes, though it is shorter than the eight-foot one Thomson saw. The head that was made for it is entirely iron because scrap metal is easy to come by now, but when metal was more scarce Mukogodo hunters would make their *punat* points of wood, with a slot carved in one end where an arrowhead could be slipped in. One of the highlights of the archaeological survey in which I participated in 1992 was the discovery of an old wooden *punat* point on the floor of one of the rockshelters, carved with a distinctive cross-hatched design to indicate its owner. Mukogodo men who are old enough to have seen or participated in hunting with *punat*s say that a hunter or group of hunters would approach an elephant with *punat*s in hand and quivers full of points slung to their sides, thrusting as many times as they dared before running away and waiting for the poison to take effect.

Mukogodo men also used a variety of traps. Neckhold snares were placed high between trees to catch giraffes, while leghold snares were placed close to the ground to catch smaller game, including dik-diks. Older Mukogodo men also report the use of deadfall traps, in which a heavy log or rock was placed to fall on an animal that set off a trigger. Their most spectacular trap was called a *ng'ereng'et*, and it was reminiscent of a *punat*. It consisted of a heavy piece of wood with a poison-smeared point attached. It would be hung over an animal path with a trip wire below it, and when an animal passed underneath, it would fall and stab it in the back. This was an effective way to obtain large, dangerous animals such as buffaloes and rhinoceros. Some of my informants also remembered *ng'ereng'et*s being used not just for trapping but also symbolically as boundary markers between the territories of different lineages. One lineage would put its *ng'ereng'et* on one side of the tree, typically a wild olive tree, and the other would place its on the other side.

All of this hunting and trapping sometimes resulted in more meat than the small Mukogodo residential groups could consume quickly. They therefore preserved meat by cooking it until it was very dry and mixing it with fat, similar to the pemmican made by some Native Americans. This mixture, called *lporrda* in Maa, was then placed in a container and stored in a cave. Thanks to *lporrda* and stashes of crystallized honey, Mukogodo families were usually able to avoid hunger even when their favorite foods were hard to find. But they did have a list of famine foods, species they normally rejected but could turn to in times of need. These included baboons and other monkeys, rabbits, and zebras. Although the only reason I was ever offered for the rejection of primates was simply that they are disgusting, my Mukogodo informants had very specific reasons for rejecting rabbits and zebras. Rabbits have footprints that resemble those of dogs. Dogs are in turn eaten only in times of great distress because they will eat virtually anything, including feces. Zebras are normally off the menu because they are so similar to donkeys (indeed, the Swahili name for zebra is *punda milia*, or striped donkey), which are taboo to many Maa speakers and other East Africans for a reason similar to the taboo on eating elephants among three of the four Mukogodo clans: just as elephants are like people because their mammary glands are arranged like a woman's breasts, donkeys are like women because they both carry things. Nevertheless, excavations of the top layers of Mukogodo rockshelters revealed a few zebra, baboon, and other bones from species that were normally taboo to Mukogodo. Those bones could have been deposited by a nonhuman carnivore, or they could be the result of an episode of food shortage while the Mukogodo were hunters, gatherers, and beekeepers.

The emphasis in this account of Mukogodo subsistence is on honey and meat because that is what the Mukogodo themselves always say when asked about their old diet: "Meat and honey only." However, when asked specifically about plant foods they do report that some were collected, mainly by women, and consumed, though apparently not very enthusiastically. The list includes several root species, some fruits, and a couple of leafy species. Many of these are still eaten occasionally today, but they do not constitute a major part of anyone's diet. The most commonly consumed wild plant these days is a dark green leaf called *nterere* (*Amaranthus hybridus*), but my most knowledgeable Mukogodo informants reported that its consumption is a new phenomenon and that they did not eat it as children in the caves. This may be because it grows best in abandoned livestock pens, which of course were few and far between when the Mukogodo were primarily foragers. *Nterere* tastes something like spinach, and it is quite good when mixed with another modern Mukogodo staple, maize meal mush.

Mukogodo foragers had one other source of food: domesticated livestock. My informants report that some families would keep a few sheep and goats in their rockshelters with them, which they used for milk and meat. These were very small herds, a handful of animals at the most. This is confirmed by the surveys and excavations of the old rockshelters, a few of which contained manure deposits where small pens once stood. Given the small numbers of domesticated animal bones found in the rockshelters relative to wild species like hyrax and dik-dik, it is unlikely that these small herds were much more than a supplement to a diet that was primarily based on honey and wild meat. The rockshelters also contain a few cattle bones, but these are likely to be animals that were obtained from neighboring pastoralists by trade or theft and quickly eaten because the rockshelters were mostly inaccessible to cattle, and even those that cattle could reach were too small to contain more than one or two of them. The incorporation of small numbers of domesticated livestock into the Mukogodo subsistence system fits with a recent realization among anthropologists who study hunter-gatherers that "pure" hunter-gatherers are rare. The Mukogodo did not apparently have any sort of ideological commitment to hunting and gathering as a way of life to the exclusion of other sorts of subsistence. Rather, they were willing to do what was necessary to make a living, provided it was not too disruptive to their existing routine. Despite the presence of a few sheep and goats in some of the rockshelters from time to time, it is clear that the Mukogodo subsisted primarily on honey and wild foods until well into the twentieth century.

SOCIAL AND
RELIGIOUS LIFE IN THE FOREST

While Mukogodo have broken from their foraging past in terms of subsistence, there are many ways in which their social institutions and practices continued through the transition to pastoralism right up to the present day. Because of this continuity, this section is written in a combination of past and present tenses.

Lineages, clans, and marriage

One of anthropology's great accomplishments is the elucidation of different systems of kinship, descent, and marriage around the world. A series of influential ethnographies written mainly by British anthropologists showed that segmentary descent systems are particularly common in that continent. East African pastoralists in particular are associated with the patrilineal version of such a system. What all of this means is that descent, and hence membership in a descent group as well as inheritance, is reckoned through male links only: an individual is born into his father's descent group and inherits property or access to property, and sometimes other legal rights and responsibilities, through that same link. Descent groups created in this way are related to each other through a series of ever-deeper genealogical connections, which creates a system of segments, with smaller segments forming parts of larger segments. Such segmented systems sometimes have several levels. Anthropologists use the word *lineage* to refer to a relatively small segment in which, at least according to the textbook definition, all members have known links through males back to a common male ancestor whose identity is known. Lineages can, in turn, be connected through deeper genealogical connections into larger segments called *clans*. In clans, the focal ancestor may not be known by name and links back to him might be impossible to specify. Extra levels in such a segmented system are given additional labels, such as *phratry, minimal* and *maximal lineage, subclan,* and so on. It is usually the case that in patrilineal systems, postmarital residence is patrilocal, that is, a newly married couple usually lives with the husband's kin.

For the most part, the Mukogodo fit this pattern very well. They have a patrilineal, segmentary descent system consisting of four clans that are further broken down into thirteen lineages, and postmarital residence was and still is most often patrilocal. A summary of the system is shown in Table 2.1. These units were important in the lives of Mukogodo when they were hunter-gatherers for two main reasons: access to territories and restrictions on marriage partners. As explained earlier in this chapter, a man had rights of access to his own lineage's territory, but had to ask permission before using resources from another lineage's territory. Perhaps most important, all members of one's lineage of one's own generation were and still are referred to by the same terms used for siblings, and sex and marriage with them was considered incestuous. Therefore, one had to find a mate from outside one's own lineage. Anthropologists call this *lineage exogamy,* and it is a very common pattern. As we have seen earlier, the clan system also had some relevance to the symbolic issue of food taboos, with members of all but the Sialo clan refusing to eat elephant meat as well as some other wild species. Although some anthropologists now question whether these kinds of systems exist on the ground the way they do in the ethnographies and textbooks, Mukogodo do indeed identify lineages, usually referred to simply as "brothers" (*lalashera*) and clans, usually referred to as *il-gilat* (singular: *ol-gilata*).

The official rules of the system were patrilineality, segmentation, patrilocality, and lineage exogamy. For the most part, Mukogodo during the hunting and gathering period seem to have taken those rules seriously and largely followed them. However, it is important to note that even when rules are important to people, understanding the rules is not quite the same as understanding their actual behavior. My informants' recollections make it clear that even though the rules were taken seriously, they could be and were broken, or at least bent when circumstances made following them impractical. As we will see more clearly in later chapters, this willingness to bend and even occasionally break important social rules plays a role in the maintenance of the Mukogodo's low status in the eyes of other Maa speakers.

I can provide a few illustrative examples of such bending and breaking of the rules. The main rule of patrilineality—lineage membership and inheritance patterns determined solely by male links—can be broken in a variety of ways. A fairly common occurrence is for a young woman to have children before she is married. Most women, even those who have already had children, do eventually get married, and such children are adopted by the husband, regardless of whether he is the biological father. Another possibility is for such women to never marry, but rather to remain members of their father's household and to bear children in her father's name who are then members of his lineage despite the fact that their only link to the lineage is through a woman, not a man. This does not imply, by the way, any father-daughter incest, which Mukogodo find abhorrent. Rather, the woman is free to have sex with whomever she chooses outside her lineage, meaning that the children's biological fathers are not in the same lineage as her offspring. Yet another way for people to become members of a lineage despite having no male ties to it occurs when women are widowed. Because women usually get married in their teens while men start marrying no earlier than their early twenties but can continue until

Table 2.1. Mukogodo clans and lineages during the transition to pastoralism.

Clans	Member lineages
Orondi (Herok'te)[1]	Matunge Leitiko (includes Pokisa) Pardero Losupuko (Leupi)
Sialo (Re'che'hu)	Sakui Parmashu Moile Nantiri Lioini
Ol Doinyo Lossos (Moror)	Lentolla
Luno (Kiperper)	Liba (also known as Nukur)
Lineages with no clan affiliations	Biyoti Suaanga

NOTE: This list differs slightly from one previously published by Heine (1974/75). For an explanation of the differences between Heine's list and this one, see my dissertation (Cronk 1989a: 64–66). This list includes those lineages whose members spoke Yaaku and went through the transition from hunting and gathering to pastoralism. Since that time, some families with no history of speaking Yaaku or foraging have been accepted by most Mukogodo as *Mukogodo taata* ('Mukogodo now'), and two of the lineages listed in the table have ceased to exist. For those reasons, this list is not considered a definitive statement about who is and who is not Mukogodo.

[1]Mukogodo informants remember some of these descent groups as having had different names in Yaaku than in Maa. Yaaku names are given in parentheses.

they are elderly, widowhood is common. Widows do not usually remarry. Rather, they remain members of the lineage into which they married, and they continue to have children that are putatively those of the dead man. This became clear to me while conducting the census and genealogical interviews. Occasionally I would come across a man who had died, say, ten years ago, but who had children who were only two or three years old. Given the absence of sperm banks in Mukogodo, I knew that there had to be some sort of legal fiction involved! And, indeed, my informants confirmed that a child may be legally the offspring of a dead man while biologically the offspring of his or her widowed mother's lover.

The Mukogodo also violate rules they do not even have, if such a thing is possible. What I mean by this is that anthropologists have established definitions of concepts like *lineage* and *clan*. Lineages are supposed to be descent groups with members who have known genealogical links back to a known ancestor. Clans are supposed to be descent groups in which such links and such founding ancestors may be not entirely known. In a segmentary system, lineages are supposed to be nested within clans, with more than one lineage in each clan. Those definitions are important for anthropologists because they allow them to have clear discussions about descent systems. But there are Mukogodo lineages and clans that do not strictly fit these definitions. Although my genealogical informants were able to identify founding ancestors for most of the thirteen lineages, some have been forgotten, as have some of the ties of some branches of some of the lineages back to the lineages' roots. Clans are supposed to consist of bundles of lineages, all of which share common roots, but in the case of at least one of the Mukogodo clans, Orondi, this is well known not to be the case because the Leitiko and Matunge lineage founders were adopted by that clan. Because clans are supposed to be bundles of lineages, each clan should presumably have more than one lineage, but this is also not true for two of the four Mukogodo clans. When clans are being discussed, people refer to the Luno and Ol Doinyo Lossos groups. But when lineages are being discussed, people use the terms *Liba* and *Lentolla*, but they are referring to exactly the same groups of people because the only lineage in Luno is Liba and the only lineage in Ol Doinyo Lossos is Lentolla. According to the textbooks, neat segmentary system are also not supposed to have danglers and outliers, but the Mukogodo system has them: the Biyoti and Suaanga lineages, both now extinct, are not remembered as having been members of any of the clans.

The rule of lineage exogamy, though taken very seriously indeed, is also known to have been violated at least twice. In the course of my genealogical interviews I came across two instances of individuals from the same lineage marrying. In one case, my genealogical informant simply explained that it happened many years ago, perhaps around the turn of the twentieth century, when the population was small and eligible mates were not so easy to find. Given that the lineage was a large one, perhaps including people from neighboring groups who had been adopted, a single incident of lineage endogamy was tolerated as a practical necessity. Another instance of the same phenomenon makes for a better story, one now told with relish by the descendants of the people involved. The story goes that, many decades ago when they were still living in rockshelters, a young man and young woman, both from the Parmashu lineage, fell in love. Rather than following the rule of lineage exogamy, they eloped, setting up housekeeping on their own in a rockshelter separate from those of the rest of the lineage members. Marriages based on love rather than on familial and economic arrangements were and still are the exception rather than the norm, which may explain why this story is so fondly remembered by some people. Seeing that the marriage was not going to be easy to break up, the members of the Parmashu lineage decided to accommodate it in a very clever way: they simply broke the lineage into two new lineages rather than break up the couple. The members of the lineage who were most closely related to the husband in the young couple remained Parmashu, while those most closely related to the wife changed their name to Sakui, so that the marriage could no longer be considered a violation of the rule of lineage exogamy. Ever since that time, these two lineages have intermarried frequently, providing an example of how an apparently rigid system can, when necessary, be quite flexible.

The rule of postmarital residence is also sometimes violated. While the most common pattern is indeed for a newly married couple to live with the husband's kin rather than with the wife's, exceptions do occur. However, in the few cases I know well of men living with their in-laws the men are treated poorly and given little respect or consideration, so it is clear why most men try to avoid such a situation. Another rule is that when a couple marries the man must pay something to his wife's parents, which anthropologists call *bridewealth* or *brideprice*. During their time as foragers, a normal bridewealth was a few beehives. These days bridewealths are normally paid in livestock, and as we will see in a later chapter this difference in bridewealth payments is crucial to an understanding of Mukogodo history. Some of my informants reported that even when they had almost no livestock a man would always give one sheep to his mother-in-law, but others argued that this was just an imposition of modern practices, borrowed from Maa-speaking pastoralists, on the past. Those informants held that bridewealths in the past actually consisted entirely of beehives, though sometimes a particular beehive would be called "sheep" and given to the mother-in-law in mimicry of the Maasai custom.

Another rule associated with marriage these days is that a bride is expected to have had her clitoris removed in a ceremony that usually occurs soon after her first menses. Clitoridectomies and similar operations on female genitalia are common though not universal in some parts of Africa as well as elsewhere in the world. Maa speakers refer to these operations using the same term that they use for male circumcision, though it is actually much more drastic than the procedure performed on males because it involves removal of the entire clitoris, an organ homologous to the penis, rather than just the hood of the clitoris, which is analogous to the foreskin of the penis. It is unclear whether clitoridectomies were performed on Mukogodo girls when they lived in the rockshelters. My own informants from 1985 through 1987, who considered sex with a woman with an intact clitoris to be disgusting, insisted that their female ancestors had indeed all been "circumcised." However, D. G. Worthy, a British colonial official who lived in the Mukogodo area for a brief time in the 1950s, reported that the practice had been introduced only recently. The issue of which of these accounts might be correct will be revisited in Chapter 4.

Age sets
In addition to a segmentary descent system, another common feature among East African pastoralists is an age-set system. Here again the Mukogodo fit the regional pattern fairly well. Many societies have age grading systems, in which men and sometimes women go through a series of culturally recognized stages in life, usually with important ceremonies marking the transitions between stages. Among Americans, high school and college graduations serve as an age grading system, and some groups in America also have their own ceremonies to mark major transitions in life, such as bar mitzvahs and bat mitzvahs among Jews and *quinceañeras* among some Latinas. An age-set system is like an age grading system, but in addition to marking the stages in the lives of individuals it also takes people who are going

through life's stages at more or less the same time and gives them a group identity. Mukogodo have been following the age-set system of East Africa's Maa-speaking peoples since about the middle of the nineteenth century, making it one of the first aspects of Maasai culture to be adopted by the Mukogodo (see Table 2.2). The key event in this system is circumcision, which begins the transition of a male from a boy to a *murrani*, the first stage of adulthood. Later, a *murrani* will become an elder. Until recent years, circumcision was usually performed when men were older teenagers, but these days it is common for it to be performed when boys are in their early teens because this fits better with their school schedules. About every fifteen years a new age set is named, and the men who are circumcised during such a fifteen-year period all identify themselves as part of the same age set, such as Kiroro, Kishille, or Kimaniki. The age sets are further subdivided into the "right hand" (*tatene*), meaning those circumcised earlier in the fifteen-year period, and "left hand" (*kedianye*), meaning those circumcised later in the period. The Mukogodo do not choose the names of the age sets or the timing of the transitions between age sets themselves. As you can see in Table 2.2, at one time they followed the names given by the Maasai, but they have since switched and now follow the lead of their Samburu neighbors to the north. Table 2.2 also shows that the age sets have different names as *murran* than as elders, though it is perfectly acceptable and very common to continue to refer to elder men by the name their age set used when they were *murran*. Women go through a ceremony that is analogous to circumcision in men, though more extreme in terms of the surgery involved, but they are not organized into age sets in the same way as men. Rather, a woman is associated with the age set of her husband, regardless of the difference between their ages.

As I explained in Chapter 1, the word *murran* is often translated as "warriors," but it actually derives from the Maa word for circumcision. The idea that they are warriors dates from precolonial and colonial times, when Maasai *murran* did indeed form large armies and engage in military campaigns to defend their lands and herds and to obtain those of others. Even today *murran* carry spears, knives, and clubs and engage in some livestock raiding and defense of their families' herds. Despite their willingness and ability to engage in violent conflict when necessary, the culture of Maa speakers is actually one that emphasizes peacefulness and a sort of quiet resolve and inner strength rather than any sort of outward fierceness or bravado, which makes the translation of *murran* as "warriors" not only inaccurate in terms of its literal meaning but also misleading in terms of how Maa speakers see the role of the men in the *murran* age set. These days *murran* are responsible for the most difficult herding assignments, while also finding time to primp, spend time with their girlfriends, and, increasingly, get jobs elsewhere in Kenya. Those who stay home often wear their hair long in a style that is a classic ethnic marker of Maa speakers (see Figure 2.7 for a striking example). Those who leave for work elsewhere in Kenya, which nowadays includes most young men, usually cut their hair short, wear Western-style clothing, and eschew jewelry and body modifications such as distended earlobes.

Table 2.2   Mukogodo age sets.

Approximate circumcision dates	Mukogodo age-set names	Corresponding Maasai age-set names [1]	Corresponding Samburu age-set names [2]
c. 1850	*Nyankusi*	*Nyankusi*	Kiteku
c. 1865	*Peles, Marikuni*	Merisho, Aimer, *Peles*	Tarigirik
c. 1880	*Talala, Terito*	*Talala*	Marikon
c. 1895	*Merisho, Nyankusi*	Mirisho, Tuati	Terito
c. 1912	*Meruturot, Tareto*	Meiruturut, Tareto	Merisho
c. 1921	*Tiyeki, Kileko*	*Tiyeki, Terito*	Kileko
1936–1947	*Mekuri, Nyankusi*	Kalikal, *Nyankusi*	Mekuri
1948–1959	*Kimaniki, Kirimat*	*Kiramat*, Terekeyiani, Seuri	*Kimaniki*
1960–1975	*Kishille, Kiyapo*	Keruti, Kiseeyia, Kitoipi	*Kishille*
1976–1989	*Kiroro*	Kishili	*Kiroro*
1990–	*Meoli*		*Meoli*

NOTE: This is an extreme simplification of a very complicated picture. Many different names exist among Maa speakers for the various age sets, and the correspondences among age sets across different ethnic groups are quite rough. Some names are in italics to emphasize the shift that occurred in Mukogodo age-set nomenclature from Maasai names to Samburu ones at about the time of the Tiyeki age set.

[1]Maasai age set names are from Mol (1979, 1996).

[2]Samburu names are from Spencer (1965, 1973) and Bilinda Straight's web site.

Figure 2.7   A Mukogodo murrani's hair and jewelry.

As with the kinship system, Mukogodo adherence to the rules of the Maa speakers' age-set system is sometimes loose. Unlike Samburu, they do not perform circumcision or other transitional ceremonies involving many men at once. Rather, such ceremonies usually involve just one or two initiates. Although most Maa speakers will tell you that *murran* are not allowed to marry, Mukogodo *murran* typically marry in their early twenties if they can afford the bridewealth. Another aspect of this system is that the men in the current *murran* age set have a special relationship with the men in the age set two sets older than them. Men in the older age set are known as the "firestick elders" of the *murran*. For example, the Kishille are the firestick elders of the *murran* in the Meoli age set. Most Samburu would say that it is important that the firestick elders not be the fathers of any current *murran*. Although the Mukogodo recognize the firestick relationship and consider it important, they disregard the idea that firestick elders cannot have *murran* sons, and it is common to find Tiyekis with Kimaniki sons, Mekuris with Kishille sons, Kimanikis with Kiroro sons, and so on. Yet another aspect of the Maasai age-set system disregarded by the Mukogodo concerns wife sharing. Perhaps to enhance the solidarity among men in a given age set, Maasai women married to men in a particular age set are permitted to have sex with other men in that same age set. Mukogodo do not follow that custom, and my informants report that they never did.

Religion

Unfortunately, little is remembered about the religious life of the Mukogodo when they were hunter-gatherers. Bernd Heine, the linguist who has worked in the Mukogodo area since about 1969, reports that the Yaaku language contains words for both "god" (*yecheri*) and for a god of rain, but my informants reported that they believed in only one god. The British colonial official D. G. Worthy reports that God was believed to live atop Mount Kenya, and my oldest Mukogodo informants agreed with that. My cave-dweller friend LeKitiman still strongly believed in the presence of God on top of Mount Kenya, and he insisted that if you were to climb to the top of the mountain you would be swept down by strong winds. I decided not to let him know that I had actually climbed Mount Kenya twice and that many other people climb it, and safely climb back down, virtually every day.

The holiest place in the Mukogodo area was the top of Ol Doinyo Lossos, the most visually striking if not quite the highest peak in the region. The leader of a family would climb to the top of Ol Doinyo Lossos and make offerings to God of honey, blood, fat, and milk. Some say that offerings were made simply by leaving the food at the peak, while others said that sometimes honey and water were mixed and then shaken onto the ground. Worthy's report that these offerings were made for things like rain, peace, honey, and other foods was confirmed by my informants. Worthy also reported that sheep were sacrificed on top of Ol Doinyo Lossos, but my informants could not confirm that. In addition to the top of Ol Doinyo Lossos, there were other, less important holy places in the forest, including a particular water source, a small hill in the Siekuu Valley, and a particular tree called Hindadai. At Hindadai, the contents of a slaughtered animal's stomach could be rubbed on the tree as an offering.

Many Maa-speaking groups have ritual specialists known as *loibonok* (singular: *loiboni*). Today there are no Mukogodo *loibonok*, but my informants remember that a member of the Moile lineage was one during the cave period. However, they disagreed on which particular individual was the *loiboni*, so perhaps there was more than one. He is said to have prepared charms to help warriors on their raids against neighboring peoples.

UNDERSTANDING
MUKOGODO AS FORAGERS

Because for many millennia all humans were hunters and gatherers, living hunter-gatherers have a central role in anthropological theory. Anthropologists have developed a variety of ideas to understand both similarities and differences among foragers around the world. In this section I will relate what we know about how Mukogodo lived as foragers to theories about hunter-gatherer social organization, diet, prey selection, and the world system.

Mukogodo as delayed-return foragers

In order to describe the diversity among the world's hunting and gathering peoples, anthropologists have developed several different typologies. James Woodburn's distinction between "immediate-return" and "delayed-return" foragers is particularly helpful in understanding Mukogodo and other East African highland hunting and gathering peoples. Woodburn himself studied the Hadza of Tanzania, a classic example of immediate-return foragers. Hadza do not invest time in any large or elaborate structures or tools for foraging, they do not store food, and they consume what they hunt and gather more or less immediately— hence the label *immediate-return foragers*. Hadza social organization is also typical of immediate-return foragers: small, mobile bands with flexible group membership and little in the way of territorial defense. Other well-documented immediate-return foragers, such as the Ju/'hoansi of Namibia and Botswana, have similar patterns of foraging and social behavior.

The contrast with Mukogodo foragers could not be more stark. As we have seen, Mukogodo foragers invested a great deal of time and energy in equipment, such as large traps and particularly beehives. They defended territories that were important chiefly for beehive placement. They stored food in the forms of cooked meats and crystallized honey. All of these are good examples of "delayed returns," that is, investments of time, energy, and materials that will not pay off until some time in the future. Mukogodo social organization also reflects this strikingly different subsistence base: formation of descent groups associated with territories, residence determined primarily by descent group membership, and payment of bridewealth as a requirement for marriage. Mukogodo foragers shared all of these features with other East African highland foragers, particularly the Okiek. Other delayed-return foragers around the world display similar patterns, though the resources they rely upon are often quite different. For example, Native Americans in California such as the Pomo depended greatly upon acorns, while those on the Northwest Coast such as the Haida and Tsimshian relied heavily upon fish. Because the investments such peoples make in foraging equipment and food storage are analogous in many ways to the investments food producers put in their fields, crops, and livestock, it is not surprising that the social organization of delayed-return foragers is much more like what anthropologists expect to see among food producers than what they typically imagine hunter-gatherer life to be like.

It is important that all anthropologists, but particularly those who focus their attention on hunter-gatherers, recognize the existence of delayed-return foragers and find ways of incorporating them into their attempts to theorize about hunter-gatherers generally. Despite the fact that immediate-return foragers like the Hadza and Ju/'hoansi have dominated anthropological thinking about hunting and gathering peoples, delayed-return foragers have undoubtedly existed alongside immediate-return systems for many millennia. Even in recent times—say, in the nineteenth century—a census of the world's hunting and gathering peoples would have revealed that the number of people living in societies based on delayed-return foraging was far greater than those living in societies based on immediate-return foraging. Furthermore, archaeologists have uncovered signs of delayed-return foraging and social complexity from periods before the domestication of plants and animals. The implication is that a better understanding of what human life was like when the whole world was occupied by hunter-gatherers would result from closer examination of delayed-return foragers like the Mukogodo.

Diet and division of labor

My Mukogodo informants were in agreement about their diet as foragers: "meat and honey only." As we have seen, they did in fact eat some plant foods, but not many in comparison to meat and honey. This appears to have been a nutritious and adaptive combination of food types. Although we all need protein in our diets, University of Michigan anthropologist John Speth and Katherine Spielman of Arizona State University have pointed out that eating too much protein and not enough other foods, such as carbohydrates and fats, can cause serious health problems. A diet that provides more than 50 percent of one's calories in the form of proteins can cause a sort of protein overdose, leading to symptoms such as dehydration, electrolytic imbalance, calcium loss, elevated blood ammonia levels, and hypertrophy of liver and kidneys. The wild tropical mammals to which Mukogodo foragers had access were quite lean and therefore unable to provide much in the way of fat as an alternative source of calories.

Enter honey, a source of concentrated and easily digested carbohydrates. University of Maine anthropologist Kristin Sobolik has suggested that honey was a key part of the nutritional adaptation of East African highland foragers like the Mukogodo because it enabled them to avoid overdosing on protein. This may have made particular sense in forested environments, where flowers are common but where much of the plant biomass is locked up in inedible forms such as wood. Honey's tremendous importance to the health of people like the Mukogodo helps explain why they invested so much time and energy in beehive construction and territorial defense.

Mukogodo reliance on meat and honey also helps explain their sexual division of labor. In the 1960s it was discovered that among the Ju/'hoansi women provided the majority of the calories, mainly in the form of plant foods such as nuts and tubers. Anthropologists quickly jumped to the conclusion that the Ju/'hoansi pattern is the standard one for human foragers in the tropics. We now know that not to be the case. Other well-studied tropical foragers, such as the Ache of Paraguay, receive most of their calories from animals and other foods obtained by men, not women. As we have seen, Mukogodo men also provided the majority—perhaps almost all—of the calories consumed, mainly in the forms of meat and honey. Women had plenty of work to do, to be sure, but their role as food collectors was minor compared to women in some other foraging groups.

Small game hunting

For many years, anthropologists assumed that men in foraging societies hunt to provide themselves, their wives, and their children with meat. But, as Kristen Hawkes of the University of Utah has pointed out, in many foraging societies the meat men bring home is distributed among the entire camp, with no preference for the hunter's wife or children. Hawkes and her colleagues have documented this pattern among, for example, the Ache of Paraguay and Hadza of Tanzania. Judging from the archaeological record, which is full of evidence of big-game hunting by prehistoric humans, this is a pattern that might be rather typical of human foragers. Hawkes argues that we must think of hunting as something other than male parental behavior. This is because men in hunting and gathering societies typically forego small game and other relatively reliable resources they could direct towards their own wives and children; choosing instead to pursue big game that is unpredictable and widely shared. One possibility is that big game hunters engage in long-term reciprocity, sharing meat with those who have shared with them in the past. But detailed studies of food-sharing patterns in foraging societies do not support that model, either. A typical pattern is for certain men to be consistently better hunters than others and for there not to be the long-term balance among different hunters that would support the idea of reciprocity.

So why do men in so many foraging societies spend their time in risky pursuit of big game when they could be collecting foods, like plants, honey, and small game, that can reliably be found, that are not widely shared, and that they could direct to their own wives and children? Eric Alden Smith of the University of Washington has argued persuasively that big-game hunting is a way men signal their high quality as a hunter—and, by extension, as an ally, a competitor, and a mate—to a broad audience. Even though a successful hunter's own wives and children may not benefit more than anyone else in the camp from his ability to occasionally provide large amounts of meat, the hunter himself may benefit by the mates and allies he can attract by such demonstrations of his abilities. Studies by Smith and others have shown that a variety of types of hunting and fishing persist, despite the fact that other ways of obtaining food would be more efficient, because they allow good hunters and fishers to demonstrate their skills to an audience.

Mukogodo hunting, with its emphasis on reliably obtained foods like honey and small game like hyraxes and dik-diks, contrasts sharply with the big-game focus documented among other foragers. Though they did occasionally hunt and trap some very large game, their day-to-day foraging activities appear to have been focused simply on providing food for their families in the easiest and most reliable way possible rather than on signaling to others what great hunters they were. Why? Like many aspects of Mukogodo life during their foraging period, I suspect that this difference emerges from their emphasis on honey. For big-game hunting to act as a signal to potential mates and potential allies, those people need to be able to see the signal. But the Mukogodo reliance upon honey from man-made hives led to a system of territories, patrilineages, and patrilocal residence that would have prevented big-game hunters from reaching their intended audiences. Any hunter's residential group would have consisted not of potential mates and potential allies but rather of men who, as members of his patrilineage, were already his allies, their wives, and women who were off limits as mates due to the rule of lineage exogamy. Occasional displays of one's hunting ability would have been a good idea if people from other lineages were in a position to learn about them, but on a day-to-day basis it would have made more sense to focus on resources that could be depended upon to keep oneself, one's wife, and one's children well fed.

Rural proletarians or independent contractors?

It was once common for anthropologists to portray hunter-gatherers as if they were living fossils, pristine remnants of a time when all humans shared their way of life. This view was strongly challenged in the 1980s by anthropologists who used archaeological, historical, and other sorts of evidence to argue that many hunter-gatherers were not pristine at all. Instead, they argued, today's hunter-gatherers are products of the world system who can be fully understood only in terms of their role within that system. The hunter-gatherer revisionists argued that foraging peoples are simply the poorest of the poor, the most rural of the rural proletariat of a worldwide division of labor.

The revisionist critique is a powerful one that all students of hunter-gatherers must take seriously. It has provided some valuable insights into some of the world's most famous hunting and gathering peoples. But the critique and the arguments surrounding it are nothing new to people who study East African highland foragers like the Mukogodo, about whom essentially the same debate has been going on for decades. This debate can be clarified with the help of a distinction made by James C. Scott, a political scientist at Yale University, between "public" and "hidden" transcripts. The public transcript is the version of reality that is acknowledged openly where dominants and subordinates interact. It describes the social order and provides reasons why people, including subordinates, should think that it is good for all and certainly unavoidable and unchangeable. But, as Scott points out, the public transcript, "where it is not positively misleading, is unlikely to tell the whole story about power relations." The hidden transcript, in contrast, is the version of reality shared among the subordinates when no representatives of the dominant group are there to hear it. Because it is hidden, it is inherently difficult to study. It often takes disguised and anonymous forms, such as jokes, folk tales, and graffiti.

Talking to Maasai and Samburu about *il-torrobo* gives you the public transcript. For them, the foragers are simply *il-torrobo*, the lowest and most despised parts of their system (that system is more fully described in Chapters 3 through 6). Maasai and Samburu emphasize those *il-torrobo* who are failed pastoralists, forced into hunting by circumstances, rather than those whose ancestors have been foraging and keeping bees for centuries. Foraging is thus portrayed as more of a backup plan than a complete way of life. From the pastoralists' point of view, the lives of *il-torrobo* have meaning only insofar as they serve their pastoralist betters by providing forest products such as honey wine and dangerous and polluting services such as circumcision. The idea that the foragers might have an identity and existence that is independent of the pastoralists and that even precedes their arrival in the area is not entertained.

The pastoralists' view is well represented in the scholarly literature. The nineteenth-century explorer Joseph Thomson, for example, described Dorobo as "species of serf" who have "nothing like tribal life among them" and who are "treated accordingly." More recently, Cynthia Chang has argued that "at least from the mid–1800s onwards, Rift Valley hunters and gatherers have consisted largely of disenfranchised pastoralists and farmers, rather than being descendants of ancient populations who have hunted since 'time immemorial.'" Chang points out that her viewpoint "is not based upon early ethnographic sources on Dorobo" but rather on "the travel journals of the late-nineteenth-century British explorers."

Talking to Mukogodo and other foragers and former foragers gives you the hidden transcript. While recognizing that the Maasai and Samburu look down upon them, they reject the *il-torrobo* label. They are the centers of their own worlds, worlds in which they were the first inhabitants, worlds in which Maasai are just the latest in a long series of powerful but ephemeral groups to pass through. They point out that the pastoralists need the foragers more than the foragers need the pastoralists. While Maasai and Samburu are dependent upon foragers for such essentials as honey wine and their work as circumcisers, foraging and beekeeping is a complete way of life, one that predates the arrival of pastoralism in East Africa. From the hunter-gatherer point of view, their residence in the forest and lack of livestock result not from forced marginalization by Maasai, but from their own free choice. Aspects of hunter-gatherer behavior toward Maasai that may look to Maasai or to an outsider as deference by the hunter-gatherer or domination by Maasai often look quite different from the point of view of the hunter-gatherer. For example, Okiek and Maasai normally use the Maa language when speaking with one another. Corinne Kratz, an anthropologist at Emory University who has studied the Okiek for decades, explains that for Okiek, this is merely a convenience because while most Maasai cannot speak Okiek, most Okiek can and happily will speak Maa, a language that they even incorporate into some sacred rituals. Similarly, Kratz says, relationships between Maasai and Okiek individuals that a Maasai might describe in terms of patrons and clients are usually described by Okiek as merely friendships.

Perhaps nothing expresses the Okiek hidden transcript better than a story they told ethnographer Roderic Blackburn about an Okiot (the singular form of Okiek) and two Maasai warriors. The Okiot was returning from a trip to collect honey when he was stopped by the Maasai, who told him that they were going to kill him. He asked to be allowed to eat his honey so that he could die satisfied. As he began to eat, he asked his captors, "Do you eat honey?" They did, and while their hands were covered with the liquid the Okiot quickly washed his hands with dirt, grabbed one of the Maasai's swords and stabbed him. The other Maasai, unaware of the beekeeper's trick of washing hands with dirt, tried to grab his spear, but could not because his hands were too slippery with honey. The Okiot stabbed him, too, picked up his honey, and left. Thus, an Okiot and his honey can outwit even two threatening, spear-wielding Maasai.

A complete picture can be created only by understanding both the public and hidden transcripts. At the same time that the pastoralists' view of them was and still is an important fact of life for East Africa's highland foragers and former foragers, it did not and does not define them. A full understanding of such groups can be obtained only if we recognize both their independence and their position within the wider regional and world systems.

CONCLUSION

Perhaps what is most impressive about the culture and language of Mukogodo foragers—beekeeping, hunting, trapping, and gathering—is its *richness*. Though Mukogodo did absorb some refugees from pastoralism, the skills they were taught were not those of mere refugees. Making a living in the forest involved an elaborate and complex body of knowledge and the language with which to express it that had taken centuries to develop. Mukogodo foragers had knowledge and skills necessary to maintain themselves, their culture, and their language for many centuries.

This is an important point if we are to understand why the Mukogodo stopped being foragers and started instead to keep livestock. If we see them as simply the very poorest members of a pastoralist world who happened to become a little less poor, then the transition to pastoralism is not really a transition at all, and thus not something that needs to be explained. But if we realize that the Mukogodo were a long-lasting, well-adapted group with its own language, culture, social organization, and subsistence patterns, all of which had served them well for centuries, then the transition is indeed a puzzle. After all, other groups of hunter-gatherers in East Africa, such as the Hadza, still have not all made the transition to food production, while still others, like the Okiek, have shifted subsistence but have retained much more of their own culture and ethnic identity than the Mukogodo. What made the Mukogodo different, what made them change so radically and so quickly, is the focus of the next chapter.

The Mukogodo foraging way of life involved an intricate relationship between their subsistence and their social organization. Lineages owned territories that were important for beehive placement, beehives were used as bridewealth, and the emphasis on beekeeping led to residential patterns that encouraged a focus on small game. These kinds of interrelationships are a major theme of anthropology, which prides itself on being the most holistic of the social sciences. The next chapter will continue to emphasize these sorts of connections between subsistence and social behavior because it is in those connections that we will find the reasons why the Mukogodo so quickly abandoned their centuries-old foraging way of life, their language, and their religion.

RECOMMENDED READING

Matthias Brenzinger, Bernd Heine, and Ingo Heine's *The Mukogodo Maasai: An Ethnobotanical Survey* (Rüdiger Köppe Verlag, 1994) is an encyclopedic treatment not only of Mukogodo knowledge about plants but also their language and the culture of beekeeping. Robert L. Kelly's *The Foraging Spectrum: Diversity in Hunter-Gatherer Lifeways* (Smithsonian Institution Press, 1995) is an excellent overview of the anthropological study of foragers. James C. Scott's important distinction between "hidden" and "public" transcripts is explained in his book *Domination and the Arts of Resistance: Hidden Transcripts* (Yale University Press, 1990).

3

From Mukogodo to Maasai

One day while hiking back to Kuri-Kuri from a visit to some families living in the forest, I met a group of women returning from a shopping trip in Don Dol. After we went through the rather lengthy greeting that is customary in Maa, we chatted about our days. One of the women explained that she was bringing back *ele cani* for a sick old woman back home. In that context, *ele cani* means "this traditional herbal medicine," so I expected her to reach under her cloak and pull out a handful of roots or bark. Instead, she showed me a bottle of Coca-Cola. Given that Coke consists of water, sugar, and caffeine, it probably did make the old woman feel a little better.

All peoples are creations of the times and places in which they lived, including their contacts with other groups. Like the Mukogodo woman with the bottle of Coke, people often incorporate things from outside so thoroughly that they appear to people both inside and outside the culture to be parts of their "traditional" culture. But that appearance is often misleading. The way of life we associate with the Plains Indians of North America, for example, arose only after horses and guns were introduced from Europe. The Yanomamö Indians of South America, as isolated as they may seem deep in the Amazonian rain forest, base their subsistence on plantains, a crop unknown in the Americas until European contact. European culture itself is an amalgam of ideas from the ancient Near East, the Mediterranean, and elsewhere. Even something as classically Italian as marinara sauce would not exist without tomatoes from the Americas.

In the last chapter, we saw how a distinctive Mukogodo identity and way of life emerged and changed over many centuries as different groups arrived in East Africa, bringing with them their languages, economies, and beliefs. In this sense, the more recent history of the Mukogodo is a continuation of the past: outsiders come, Mukogodo culture absorbs some of their ideas, and what it means to be Mukogodo changes as a result. But the latest episode of Mukogodo culture change is also profoundly different in several ways. For one thing, the ultimate cause of much of the change is located not in Africa, but in Europe. Also, the changes wrought are more drastic and profound than any that have come before: complete change of language, culture, and subsistence. And finally, as we will see better in Chapter 6, it now appears likely that these most recent changes will eventually lead to the end of the notion of a distinctive "Mukogodo" ethnic identity.

WHEN DID THE TRANSITION OCCUR?

My estimate is that the Mukogodo shifted from a way of life based primarily on hunting and gathering to one based primarily on pastoralism between 1925 and 1936. I determined this through examination of written sources and interviews with Mukogodo individuals who witnessed it. For example, the settler Raymond Hook reported in 1932 that when he first met Mukogodo in 1915 they were "a miserable tribe living in clefts of the rocks and subsisting on wild yams and honey and the chase," but that since 1920 they had "learnt to build the Masai type of huts and have got together a few hundred cattle, mainly obtained by the sale of their girls to cattle owners." Also in 1932, a group of settlers described the Mukogodo as being "stock owners in a very small way, the remainder being bush and cave people pure and simple," indicating that by that time the transition had begun but was not yet complete. This was corroborated by Mukogodo individuals who were alive during the transition. A key indicator of a particular family's subsistence practices during the transitional period was whether they lived in a rockshelter. While it is possible to keep a few small stock in a rockshelter, the Mukogodo rockshelters are mostly small and difficult to access, and so are not good places to keep cattle. Therefore, a movement out of the rockshelters and into houses indicates a new reliance on livestock in general and cattle in particular. Individuals who were about ten years old when their families moved out of their rockshelters were about sixty-five years old in 1986, indicating that they moved out of their rockshelters in about 1931. Slightly younger individuals have no memories of life in a rockshelter. Considering all of the evidence together, it seems clear that the transition occurred during a brief period lasting roughly from 1925 to 1936.

THE BRITISH IN EAST AFRICA

In a sense, the roots of the most recent episode in Mukogodo history are not in places like Don Dol and Kuri-Kuri but rather in London and Berlin. By the second half of the nineteenth century, almost the entire inhabited world had come under the rule or domination of a European or European-related power, such as the United States. The Americas had been taken over by the Spanish, Portuguese, British, and others. Much of Asia had been colonized by countries like Britain, France, and the Netherlands. Most of the Middle East was ruled by the half-Asian, half-European Ottoman Empire. Vast stretches of Asia and portions of North America were ruled by an expanding Russian Empire. Sub-Saharan Africa, most of which remained not only uncolonized but unexplored by Europeans until the second half of the nineteenth century, was the last major exception to this pattern.

The colonization of Africa by Europeans got a late start thanks to a number of factors, including tropical diseases and the military strength of some African societies. But by the late nineteenth century, a rush was under way to claim vast areas of the continent for old European empires like Britain and France as well as for upstarts like Germany and Italy. By the turn of the twentieth century, the entire continent was at least nominally under the control of one or another European power, with the exceptions of Liberia in the west and Ethiopia in the east. The portion of East Africa that included the Mukogodo area became part of the British East Africa Protectorate, later renamed Kenya Colony.

The colonizing nations took varying approaches to their new territories. In some, like Nigeria, many local rulers were left in place to administer their formerly independent territories on behalf of the colonial power. Some were ruthlessly exploited for their resources and labor, the most notorious example being Belgian Congo, where millions died in the first few decades after colonization.

Initially, British authorities were at a loss for what to do with Kenya and, most important, how to make it pay for its own administration. Before the twentieth century, the British saw Kenya mainly as an obstacle between the ports on the Indian Ocean and the real prize of East Africa, Uganda. Eventually they decided on the same approach for Kenya that had worked in North America, Australia, and New Zealand: make it a "white man's country," a land for European settlers to live in and rule over. The main attraction for the settlers was Kenya's agricultural potential, mainly in the beautiful central and western highlands. For European settlers, the Kenyan highlands held out a promise of tremendous agricultural productivity, a delightful climate, and the creation of a socioeconomic system with Europeans firmly in control. Huge areas (see Figure 3.1) were set aside for European settlement. Of course, those areas were already occupied by Africans, who were forcibly moved out of the way and set up in a system of Native Reserves, not unlike the reservations being set up at about the same time in the United States to contain American Indians. In central Kenya, the people displaced by the alienation of what became known as the White Highlands included both Maasai and members of several large Bantu-speaking agricultural groups, including the Kikuyu (or Gikuyu), Embu, and Meru. When those peoples were displaced by the British, they in turn displaced other people, and a sort of domino effect occurred with one group displacing another, and so on down the line.

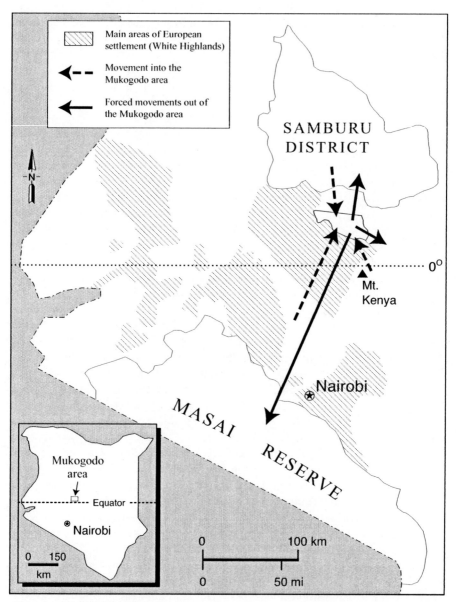

Figure 3.1   *Map showing the White Highlands and migrations in and out of the Mukogodo area during the colonial era.* MIKE SIEGEL, RUTGERS CARTOGRAPHY LAB.

THE NON-MUKOGODO
PEOPLES OF MUKOGODO DIVISION

A few of these displaced peoples ended up living in the Mukogodo area. Their origins were diverse, but what they had in common was a pastoralist subsistence base, the Maa language and other aspects of Maasai culture, and recent residence elsewhere. The main groups that ended up in Mukogodo were the Ilng'wesi, the Mumonyot, and the Digirri. Many Samburu families also traveled into the Mukogodo area from the north, sometimes settling down. The LeUaso, a group with which most Mukogodo have little contact, appear to have lived in and around the western part of the Mukogodo area for as long as anyone can remember. Although this book is not about these non-Mukogodo peoples of the Mukogodo area, they have had such a large impact on Mukogodo history that it is worthwhile giving at least a brief sketch of each of them. The information here on the Ilng'wesi, Mumonyot, and Digirri is from my interviews with people from those groups and the work of Urs Herren, a Swiss anthropologist who has studied the non-Mukogodo peoples of Mukogodo Division. Paul Spencer's books are the main source of my information on the Samburu, and my sketch of the LeUaso is from works by Herren and Spencer.

Ilng'wesi.   The Ilng'wesi, whose name means "the wild animals," originally lived as hunters on the northeastern flank of Mount Kenya. Unlike their Mukogodo contemporaries, however, they did not routinely eat hyrax or keep bees. At that point they lived close to the Meru, a large Bantu-speaking agricultural group. Jeffrey A. Fadiman, who has recorded the oral history of the Meru, reports that Meru remember establishing an alliance with the ancestors of the Ilng'wesi, whom they called the Mwethi, as long ago as the 1750s. The Ilng'wesi also absorbed people with roots among the Maasai, Boran, Rendille, and Samburu. By the time they came into regular contact with the Mukogodo in the late nineteenth and early twentieth centuries, the Ilng'wesi subsisted primarily on livestock and spoke Maa, though some Ilng'wesi maintained contacts among the Meru and some knowledge of the Meru language until quite recently. These days, Ilng'wesi live mainly in the southeastern portion of Mukogodo Division.

Mumonyot.   The Mumonyot started in the late nineteenth century as a remnant of the once powerful Laikipiak Maasai, who were dispersed following their defeat by other Maasai groups. Following that defeat, the Mumonyot went through a period when they had few or no livestock and so had to learn hunting skills and obtain hunting equipment from the Mukogodo. Unlike the Mukogodo, however, they did not keep bees or eat hyrax. By the early twentieth century the Mumonyot had, like the Ilng'wesi and Digirri, obtained livestock and were primarily pastoralists, so their time as hunters was quite brief. Although at that time they moved around a large portion of what is now eastern Kenya, these days

Mumonyot families live mainly in the portion of Mukogodo Division that is just west of the Mukogodo forest.

Digirri.   In the nineteenth century, the core of the group now known as Digirri lived as Kalenjin-speaking hunter-gatherers in the area between Mount Kenya and the Nyandarua Range (also known as the Aberdares), southwest of the Mukogodo area. Unlike the Mukogodo but like the Mumonyot and Ilng'wesi, they were not beekeepers. The Digirri absorbed quite a few Maasai and obtained livestock, mainly by trading elephant tusks, eventually moving north and settling in what was to become Mukogodo Division. By the late nineteeth or early twentieth century they were living as Maa-speaking pastoralists and following Maasai-style age-set and other customs.

LeUaso.   The name LeUaso means "of the river," indicating the fact that they live in the westernmost part of Mukogodo Division along the Uaso Nyiro, or Brown River. In the nineteenth century, the LeUaso lived as beekeepers, hunters, and gatherers and maintained a close relationship with the Laikipiak Maasai. The LeUaso rival the Mukogodo as both the poorest people in the region in terms of livestock and the most dedicated beekeepers. Although some of my oldest informants remembered having problems with beehive theft by LeUaso, Mukogodo and LeUaso generally have had very little contact with each other, and the two groups have had little impact on each others' histories.

Samburu.   The Samburu are a large group of Maa-speaking pastoralists who live across a broad swath of northern Kenya centered on Samburu District. Some Samburu have very large herds of cattle, goats, sheep, and camels, and they constitute the elite among Maa speakers in northern Kenya. According to British colonial documents, the first Samburu to move south into the Mukogodo area probably arrived in the 1920s. Some of these families have lived there ever since and are now regarded by most Mukogodo as more Mukogodo than Samburu. Most of the Samburu living in Mukogodo have married the local people, and some have even started keeping bees and using the dialect of Maa that the Mukogodo speak rather than that of the Samburu.

The creation of the White Highlands had the unintended effect of sending some of these groups, most notably the Ilng'wesi and the Digirri, into the Mukogodo area. The Ilng'wesi were displaced both by European settlers and by Meru farmers who had been displaced by other settlers, while the Digirri were displaced mainly by European alienation of their usual territory. The connection between the alienation of land for European settlement can be understood in some detail thanks to official testimony collected by the colonial authorities in the early 1930s. The testimony was collected as part of an investigation by the Kenya Land Commission, also known as the Carter Commission. This commission had been established to document and assess competing claims to land, most of which were a result of the alienation of land for European settlement. Testimony given to the commission is now one of our best sources of information about Kenyan history. The testimony to the commission by representatives of the Digirri and Ilng'wesi supports the idea that both groups had arrived recently in the Mukogodo area due to European alienation of land. The Digirri representative, Rono Ole Kifaru, specified that they "originally occupied land on the north bank of the Ahoni River, but when this was alienated to Europeans" they moved to their old hunting grounds in the west of the Mukogodo area. The Ilng'wesi representative, Mungai Ole Theorori, identified the alienation of land for European settlement around Nanyuki, just south of the Mukogodo area, as the main impetus for their movement into Mukogodo.

Somewhat belatedly, this side effect of European settlement was acknowledged by colonial officials familiar with the area. For example, D. G. Worthy, district officer in Mukogodo in the late 1950s, wrote that "the results of European pressure and settlement were that the Ndigiri [Digirri] moved gradually north until they came to settle in the area called Ol Choki which lies partly within and partly to the west of the present Mukogodo area." Worthy also cites the pressure of European settlement as a reason for the Ilng'wesi movement in the Mukogodo area: "pressure first by the Meru and then by the European settlers caused the Il Ngwesi gradually to move in a North-Westwards direction toward and into the South-East corner of Mukogodo they now occupy." Thus, the domino effect caused by creation of the White Highlands put Mukogodo into steady contact with these groups for the first time, giving them chance to interact and, most important, to intermarry.

IL-TORROBO, "DOROBO," AND TORROBO

To explain the rest of Mukogodo history, we first need to take a digression into the ethnic and status labels used by Maa speakers. First, let's look at the word *Maasai*. It is an ethnic label, to be sure, but to Maa speakers it is much more than that. The label carries with it not only a suggestion of what language a person speaks and other aspects of his or her culture, but also information about subsistence and, most important, status. Pastoral Maasai see themselves as being at the peak of a socioeconomic hierarchy defined by language and subsistence practices. Simply put, Maa speakers have more prestige than speakers of other languages, pastoralism is more prestigious than farming, and farming, though less desirable than pastoralism, is more prestigious than hunting and gathering. Groups that conform closely to this pastoral, Maa-speaking cultural ideal can claim greater prestige than groups that violate it either by speaking a different language or by engaging in subsistence activities other than pastoralism.

Different groups of Maa speakers conform to this ideal to different degrees. The Maasai themselves exemplify the ideal because they speak Maa and subsisted, at least until recently, mostly on their livestock. Even though they are not usually called Maasai, the Samburu of northern Kenya also have high status thanks to their recent history of conformity with the ideals of Maa speaking and pure pastoralism. The Ilchamus of the Lake Baringo region in Kenya, though still usually considered Maasai, deviate from the ideal by eating fish, which most Maa speakers consider repugnant. The Arusha Maasai of Tanzania, though still Maasai, violate the ideal by growing crops.

Maa speakers usually refer to Mukogodo, Mumonyot, Ilng'wesi, Digirri, and LeUaso, as well as a variety of groups in other parts of Kenya and Tanzania, not as Maasai but as *il-torrobo* (singular: *ol-torroboni*). *Il-torrobo* has been anglicized as "Dorobo," also spelled Ndorobo, Nderobo, Wandorobo, Wanderobo, and Torrobo. In this book I use the spelling *il-torrobo* when referring to how Maa speakers use the term and "Dorobo," the most common spelling in British colonial-era documents, when referring to how British administrators and colonists used it. Anthropologists use the "Torrobo" spelling when using the word for their own purposes, which I will also do. Thus the spelling of the word will serve as an indicator of whether I am using the word as it is used by Maa speakers, as it was used by the British, or as it is used by anthropologists.

The origins of the term *il-torrobo* are obscure. It has been suggested that it comes from the Maa word for "short," *dorop*; the Maa word for tsetse fly; a combination of the Maa words for bees, *lotorok* with the word for cattle pen, *bo*, referring to people who keep bees rather than livestock; and the word *darabe:da*, meaning "forest" in the language of the Datog of Tanzania. Whatever its origin, it is clear that the meaning of *il-torrobo* to Maa speakers is essentially derogatory, being used to refer to poor people who must live like wild animals, that is, by hunting and gathering, rather than from domesticated plants and animals. The label has a way of sticking with people through the generations so that even groups that have not hunted for decades may be labeled *il-torrobo*.

In the minds of Maa speakers *il-torrobo* are associated with a variety of negative concepts, including offensiveness, meanness, poverty, cowardice, womanhood, degradation, imperfection, degeneration, and contamination. *Il-torrobo* are associated in a Maasai myth with an original fall from grace, in which *ol-torroboni* is said to have shot an arrow to sever the cord connecting heaven and earth, down which God had been sending cattle. Other Maasai stories use *il-torrobo* as negative models to teach lessons about envy and selfishness. Alfred Hollis, who studied the Maa language and Maasai folklore early in the twentieth century, recorded two such stories. "The Two Dorobo" is a tale of treachery and deceit between two brothers in which one brother, jealous at the other's hunting success, first puts his brother's eye out and then attempts to kill him, only to be killed himself when his plot is discovered. "The Dorobo and the Giraffe" is about one man tricking a hunter into giving him all the meat from a giraffe in retaliation for the hunter's selfishness. John Galaty, an ethnographer of the Maasai from McGill University, suggests that the idea of *il-torrobo* is so antithetical to the Maasai image of themselves that it acts as a kind of symbolic "antipraxis," helping the Maasai to define themselves more clearly. One of Galaty's informants even went so far as to list these three key differences between *il-*

torrobo and Maasai: *il-torrobo* smell like urine and feces, they were reared without cattle and eat wild animals, and they speak Maa imperfectly. According to a Samburu man I spoke to recently, *il-torrobo* are treacherous little people who will shoot you with their bows and arrows if you walk through their forests. This pattern of denigration of foragers by pastoralists is widespread in Africa.

Maa speakers apply the term *il-torrobo* to all hunters and gatherers, not as a tribal label so much as a class designation. British colonialists, however, did not understand that it referred to status and subsistence patterns, mistaking it for a legitimate ethnic label. Following the lead of the pastoralist elites of the Maa-speaking world, the British referred to the Mukogodo and many other groups as "Dorobo." This kind of mistake, in which one group is smeared by the derogatory label given to it by its neighbors, is commonplace in the history of colonialism. As a result, anthropologists have become accustomed to learning new names for groups they have studied or read about. The word *Eskimo*, for example, is considered derogatory by the people it is used to refer to because it means "eaters of raw meat" in the language of their neighbors. Today, we call those people what they call themselves, Inuit. Similarly, I grew up in southern Arizona referring to the Native Americans in a large reservation nearby as "Papago." But in the 1980s the people on the reservation decided to abandon that name, which means "bean eaters," and use instead their preferred name, Tohono O'odham, meaning "people of the desert."

Because they were all referred to by the same term, most British jumped to the conclusion that all "Dorobo" somehow formed a single "tribe." The British view of "Dorobo" as a single tribe reflects a widespread belief among European colonialists in Africa in the reality and fixity of various "tribes." These days, anthropologists disparage that kind of thinking as "essentialist," meaning that it focuses too much on the search for what a particular group has in common—its "essence"—and pays too little attention to the variability within groups and the often very porous boundaries between them. But essentialism is an easy way to think and a simpler basis for colonial policy than would have been possible had the British recognized the complexities and subtleties of ethnic identity among their new subjects. Although the essentialist view of ethnicity and tribal identity is always misleading, it is particularly inappropriate in the case of the Dorobo. Rather than living in a single contiguous region like a proper tribe, they were scattered across the map in a variety of small, isolated groups, many of whom knew nothing of one another's existence. Unlike typical "tribes," which were often defined in terms of a common language, the various Dorobo groups spoke no single language. Rather, some spoke Maa, some Kalenjin, some Kikuyu, and, of course, one group spoke Yaaku. Finally, the boundaries of "Dorobo" groups are especially variable, with people continually joining and leaving them depending on their successes and failures as livestock keepers. In short, it would be hard to find a label that is less appropriate as an ethnic label than "Dorobo."

Despite how little the "Dorobo" resembled a tribe, British officials struggled throughout the colonial period to treat them as one. It is clear from colonial records that this caused quite a few administrative headaches. For example, one British colonial official remarked upon the difficulty he found during a safari along the Kenya–Tanganyika border of telling lapsed Maasai from "true Wandorobo," while at the same time persisting in the belief that "Wandorobo" (a Swahili plural form of "Dorobo") was a legitimate category to begin with. Later, a colonial administrator traveling in the Laikipia area noted in a telegram to another administrator the frustration he felt in trying to fit a particular "Dorobo" group into a predetermined pigeon hole, grumbling that these anomalous people "should be called upon to explain their origin and to quote to whom they were known and what their language."

Although a good case could have been made to abandon the idea that "Dorobo" had any legitimacy as a tribal label, this was not done. The tenacity with which the British clung to the "Dorobo" notion may be explained by the important place "Dorobo" came to have in the ideology behind British colonialism in Kenya. Many administrators and some settlers believed that "Dorobo" had been systematically victimized by members of other, more powerful tribes, particularly Kikuyu and other Bantu-speaking agricultural groups. The image of victimized Dorobo became an important element in the British justification of the creation of the White Highlands in Kikuyu-dominated areas of central Kenya. This grew out of the fact that the Kikuyu case for the legitimacy of their claims to sections of the White Highlands rested in part on the idea that they had purchased much of the land from its hunter-gatherer owners, people they called Asi or Athi and Agumba. Much of the work of the Kenya Land Commission in the early 1930s concerned exploring the legitimacy of these claims, and much of its subsequent report is devoted to a contemptuous and mocking dismissal of most of them.

Elspeth Huxley, who is best known for *The Flame Trees of Thika*, an autobiographical account of European settler life in Kenya, summarized the settler point of view in a history of Kenya colony that she entitled *White Man's Country*:

> Most of the Kikuyu country was said by the Wakikuyu themselves to have been occupied until relatively recently by Wandorobo tribes called the Asi and the Agumba. It is only in modern times that the Wakikuyu came down from the north and dispossessed these little hunters. So even that part of the disputed land which was in temporary native occupation in 1904 can hardly be said to have belonged to the Wakikuyu. They had taken it from somebody else only a few years before. For some of it—although for by no means all—they paid a fee in goats. So recent was the invasion of Dorobo territory that many of the goat transactions were, according to the Wakikuyu themselves, only partially completed when the British took over the administration of the country.

Huxley's language is worth noting for what it reveals about the settlers' view of the situation. While "these little hunters" are said to have been "dispossessed" of their lands through a Kikuyu "invasion" of their territories, the British are described as merely "taking over the administration of the country." In this way, the British settlers and their supporters could depict themselves not as having invaded and displaced peoples with longstanding claims to the land, but rather as defenders of the powerless Dorobo against invading Bantu hordes that had arrived only recently.

If "Dorobo" were somehow worthy of protection to the British, the Mukogodo, who lived in rockshelters and spoke a unique language, were special. They were, as colonial administrator C. A. Cornell declared in 1924, "of pure Nderobo stock," and, as a settler called them a few years later, the "true Dorobo." The protective attitude of administrators toward Mukogodo is evident in testimony given before the Kenya Land Commission by R. G. Stone, provincial commissioner of Northern Frontier Province, in an attempt to counter the testimony of settler Raymond Hook, who depicted the Mukogodo area as one in need of "improvement": "Com. Hook stated that some years ago the Mukogodo were—I think he used the term—a despicable race, but that they now own huts and stock. That appears to me to indicate considerable progression. That is a thing which the administration of this country encourages." K. G. Lindsay, another colonial official familiar with the Mukogodo area in his capacity as district commissioner of North Nyeri District, also testified in defense of Mukogodo:

> Finally I would make a special plea on behalf of the Dorobo for a permanent reservation which they can call their own.
>
> They have the making of a useful section of the community, but for years they felt insecure in the tenure of the grazing areas left to them. They ask for little, and, having in the past been driven like chaff before a wind of progression, now merit some recognition for themselves.

The result was the creation of the Dorobo Reserve, now known as Mukogodo Division, as a safe haven for "true Dorobo" such as Mukogodo.

Later colonial administrators continued the tradition of defending Mukogodo from other groups. D. G. Worthy, district officer in Mukogodo for almost a year during the late 1950s and a prolific writer of reports on the peoples of the Mukogodo area, argued that Mukogodo may have been victims of the same sort of Bantu expansionism that had victimized "Dorobo" in central Kenya: "There is reason to believe that in the past the Mukogodo did in fact derive from the North and West of Mount Kenya. If this theory is correct then the Mukogodo must have been expelled by the Bantu invasons [sic] that brought in the Meru and Kikuyu people." Although Worthy does not explain the source of this idea, it does fit with Meru traditions regarding the Mukogodo. In his "Handing Over Report" to his successor as district officer, J. Rowlands, Worthy argued that it was "a prime necessity that at all times, the priority of the Dorobo interests be emphasized and wherever possible, a Dorobo be appointed to a post in preference of an alien." Years later, Worthy repeated this general idea in a letter to me: "These Wanderobo were people who were and presumably still are the victims and prey of more powerful groups. We sought in the nineteen fifties to give them a chance to retain their very unusual identity as people who predated the later migrations."

ETHNIC TIDYING

The phrase *ethnic cleansing* entered English as a cynical euphemism used to describe efforts to purge portions of the former Yugoslavia through forced migrations and mass murder. British policies toward the people of Kenya were by no means the equivalent of ethnic cleansing, but they were still based on the belief that ethnic identities are essential qualities of people and that people who share an ethnicity should live with one another and apart from people of other ethnicities. Because the British are fond of tidiness in many respects (for example, the British equivalent of the U.S. "Keep America Beautiful" advertising campaign is "Keep Britain Tidy"), I have coined the phrase *ethnic tidying* to describe British colonial policies toward the peoples of Kenya.

The essence of ethnic tidying was quite simple: identify a limited number of discrete ethnic units in the colony, associate certain parcels of land with those ethnic units, and ensure that people live in the areas where they have the most cultural affinities. This policy bore many similarities to the United States government's creation of a system of reservations for American Indians. In Kenya, the result was the creation of a series of tribal reserves, including the Dorobo Reserve (now Mukogodo Division) and the Maasai Reserve in southern Kenya, and the forced movement of people into those reserves. People who did not fit the ethnic profile of a particular reserve were moved to another that administrators deemed more appropriate.

Ethnic tidying was not simply a matter of creating a neat and simple ethnic landscape. Another goal was to limit the amount of land associated with particular ethnic groups and so to increase the land available for European settlement and related infrastructure, such as railroads and highways. How the British accomplished those goals can be seen in the history of their treaties with Maasai leaders. Before the arrival of the British, Maa-speaking peoples were distributed in a more or less continuous swath across East Africa from Kenya's Ndoto Mountains and Lake Turkana in the north, where they are represented by such groups as Ariaal and Samburu, down through the Great Rift Valley and into eastern Tanganyika (now Tanzania), where they are represented by Parakuyo. In the center of this distribution was the main body of the pastoral Maasai. This continuous distribution of Maa speakers was split in two as a result of British colonial policies in the early twentieth century. This bifurcation occurred in two stages. The first Maasai Treaty of 1904 created two reserves, one on the Laikipia Plateau north of the new railway and another south of the railway. The subsequent Maasai Treaty of 1911 eliminated the northern reserve and obligated the Maasai to move to an expanded southern reserve (today's Kajiado and Narok Districts).

The Mukogodo area was a problem for this policy. As we have seen, the alienation of land for European settlement led to the movement of Maa-speaking pastoralists into the Mukogodo area. Such movements filled the Mukogodo area with people who appeared to belong either with the Meru to the southeast, in the Maasai Reserve to the south, or in Samburu District to the north, along with people such as the Mukogodo themselves who seemed to be "true Dorobo" and thus in need of some sort of reserve of their own. Some colonial officials, perceiving some similarities between Mukogodo and other Cushitic speakers such as the Galla in northern Kenya, suggested making the Mukogodo area part of the Northern Frontier Province. However, the status of the Mukogodo in British eyes as "true Dorobo" and the importance of that identity as a justification for the alienation of land for European settlement served to protect Mukogodo from such forced movements and encouraged the creation of the Dorobo Reserve, where they hoped to protect Mukogodo from Maa speakers and others.

If the Mukogodo were to be protected, then at least some of the non-Mukogodo peoples had to leave. Accordingly, British authorities deported Digirri, Ilng'wesi, LeUaso, Mumonyot, and Samburu to other parts of Kenya a total of twenty-one times between 1912 and 1959. The LeUaso were deported only once, in 1935 to Samburu District, but in the late 1950s there was an additional attempt on the part of the local administrators to move LeUaso to Samburu District. That attempt was foiled by a report by the anthropologist Paul Spencer that undermined the idea that the LeUaso had affinities to the Samburu. According to Spencer, moving people out of the Dorobo Reserve had become such a popular pastime for local officials that it was derided as "the Doldol [that is, Don Dol] administrators' sport," and other officials sometimes refused to go along with it, particularly when it involved a group for which no other area felt any responsibility. Mukogodo, their status as "true Dorobo" unassailable, were the only people the administrators never attempted to deport from the Dorobo Reserve.

BRIDEWEALTH INFLATION

If the goal of British administrators was to protect the Mukogodo from contact with and influence from Maa-speaking pastoralists, it is fair to say that the policy was an utter failure. The net effect of British colonial policies was, in fact, just the opposite. British alienation of land for European settlement forced several groups into contact with the Mukogodo for the first time. This gave them the opportunity to interact and, most important, to intermarry. And the British policy of deportations had the unintended effect of encouraging intermarriage between Mukogodo and the Maa speakers. Such marriages provided a couple of important benefits, especially to the non-Mukogodo. First, it gave them additional support for their claim to have extensive local ties in the Mukogodo area. Second, it gave them Mukogodo affines (relatives by marriage). As soon as they could, the deportees returned, often having left their livestock with their new Mukogodo affines. As the colonial administrator D. G. Worthy noted with frustration, "Each time the Mumonyot Masai were removed from the Mukogodo area, their relations by marriage helped them return." Worthy reported that he "had to be constantly on the alert for Samburu returning secretly and being hidden by their Dorobo relations by marriage." The resulting failure of any of the deportations to take hold was the main reason why there were so many of them. Because the Mukogodo transition to pastoralism appears to have been largely complete by 1936, only those moves conducted before the late 1930s can be seen as contributing to that transition. But this still leaves eleven forced moves that encouraged marriages between Mukogodo and non-Mukogodo.

This combination of opportunity and motive that was inadvertently created by British policies is reflected in rates of marriage between Mukogodo and non-Mukogodo. While Mukogodo have no memory of marriages with non-Mukogodo before 1900, in the first four decades of the twentieth century six times more Mukogodo women married non-Mukogodo men as Mukogodo men who married non-Mukogodo women (forty-two vs. seven, respectively; see Figure 3.2). Non-Mukogodo men made attractive sons-in-law in part because they were able to offer livestock as bridewealth, while most Mukogodo men could offer only the traditional beehive bridewealth. The number of Mukogodo women married in exchange for livestock bridewealths began to exceed those married in exchange for beehive bridewealths in the decade following 1909, and the last beehive bridewealth was paid in approximately 1931 (Figure 3.3). After that date, only livestock were acceptable to Mukogodo parents as bridewealth for their daughters.

The change from beehives to livestock represents not only a shift in the type of bridewealth but actual bridewealth inflation because the exchange value of the livestock given in a typical livestock bridewealth was much greater than the value of the beehives given in a typical beehive bridewealth. The traditional exchange value between hives and livestock was one hive for one goat or sheep, while one head of cattle was worth several small stock. Hives were also at a disadvantage because they were never really in short supply. Any man could make a hive if he really needed one, while no man could create his own livestock no matter how hard he tried.

For many Mukogodo men the problem contained its own solution in that a simple way to obtain livestock was to marry one's daughters and sisters to non-Mukogodo pastoralist men. Nevertheless, many Mukogodo men during this period had to delay marriage until late in life due to a lack of livestock, and between a quarter and a third of the men who entered the marriage market during this period never married at all (Figure 3.4). Colonial-era census data show that one result of this pattern of out-marriage was an unusually male-biased sex ratio in the adult population. Because Mukogodo women were marrying outsiders at a much higher rate than Mukogodo men, the adult Mukogodo population was only 28.6 percent female, the adult populations of the non-Mukogodo groups in the area (Mumonyot, Digirri, and Ilng'wesi) were approximately balanced between men and women, with between 48.4 percent and 51.9 percent females in their adult populations.

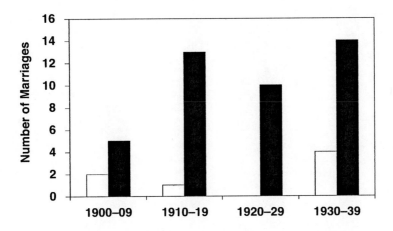

Figure 3.2   Marriages between Mukogodo men and non-Mukogodo women (white bars) and between Mukogodo women and non-Mukogodo men (black bars) during the early twentieth century.

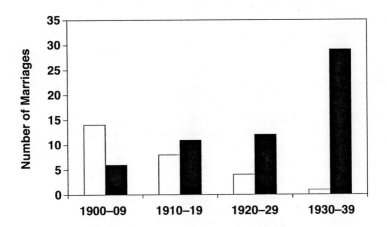

Figure 3.3   Forms of bridewealth payments during the early twentieth century. White bars represent beehive bridewealth payments and black bars represent livestock bridewealth payments.

In short, the high rate of intermarriage between Mukogodo and non-Mukogodo generally and between Mukogodo women and non-Mukogodo men in particular ensured that the Mukogodo would become pastoralists. Mukogodo men who failed to become pastoralists failed to marry and thus, given their patrilineal system of descent and inheritance, failed to produce legitimate heirs. All men in two Mukogodo lineages, Suaanga and Biyoti, failed to make the transition,

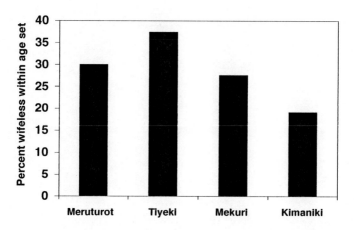

Figure 3.4   Rates of wifelessness among Mukogodo age sets during the early twentieth century.

and as a result those lineages no longer exist. Those who succeeded in getting livestock, either by marrying female relatives to pastoralists in exchange for livestock, by trading hunting trophies for livestock, or in the final years of the transition by working for Europeans and using the cash to buy livestock, were able to marry. But becoming a pastoralist for the most part meant giving up on hunting and gathering. Hunting and gathering were less necessary given the new food source, and the needs of the livestock left less time for other activities. Living in small rockshelters was no longer practical because herds were growing. And although I can attest to the fact that cattle are more agile than most people think, many of the rockshelters were inaccessible to them and good grazing was too inconvenient. As hunting and rockshelters were abandoned, other aspects of Mukogodo culture, particularly the Yaaku language and their old religion, also fell by the wayside as the Maa language and Maasai culture took their places.

ETHNICITY MANAGEMENT

Switching from hunting to herding and from Yaaku to Maa were not just practical things for a Mukogodo man to do if he wanted to make a living, marry, and talk to his new neighbors. They also were ways of shedding the stigma of the *il-torrobo* label slapped on the Mukogodo by Maa speakers. They were, to coin a phrase, efforts at ethnicity management. When the Mukogodo were living as hunter-gatherers, interacting with pastoralists but not dependent upon them for any necessities, they could afford to disregard the low opinion pastoralists generally have for hunter-gatherers in Africa. But once they became part of the world of Maa speakers their history of hunting and speaking Yaaku became a burden.

Anthropological understandings of ethnicity have tended to range between the view that there is something basic, even primordial, about ethnic identities and the contrasting view that ethnic identities are best understood as instruments used in the orchestration of social life. Both of the poles of this continuum are easy to criticize. An extreme primordialist view of ethnicity, for example, has been undermined by demonstrations of how recently so many of the world's ethnicities were created, often in the midst of local and regional political struggles. An extreme instrumentalist view is undermined by observations of how heartfelt ethnic identity is for many people, however recently it may have been constructed, and how difficult it often is to switch from one ethnic identity to another. Somewhere between these two extreme positions has emerged a more nuanced and sophisticated understanding of ethnicity as a multifaceted phenomenon that can appear in one instance as an instrumental social construction and in another as an obligatory fact of existence. Perhaps the easiest path through this conceptual maze is to recognize that, in accordance with the instrumentalist view, markers of ethnic identity, which may include clothing, hair styles, jewelry, languages, and accents, are indeed instruments used in social interaction; specifically, they are signals of ethnic group membership. But markers of ethnic identity are not just *any* sort of signal. Rather, signals that are reliable markers of ethnic group membership must be difficult to fake: it must be hard for people who do not have a good claim to membership in a particular group to send convincing signals of their membership in that group. For example, with my light brown hair, green eyes, pale skin, Anglo name, poor command of Spanish, and ignorance of the many nuances of Mexican culture, I would have a hard time convincing anyone that I am Mexican (though I was once mistaken for a German tourist while studying a map in San Francisco). If ethnic markers were easy to fake, they would be useless as markers of group membership, people would be free to change them at will, and ethnicity would lose most or all of its importance to people. Thus, as signals of group membership, markers of ethnic identity do have an instrumental quality, but they are only reliable as markers of group boundaries to the extent to which they also have a hard-to-fake quality that may give them an appearance of being primordial or even essential.

It is clear from the colonial records that Mukogodo and their neighbors were well aware of the instrumental qualities of ethnic labels. The testimony of representatives from the Mukogodo area before the Kenya Land Commission in the early 1930s is particularly revealing. Apparently appreciative of the protective attitude of British administrators toward "Dorobo" and despite the term's negative connotations to Maa speakers, the Digirri, Ilng'wesi, and Mukogodo representatives went so far as to use this hated term for themselves in their testimony. The Digirri representative testified that "We are pure Dorobo—not Masai." Similarly, the Ilng'wesi representative reported "We are of pure Dorobo extraction. We are not Masai or Meru." The Mukogodo representative agreed that the Mukogodo, Digirri, and Ilng'wesi "are all Dorobo" and even "clans of the one tribe," emphasizing that "by race we are Dorobo" and that the Mukogodo "have no affinity with the Masai and speak a different language."

The instrumental quality of such declarations of "Dorobo" status is made clearer when we realize that the Mukogodo representative Silangei Ole Matunge, unlike almost all other Mukogodo and also unlike the Digirri and Ilng'wesi representatives present at the commission's native evidence session at which they all spoke, could have legitimately claimed to be Maasai, not "Dorobo." This is because, as explained in the previous chapter, his lineage was one of two of the thirteen Mukogodo lineages to have been founded by impoverished Maasai individuals who took refuge among the Mukogodo in the nineteenth century. The fact that he chose not to do so and instead identified himself as a "Dorobo" is evidence of his sophisticated understanding of the importance of that label in the minds of the British administrators. It should be noted that it was not enough to claim "Dorobo" identity to avoid deportation to another tribal reserve. In addition to the non-Mukogodo peoples of the Mukogodo area, other "Dorobo" groups in other parts of Kenya were also moved to areas where they were believed to have greater cultural affinities, including areas set aside for Kalenjin, Kikuyu, and Maa speakers. The Mukogodo were left in place largely because of their unique language. Ironically, as we have seen, other British policies were leading to a replacement of that language by Maa.

The strategic and deliberate quality of Mukogodo pronouncements about their "Dorobo" status is made even clearer when we contrast it to other groups that had nothing to gain from declaring such a status and a lot to lose in the eyes of their Maa-speaking neighbors if that were to become their permanent and official label. The "Dorobo" of the Matthews Range in Samburu country north of Mukogodo are one such group. That group, referred to in colonial records as the "Wamba Wandorobo" because they lived near the town of Wamba but more properly known as the Suiei, were discussed in a 1947 memo from the district officer in their area to his boss, the provincial commissioner. After describing their current situation, he added the following side note:

> An interesting point which cropped up on my last safari to Wamba
> was that the Wandorobo asked to be called by the name SWEI, which
> they say is their proper old name and they dislike being called
> Wandorobo. I am not quite sure of the significance of this though it
> appears to be a "nationalistic" move. I will look into it further.

OTHER POSSIBLE
REASONS FOR THE TRANSITION

Transitions from one sort of subsistence to another—from hunting to herding, from herding to farming, from farming to wage labor—occur frequently and for a wide variety of reasons. The available evidence suggests that the key to understanding the Mukogodo transition was intermarriage with their new Maa-speaking pastoralist neighbors and bridewealth inflation, but other explanations are worth considering briefly.

Improved standard of living.   Given that human history has witnessed a general and widespread trend away from hunting and gathering and toward food production, including pastoralism, it is conceivable that food production provides some sort of broad improvement in standard of living that makes it attractive to people. However, the more we learn about such transitions, both among living peoples and in prehistory, the less likely this seems. In fact, the diets of hunter-gatherers tend to be healthier than those of food producers. Hunter-gatherers tend to eat lots of lean meats and high-fiber vegetable foods, just as physicians say we all should. Indeed, the health benefits of such a diet are thought to be due to the fact that our species evolved to eat such foods. Food producers, on the other hand, tend to rely upon a small number of foods, often relatively unhealthy starchy ones. Food producers also tend to suffer more from diseases and other ailments than hunter-gatherers. Some, such as tooth decay, are directly attributable to the diets of food producers. Others are carried by livestock and transmitted to humans. Smallpox, for instance, was carried by cattle before it jumped to humans, and very recently mad cow disease, more technically called bovine spongiform encephalopathy, was found to cause brain-wasting Creutzfeldt-Jakob disease in humans. Food producers also tend to live in larger communities and have higher population densities than hunter-gatherers, which makes them more vulnerable to infectious diseases generally. But perhaps, despite the health costs of food producing, the work load is so much easier that it seems worth it to people to make the switch. This, too, seems to be a myth. Studies since the 1960s have shown that hunter-gatherer workloads are generally not as high as those in food-producing societies. My Mukogodo friends who were alive during the transition have mixed feelings about the transition to pastoralism and its impact on their daily work lives. Some waxed nostalgic about the rockshelter days, remembering fondly that all they needed to do for food was go into the wilderness and find it, while nowadays they must do a lot of work just to maintain their herds from day to day. Others thought that life is easier with livestock because one's food source is right at home rather than out in the bush. Nothing like a consensus ever emerged from such discussions, making me think that the transition did not offer any really clear-cut benefits in terms of work loads.

Before very recent times and in particular the advent of modern means of birth control, improvements in the material conditions of life normally led to higher reproductive rates. In general, food producers, despite the health problems associated with their way of life, do have higher reproductive rates than hunter-gatherers. If, as the theory of natural selection would have it, differential reproduction is what drove the evolution of our and all other species, then perhaps the most fair way to assess the impact of the Mukogodo transition to pastoralism on their standard of living is to look at reproductive rates. This approach also does not offer much support for the idea that they made the switch to improve their standard of living. The upper part of Figure 3.5 shows data on number of children per Mukogodo woman before, during, and after the transition. The regression line, which summarizes the central tendency of the data, has an upward slope, which at first glance suggests that there might indeed have been an improvement in female reproductive success due to the transition to pastoralism. But a closer look suggests otherwise. The lower part of Figure 3.5 shows those same data divided into two categories: women for whom a beehive bridewealth was paid and women for whom a livestock bridewealth was paid. The regression line is positive even for those women who had their reproductive careers entirely or almost entirely before the transition was under way, suggesting that if these data are good then something other than the transition must have been causing an improvement in female reproductive success. This, however, seems unlikely. The individual in the upper left hand corner of that graph, marked with an asterisk, is the wife of the founder of the lineage, Leitiko, for which I had my very best genealogical informant, Stephen Lereman LeLeitiko. Stephen Lereman's knowledge of local history was so detailed that even people from the non-Mukogodo groups in the area suggested that I ask him about their history. Notice that the woman who helped found his lineage in Mukogodo appears to have had eight children. Either she had a lot more children than other Mukogodo women at that time, or Stephen Lereman's memory is simply better than those of my other genealogical informants. My guess is that the apparent upward slope in female reproductive success among the Mukogodo is simply an artifact of the way that people, particularly those women who lived back in the nineteenth century, have been forgotten over the years. If I had had thirteen genealogical informants with knowledge as encyclopedic as Stephen Lereman's about their lineages, the regression lines would probably be flat, indicating no improvement in female reproductive success or in standard of living as a result of the transition to pastoralism.

Given the poor quality of the data on Mukogodo reproductive rates before recent times, perhaps a better way to address this question would be to compare hunter-gatherers for whom we have good demographic data to the Mukogodo after the transition to pastoralism. This also does not provide much support for this hypothesis. Based on the female reproductive histories collected by Beth and an estimate of infant mortality rates based on Kenyan census data, I estimate the average number of live births per Mukogodo woman since the transition to pastoralism to be about 6.9. This is within the range for numbers of live births per woman in hunter-gatherer societies, which range from less than four to more than eight. It remains possible that Mukogodo women have given birth to more babies on average after the transition, but the existing data certainly do not make this a convincing explanation of why the transition occurred.

Food shortages.   Another possibility is that the Mukogodo experienced some sort of food shortage that encouraged them to adopt pastoralism. My main reason for skepticism about this is simply that none of my Mukogodo informants remembered

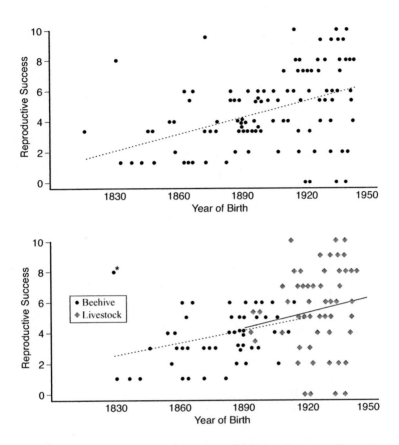

Figure 3.5   Marriage and lifetime reproductive success for Mukogodo women. The top figure shows all women, undifferentiated by the type of bridewealth their husbands paid. The bottom figure shows women separated by type of bridewealth paid. The asterisk indicates a woman discussed in the text. Because bridewealth information was not available for all women, the number of women shown in the top figure is slightly greater than the number shown in the bottom figure. MIKE SIEGEL, RUTGERS CARTOGRAPHY LAB

any such food shortage during their rockshelter days. Indeed, colonial records suggest that the area was rich with game. Charles Fannin, a government surveyor, reported in the 1930s that game was so plentiful in the area that it depleted grazing that otherwise would have been useful for livestock. British officials on safari through the Mukogodo area in 1943 reported that "the whole of this area was teeming with game, fresh tracks of elephant and rhino being seen everywhere, and giraffe must inhabit that area literally in thousands." Just west of the Mukogodo area, other British officials in the 1920s noticed that the alienation of land for European settlement was having the same sort of domino effect on animal populations that it did on human ones, causing an increase in the abundance of game in the area.

A shortage of plant foods, like a shortage of game, also seems unlikely to have led to the transition. As we saw in the previous chapter, Mukogodo foragers did not rely heavily on plant foods, preferring meat and honey. Furthermore, Mukogodo now routinely eat some wild plant foods, such as the leafy *nterere* and the berries from a plant called *lorrndo*, which my informants told me were not commonly eaten in the rockshelter days. This suggests that, had a shortage of favored plant foods occurred, they could have switched to other plants. Finally, it seems hard to believe that there was a food shortage when the Mukogodo never fully exploited their forest or the surrounding area. While most of the forest was divided among Mukogodo lineages for beehive-placement territories, a large portion of it, perhaps as much as a third, was never incorporated into any lineage's territory. This is not to say that no one ever hunted or gathered in those areas, but it does indicate that a reasonable response to a food shortage could have been an intensification of hunting, gathering, and beekeeping rather than a wholesale switch to pastoralism.

Laws against hunting.   The British colonial government in Kenya outlawed the hunting of certain species. These laws were not inspired by concerns about endangered species or biodiversity, which no one considered at the time. Rather, they were chiefly inspired by a desire to prevent African hunters from competing with European ones. If these laws were enforced in the Mukogodo area in the early twentieth century, then perhaps the Mukogodo adopted pastoralism out of a fear of prosecution and imprisonment. This, too, seems very unlikely. No colonial official was permanently stationed anywhere in the Mukogodo area until 1948, and no police post was established until 1951. Before that time, enforcement of colonial laws in the Mukogodo area was sporadic, at best, mostly consisting of the periodic forced deportations described above. Paul Spencer, the ethnographer of the Samburu, describes the Mukogodo area as having been "an unadministered paradise" for local people in the 1920s, 1930s, and 1940s because colonial officials were far away and could not "concern themselves unduly with an isolated pocket of minority groups" who lived "in difficult country." When game wardens did visit the Mukogodo area, they rarely bothered to arrest anyone. One old Mukogodo man remembered that, especially if the hunter was old, the British would usually just tell them to go away and stop hunting—"Shomo! Tapala!" (Go! Leave off!)

Furthermore, the British were mainly concerned with big-game species that were attractive to European hunters, such as elephants and rhinoceros. But as we saw in Chapter 2, most Mukogodo did not eat elephant meat, and, on those rare occasions when they ate rhinoceros meat, they did so more for its supposed medical properties than because they needed the food. The main Mukogodo food sources—small animals like hyrax and dik-diks—were unimportant to the British authorities. Since independence, Mukogodo who wished to hunt have not worried a great deal about being prosecuted. On several occasions I was aware of Mukogodo men going on hunting expeditions to kill leopards that were eating their livestock, and I was proudly shown the carcass of a lion that they had killed for the same reason. More than once, my wife and I were told that people would be happy to kill an elephant if we could help them market the tusks. Needless to say, we declined such offers. More recently, the Kenyan government has adopted a shoot-to-kill policy against elephant poachers, and I no longer receive such offers when I visit the Mukogodo area.

Pax Britannica. Colonialism has, and mostly deserves, a bad reputation, but it is possible to find some beneficial effects of the colonial period. These may include the spread of formal education and the reduction of violence between African groups due to the threat of prosecution by colonial governments. Much of the violence in East Africa has long centered on livestock raiding. The possibility exists that the Mukogodo had always wanted to adopt pastoralism but were prevented from doing so by their inability to steal livestock from others and to defend themselves from attacks from other groups. If the British effectively enforced laws against such raids, then the Mukogodo may have been given the opportunity to pursue their dream of pastoralism. This seems quite unlikely for a number of reasons. First, there is no evidence that the Mukogodo ever had any such dream. Unlike their neighbors the Mumonyot, who had only recently lost their livestock and who were keen to return to a pastoralist way of life, the Mukogodo had been living as hunters, gatherers, and beekeepers for many centuries. Presumably, they were good at it and found it an acceptable way to live. In all my interviews with older Mukogodo who lived through the transition, none of them ever expressed any sort of longing for the pastoralist way of life or any memories of frustration over their inability to keep livestock due to raids from other groups. Second, this hypothesis fails for the same reason that the previous one did: Colonial law enforcement in the Mukogodo are was almost nonexistent until well after the Mukogodo had made the transition to pastoralism. Any explanation of the Mukogodo transition must focus on events before 1936, while colonial laws were not effectively enforced in the Mukogodo area until much later.

WHY DID THE MUKOGODO
FAIL TO RESIST THE CHANGE?

When I lecture about the Mukogodo transition to pastoralism in class, students often ask why the Mukogodo did not simply get together and agree to remain hunter-gatherers and not to marry their daughters off to the neighboring pastoralists. After all, the transition was a difficult period, particularly for the men who were forced either to become pastoralists or remain bachelors. It is possible that not only those men but also the Mukogodo as a whole could have both done better reproductively and maintained their way of life if they had been able to come to such an agreement. The problem is that societies like the Mukogodo do not have any good mechanisms in place for group decisionmaking. There is no central authority, no hierarchy, no bureaucracy. Individuals can mostly do what they please. The very idea of telling a man what he could or could not accept as bridewealth in exchange for his daughter would probably never occur to people in such a society.

Even if the Mukogodo had been able to come to some sort of consensus to resist the temptations of livestock bridewealths, they did not have any way to enforce such agreements. Every Mukogodo father who received an offer of a livestock bridewealth from a pastoralist man would have been sorely tempted to take it, both because of the value of the bridewealth itself and the knowledge that, if others are facing the same choice, then it would probably be a good idea to acquire some livestock in order to be able to compete with such offers when looking for a wife for oneself or one's sons. The situation resembles the Prisoner's Dilemma game, often used by scientists to study why people sometimes cooperate and sometimes do not. In the Prisoner's Dilemma, two players must choose simultaneously between cooperating with one another or not cooperating, which is usually called "defecting." The payoffs for the game are structured in such a way that if both players cooperate, they will both receive a moderately high payoff. If both players defect, then they both receive a moderately low payoff. But if one defects while the other cooperates, then the one who defects receives a very high payoff and the one who cooperates receives a very low payoff. Because both players face the same choices, the only logical thing for either of them to do when playing this game for one round is to defect in order to avoid the lowest payoff of all. Even if Mukogodo men had been able to come to an agreement to deal only with one another and not to accept livestock bridewealths, each one of them would have been in exactly this position, knowing that they would be in a very bad situation indeed if everyone else were to break the pact by accepting livestock bridewealths while they were left with no livestock at all. The fact that the Mukogodo never even attempted to come to such an agreement may suggest that they had a good enough intuitive understanding of this problem to realize the futility of such an attempt.

THE TRANSITION IN PERSPECTIVE

Although many of the world's foraging peoples have recently either stopped foraging entirely or started mixing foraging with other types of subsistence, such transitions cannot be taken for granted. In East Africa alone, other hunter-gatherers, such as the Hadza of Tanzania, are still virtually full-time foragers. It can also not be taken for granted that subsistence transitions, when they occur, will also entail the wholesale changeover of entire suites of cultural traits, as in the Mukogodo case. The Okiek, for example, once lived very much like the Mukogodo, emphasizing beekeeping and hunting, but nowadays they do a considerable amount of farming and raise livestock. But, unlike the Mukogodo, the Okiek have not lost their language or their distinctive ethnic identity and associated cultural traits. What makes the Mukogodo different?

In the previous chapter, I described the distinction that James Woodburn has made between delayed-return foragers, like the Mukogodo before the transition, and immediate-return foragers, like the Hadza whom Woodburn himself studies. Woodburn has suggested that delayed-return foraging societies are preadapted for becoming farmers and pastoralists. The reason is that delayed-return foragers already have many of the practices and institutions that anthropologists associate more with food producers than with foragers, such as territoriality, descent groups, and bridewealth payments. In the Mukogodo case, it is very easy to see how their existing bridewealth customs made it likely that a transition to pastoralism would occur as soon as they started intermarrying with pastoralists at a high rate. Bridewealth usually means that a woman's father has considerable power over the decision about whom she will marry, and that lack of autonomy on the part of the women might also be crucial. Among immediate-return foragers, although families do frequently get involved in decisions about marriage, it is also often the case that women have considerable autonomy about whom to marry and how long to stay married. If Mukogodo women had had such autonomy and particularly if Mukogodo men were not accustomed to demanding and paying bridewealth, it is possible that at least some Mukogodo would have remained independent foragers for much longer.

Why did the Mukogodo not only change their subsistence, but also their language, religion, and so many other customs? I think that this must be a result of the very small size of the Mukogodo population, which at the time of the transition was no more than a few hundred individuals. As rates of intermarriage increased, people would have found that they could no longer count on the Yaaku language to talk to their new affines or even to their own grandchildren, who very often either were members of the neighboring Maa-speaking groups of their fathers or were learning their language from their Maa-speaking mothers. As they increasingly depended on livestock and reduced their dependence on the forest, they would also have found Maa, with its well-developed vocabulary concerning livestock and related topics, more useful than Yaaku, which was best developed in the areas of hunting and beekeeping. Yaaku speakers also could not use that language to communicate with anyone outside the group. The Okiek contrast sharply with this situation. There have always been many more Okiek than Mukogodo, giving them both an ability and an incentive to maintain their own language and identity. And because the Okiek speak a Kalenjin language rather than an isolated remnant like Yaaku, they are connected by language to larger groups of Kalenjin speakers elsewhere in Kenya.

THE LAST WORD

To summarize, the Mukogodo transition to pastoralism appears to have been an indirect, ironic, and unintended consequence of British colonial policies. Although British policies were ostensibly designed to protect the Mukogodo from Maa-speaking pastoralists, those policies in fact put the Mukogodo into close contact with Maa speakers and encouraged intermarriage with them. Mukogodo men were faced with a choice between becoming pastoralists or remaining bachelors. Bridewealth was a double-edged sword, both mandating that men seeking wives obtain livestock and giving Mukogodo families a way of doing just that. The transition was rapid, taking only about a decade from start to finish. It was also quite thorough, sweeping aside not only old subsistence patterns but also the Yaaku language and many other aspects of Mukogodo culture.

Eventually, of course, the British left. Kenya did not become a White Man's Country, and the non-Mukogodo peoples of the Mukogodo area were no longer victims of colonial efforts to tidy up the ethnic landscape. Out of curiosity, I once asked my friend Kutiniyai LeKitiman, the Mukogodo cave dweller to whom I introduced you in Chapter 1, why he thought the British had finally left. Gazing out over the Mukogodo forest from the rocky perch where we were sitting, he thought for a minute, shrugged, and said, "Keiba Enkai" ("God hates them").

RECOMMENDED READING

The Mukogodo experience of shifting from foraging to food production can be compared to other African examples presented in *From Hunters to Farmers: The Causes and Consequences of Food Production in Africa* (J. Desmond Clark and Steven A. Brandt, editors, University of California Press, 1984). A good overview of African history is provided by Roland Anthony Oliver in *The African Experience: From Olduvai Gorge to the 21st century* (Westview, 2000). Paul Spencer's classic *Nomads in Alliance: Symbiosis and Growth among the Rendille and Samburu of Kenya* (Oxford University Press, 1973) provides another example of interaction among different groups of Maa speakers as well as an appendix on *il-torrobo* groups in northern Kenya.

4

Poverty as Routine

The elderly Mukogodo who lived through the transition have mixed emotions about it. Some, particularly those old enough to remember the cave days well, wax nostalgic for the time when they spoke Yaaku and tended their hives. Though Mukogodo are mostly reserved, they can get quite emotional when the subject comes up. Matthias Brenzinger, a German linguist who has studied the Yaaku language, shared a poignant story with me that highlights the sense of melancholy that surrounds Mukogodo memories of their old way of life. One day while conducting an interview with an elderly Mukogodo man about the old language, Brenzinger played back some Yaaku phrases that the man had spoken earlier into a tape recorder. At first, the man was delighted to hear the old language, even if it was coming from a box rather than from a person. Not really understanding the principle of the tape recorder, he tried engaging it in conversation, giving the customary cheery "Eiuwuo!" response to the recorded greeting "Aichee!" But soon it became obvious that the tape recorder did not really know how to carry on a conversation in Yaaku. The man first became frustrated, then very angry, and finally he began to weep.

When the Mukogodo shifted from hunting to herding and from Yaaku to Maa, they ensured their continued existence, but at great cost. Partly the cost was cultural: they lost not only their old language but many other aspects of their old way of life as well. But there was also a social cost. As foragers and beekeepers, the Mukogodo had maintained an independent identity and a continuous way of life for hundreds, perhaps thousands, of years. Although their herding and farming neighbors might despise them, they could always count on their hunting skills and beehives to get them by, even in periods when herders and farmers were suffering so much that they had to take refuge among the Mukogodo and similar groups. Since the transition, the Mukogodo have lost that independent stance.

They are now part of a regional social and economic system of Maa-speaking pastoralists. Their specific place within that system is at the bottom. Even though Mukogodo have more possessions than when they had only their hunting tools and hives, ironically they are poorer now than ever before. This chapter documents the Mukogodo way of life as poor Maa-speaking pastoralists, explores the implications of poverty and low status for the Mukogodo, and examines some ways they have found to cope with their new situation.

TRACES OF THE PAST

Since the transition, the Mukogodo have behaved very much like Maasai, and most people traveling through the area would have been convinced by their performance. Their clothing and jewelry are in the Maasai style, they speak a variety of Maa that is most closely related to the dialect of the Maasai of southern Kenya, and they follow the religious and social customs of the Maasai. But if you stay long enough and ask the right questions, their history of being something other than Maasai can still be seen in various ways.

LANGUAGE

Given that the Mukogodo case for being "true Dorobo" in the eyes of the British was strengthened by their possession of a unique language, the rapid replacement of Yaaku by Maa is perhaps the most ironic aspect of the transition to pastoralism. The loss of Yaaku was swift. While reports from early in the twentieth century indicate that the language was still very much alive, by the time of Bernd Heine's work in 1969 all Mukogodo spoke Maa and no more than 28 percent had even a rudimentary knowledge of the old language. Heine's informants told him that the decision to drop Yaaku in favor of Maa was made at a public meeting in the early 1930s. My informants in the 1980s remembered no such meeting, though memories could easily have faded in the intervening years. If indeed the loss of Yaaku was a deliberate act and not simply a side effect of intermarriage with Maa speakers, it makes practical sense in a number of ways. First, the number of people who could speak Yaaku was quite small, necessitating that everyone be at least bilingual. Second, Yaaku was a language well suited to hunting and beekeeping, with, for example, five different words for beehive, while Maa may have been better suited to their new pastoralist economy. Third, the retention of a language other than Maa and an inability to speak perfect Maa would have been significant impediments to Mukogodo efforts to claim "Maasai" status.

Rumors persist among the neighbors of the Mukogodo that they still speak Yaaku in private, but in fact the language is quite dead. Figure 4.1 is a photograph of Yapanoi NeSakaya, who in 2001 claimed to be the last living fluent Yaaku speaker. But the Maa spoken by the descendants of Yaaku speakers does retain a few bits and pieces of the old language, some of which have been documented by Matthias

Figure 4.1   Yapanoi NeSakaya, who claimed in 2001 to be the last living speaker of Yaaku. Lee Cronk

Brenzinger. As you might expect, much of the Yaaku that has been retained concerned the quintessentially Yaaku activity of beekeeping. The Yaaku word for a natural cavity in a tree trunk where bees have a nest, *xeneb*, has become the Mukogodo Maa word *heneb*. The Maa word for the same thing, *mulug*, is not often used.

Nostalgia for Yaaku is great enough among some older Mukogodo that they will even turn Maa words into Yaaku when given a chance. Brenzinger reports that some of his informants would give the Yaaku name of a particular tree as *porohai*. But since Brenzinger knows from his very detailed work on Mukogodo ethnobotany that the Yaaku name for that tree was actually *paxa*, it appears that *porohai* is simply a Yaaku-ization of the Maa name for it, *lporokuai*. Similarly, something an old man once told me might be less a recollection of actual spoken Yaaku than an attempt to reconstruct the past by combining some faded memories with current practice. Ngunio LeKinyare, a lively and expressive man whose company I always enjoyed a great deal, told me that during the cave days Mukogodo co-wives called each other *pameren*, a term meaning "beehive giver" and "beehive receiver," because it was customary for a senior wife to give a bee-hive to the newly arriving junior wife. This, however, seems unlikely. Because *pameren* is an odd combination of the Yaaku word for beehive, *meren*, with the Maa prefix used to mark gift-giving relationships, *pa*, it seems more likely to be a sort of linguistic chimera than an actual Yaaku term.

Maa is spoken by a range of groups from northern Kenya south into central Tanzania. Like any widespread language, it has dialects and regional accents. All versions of Maa are mutually intelligible, but the differences among them can be quite striking when you get used to one and then hear another. The biggest con-trast is between the northern version spoken by the Samburu and the southern version spoken by the Maasai of southern Kenya and Tanzania. A good analogy might be with different varieties of English. If we say that the Maasai variety is analogous to British English and the Samburu variety is analogous to American English, then the Mukogodo version would be analogous to, say, Canadian English. In many respects the Maa spoken in Mukogodo is similar to that of the Maasai of southern Kenya, but Mukogodo speech is also heavily influenced by their Samburu neighbors to the north. Like Samburu, Mukogodo tend to speak rapidly, and they enjoy making fun of the slow, drawn-out speech of the Maasai of southern Kenya. Nouns in Maa are marked with prefixes like *en*, *in*, *ol*, and *il*, depending on whether they are in the masculine or feminine category and on whether they are singular or plural. Like Samburu, Mukogodo usually drop the initial vowel from their nouns, turning, for example, *ilasho* (calves) into simply *lasho*. The Maa spoken in Mukogodo also shares some phonetic features with the Samburu variety. For example, the vowel combination *oi* in southern Maa often shifts to *ei*, as, for example, when *enkoitoi* (path) becomes *nkoitei*. The Mukogodo family name Leitiko is also a sound-shifted version of the Maa word for zebra, *ol-oitiko*. The Mukogodo version of Maa has also borrowed some vocabulary from Samburu. For example, the Samburu word for morning, *tasaran*, is much more common in Mukogodo than the Maasai word, *tadekenya*.

SUBSISTENCE

Though the proportion of the Mukogodo diet that comes from honey is a small fraction of what it used to be, beekeeping is still an important activity for many Mukogodo men. Much of the honey that is now produced is used for honey wine, but some is still eaten fresh as an occasional treat rather than a staple. The shift away from honey can be seen in how people define *daa*, "food." Although "food" is a broad category, it is very common around the world for people to define the staple that they rely most upon as the quintessential "food." For the Mukogodo when they lived in caves, "food" meant honey. When my cave dweller friend LeKitiman said "Metii daa" ("There's no food"), he meant that there was no honey. He might have had quite a bit of other food, such as famine relief provided by a local mission, but nothing but honey would satisfy his quest for real "food." These days, *daa* (food) is defined not as honey but as milk, and when most Mukogodo say "Metii daa," they mean that there is no milk, or at least not as much as they would like.

As we saw in the last chapter, beekeeping went hand in hand with the system of territories controlled by lineages. As the Mukogodo obtained livestock, however, that system began to fall apart, and for most intents and purposes it no longer exists. The problem was that the territorial system made little sense for people keeping livestock. If you are responsible for livestock in an environment with as much spatial and temporal variability as Mukogodo, you need to be able to move the animals to where the forage and water supplies are best. The British administrator D. G. Worthy reported in the 1950s that one Mukogodo man tried to exclude people from other lineages from running livestock on his lineage's territory, but to no avail. No one respected his claim to exclusive grazing rights, and the territorial system mostly fell apart. Today, while it is possible to find people living on land associated historically with their own patrilineages, it is even easier to find people living on land associated historically with someone else's patrilineage. And while some older men still do tend beehives in their lineage's traditional territories, most live too far from those territories for that to be practical. Instead, they put their hives in trees surrounding their homesteads.

Although Mukogodo men no longer routinely hunt for food, many men still keep a bow and a quiver full of arrows handy. I knew one teenage boy with a special fondness for the old way of life who maintained a link to it by secretly keeping a bow and quiver stashed away in the rockshelter in which his late father had once lived. Another man, one of the forest guards, frequently carried his bow and arrows rather than the spear favored by most Mukogodo men, though the only hunting he ever did was for the rats that infested the fence around his cattle pen. Most of the hunting that men now do is for leopards that are eating their livestock. I knew of several such hunts while I was there in the 1980s, though none of them was successful. On the other hand, they did very proudly show me the very decayed remains of a lion that they had successfully killed some months before my arrival. For all intents and purposes, hunting for meat is very much a thing of the past. Only once during our time in Mukogodo were Beth or I ever served any wild meat. The dried meat was from a giraffe, and no one at the village would provide any details about how it was obtained. But the meat was so far from fresh that we suspected that it may have been scavenged rather than hunted. The only other evidence I have ever seen of recent hunting among the Mukogodo was a long leather strap used for raising beehives into trees. The owner told me that it was two years old and made from the hide of an eland, suggesting that either he or someone he knew had hunted relatively recently.

THE ROUTINE OF THE PRESENT

If you want to know how people spend their time, the best way is simply to watch them. All anthropologists do this, usually simply by taking notes as they go about their business. But, in the case of anthropologists like me who need quantitative data in order to test hypotheses, anecdotal information, no matter how detailed, is not enough. Our behavioral observations need to be obtained in systematic ways to avoid as much as possible any biases due to when or where activities take place or who usually engages in them. To accomplish this, after we conducted our census in 1985 I selected fifteen Mukogodo settlements, amounting to just under half of the Mukogodo population at the time. I divided the year into nine periods so that we would have a sample of behaviors from all seasons and then used a random number generator to select days for visits to specific settlements. About half of the chosen settlements were within walking distance of our house at Kuri-Kuri. To reach the rest of them, we had either to backpack or drive and set up camp at least a day ahead of the scheduled scan day. On the scan day, one of us would wake up in time to begin scanning at 6:30 a.m. At that time and then again every hour on the half hour until 6:30 p.m. we would attempt to account for the whereabouts and behavior, in general terms, of every individual in the settlement. We recorded both broad categories of behavior (herding, milking, child care, etc.) and details of posture and motion (sitting on a hide, standing, walking, etc.). If someone residing in the settlement was not visible, we asked where he or she was and what he or she was likely to be doing. Usually the person in question was off doing some sort of chore, such as herding the goats or collecting firewood, or visiting another settlement. When possible we would ask the person in question what they had been up to that day when we saw them at the end of the day or the next morning. We did not enter people's houses uninvited both because we wanted to respect people's privacy and because the activities that typically take place inside houses— mainly sleeping, cooking, and eating—rarely contribute directly to economic productivity and subsistence, which was our main concern. We did record behaviors taking place inside houses when we happened to be inside someone's house at the time of a scan, and we can now use those data to infer the frequencies of different behaviors for different sorts of people while they are indoors.

The result of all this work is a database with more than 30,000 behavioral observations providing a detailed picture of the economic activities of Mukogodo people throughout 1986. Perhaps even more valuable than the data that the scans provided was the way that they forced us to visit such a wide variety of settlements, including some very isolated ones, throughout the entire year, giving us not only a statistical but also a more intuitive and nuanced understanding of day-to-day Mukogodo existence. In this section, I will first describe a typical day in a typical settlement, keeping in mind that there is considerable variation among even a group as small as the Mukogodo. Then I will examine our data more closely, focusing on differences between the sexes and across all ages.

A TYPICAL DAY

The day begins about 6 a.m., when the sun is about to rise. The rising and setting of the sun are so regular near the equator that, in the Swahili timekeeping system that the Mukogodo and virtually everyone else in East Africa follows, the new day officially begins not at midnight but at sunrise, and all times are six hours off what they would be in English. Thus, 7 a.m. is *saa nabo* (one o'clock) in Maa, and noon is *saa sita* (six o'clock) (curiously, I have only ever heard Maa speakers use the Swahili *saa sita* to refer to noon rather than the Maa *saa ile*). Women are usually the first to arise, and they begin by milking cows and goats. Children also sometimes milk goats. The women then revive the fires inside their houses and fix breakfast, which usually consists of a big cup of sweet, milky tea.

After breakfast, the calves, kids, and lambs are separated from the adult animals, and children are sent herding the livestock. Girls and young boys herd the sheep and goats, while older boys herd the cattle. If a family has only a handful of cattle, they may let them wander by themselves. Men will also do some of the herding if no one else is available to do it or if the herding is particularly difficult, such as a long trip to a water source or salt lick or when they must dig deep for water, as shown in Figure 4.2. Very small lambs, kids, and even calves are often kept inside houses or inside special small, roofed pens. When the lambs, kids, and calves get a bit bigger, small children are given the job of herding them in the area near the settlement. A few families also own donkeys, which come and go without anyone herding them. The people herding the small stock will bring them back to the settlement at noon and have lunch, which usually consists of maize meal porridge and milk, but the cattle herders must stay out with the animals all day.

Not everyone's activities are so focused on the livestock. At about the same time that the livestock are leaving to graze and browse, those children who are attending school will leave for class. School attendance is sporadic, but most families who live within walking distance of a school will send at least some of their children to school some of the time. Both boys and girls attend school. People who live far from schools but who value education will sometimes send their children to live with relatives who live near one. A few adults have jobs, usually in the town of Don Dol. Some work for government ministries, such as the forest service, nonprofit organizations, or churches. Some work in small businesses such as shops and tea houses, and a few are schoolteachers. Others do not have formal jobs but instead make small amounts of cash by making charcoal for sale in town and by buying and selling hides and livestock.

While the children are herding or at school, the men who do not have jobs often spend the bulk of the day visiting friends and relatives at other settlements and entertaining guests themselves. The bulk of the day-to-day chores are handled by the women, who not only care for the children, milk the livestock, and cook the food, but also fetch the firewood, haul the water, and build the houses. Firewood and water are particularly difficult chores, and most women try to do them only every second, third, or fourth day. Women carry huge loads of wood and water long distances back to their homes, usually with a tumpline, a leather strap that runs across the forehead so that the weight is carried by the

Figure 4.2   Mukogodo men watering their cattle. Lee Cronk

spine. It is not uncommon to see women carrying as many as thirty liters of water, twenty on a tumpline and five in each hand, weighing a total of thirty kilograms (about 66 pounds). That is about as much water as in a three-minute shower, though a Mukogodo woman will make that amount suffice for her entire family for two or three days. In between their chores, the women might find time to socialize in the shade of a tree, perhaps making jewelry or decorating their milk gourds with beads while they talk and keep an eye on the children.

House building is not a daily activity, but when families move in search of grazing and water, new houses must be built. In and around the forest, cedar is used for the walls for the same reason that Westerners like to use it for closets: it repels insects. Where cedar is not available, other materials are used for the walls, such as the big aloe plants called *ldupai* that grow in the lowlands. Construction of the roof that gives Maasai houses their distinctive bread loaf shape begins with a lattice of branches, as shown in Figure 4.3. The next step is to interweave leaves from a plant called *lokerding'ai*, which, like cedar, repels insects. Finally, a mixture

Figure 4.3   A Mukogodo woman building the roof of her house. LEE CRONK

of cow dung and mud is used as a stucco over the whole structure. Only cow dung is used; goat, sheep, and donkey turds do not have the right consistency for the job. My students often wince at the idea of a house made of cow dung, but it is actually a very good building material because it contains lots of undigested grass fibers that help it hold together. This point was made clear to me one day while my mother- and father-in-law were visiting Beth and me in the field. My father-in-law, who grew up on a farm in Nebraska, had no particular fondness for dung and, like most Americans, was unenthusiastic about the idea of living in a house made out of it. One day we all were visiting our friend Mary NeLeitiko. While she made tea, my father-in-law asked Beth and me to ask her why she built her house with a mixture of cow dung and mud. She replied, "Because we are poor and so we don't have enough cows to use dung alone. We have to mix it with mud." Whether it is mixed with mud or used straight, the dung dries into a smooth and long-lasting surface, and smells fine, or at least no different from the cattle pen surrounding it.

Sitting around a Mukogodo settlement, you are unlikely to see adult men doing much work. The impression one gets is that they do very little work indeed, but a close examination of our behavioral scan data shows that not to be the case. The fact is that many Mukogodo men spent large portions of their lives, ranging from weeks to years, living away from home, earning money to send back to their families. This pattern started during the colonial period, when young Mukogodo men would get jobs working on European-owned farms and ranches to earn money to buy livestock for bridewealth payments. During the Mau Mau uprising in the early 1950s, when Kenyans who had been displaced by European settlers rebelled against colonial rule, many Mukogodo men earned bridewealth money by fighting on the British side against Mau Mau. Mukogodo men were so much help to the British in their fight against Mau Mau that at one point during the war the colonial governor, Sir Evelyn Baring, visited Don Dol and thanked them in person: "In helping the government against Mau Mau . . . you have been wise, because until Mau Mau is dead there can be no peace in the land and without peace none of you can prosper as we all wish you to." The Mukogodo involvement in the anti–Mau Mau forces came up during our first week in the field while we were conversing with Parmashu and LeSakui, the men I introduced in Chapter 1. I was trying to get some details from them about their hunting and trapping methods, but to do that I needed to clarify some vocabulary. From what they were telling me, I said to Beth that it sounded as if the Maa word that our dictionary defined as "trap"—*arresh*—really meant something more like "ambush." "Ambush, yes!" Parmashu said. It turned out that he had learned the English word during his work for the British against Mau Mau more than thirty years earlier.

These days most men work in jobs requiring little skill or training. The most common job is as a night watchman, highly in demand in Nairobi due to the crime rate there. Others work as laborers on farms and ranches. A few work in factories, a small number are in the Kenyan military and police forces, and one Mukogodo man had a very good job as a safari driver for wealthy American and European tourists.

The men who are not away at jobs get a bit busier at around 6 p.m., when the sun is beginning to set. At that time, the livestock are herded back to the camp, and lambs, kids, and calves are reunited with their mothers. While the women tend to the milking, the men survey their livestock, making sure that all their animals are there. Rather than counting their livestock, they recognize each animal as an individual and quickly figure out if one is missing or if someone else's animal has been mixed in with their herd. If an animal is missing, the men might head off into the forest, sometimes spending hours in the darkness searching for it.

After dark, dinner is served. If milk is plentiful, then that may be the only thing served, either fresh, in a curdled form called *kule naaoto*, or in tea. Maize meal porridge is also very common, and occasionally people have some potatoes and cabbage, a few wild vegetables, or perhaps some bulgur wheat obtained in a distribution of famine relief foods. Meat is eaten rarely, usually only if an animal happens to die or if there is a special occasion, such as a birth or a wedding. Most evenings are spent quietly chatting with family members indoors. If the moon is full then it is possible to see almost as well as during the day, and people take advantage of the light by staying up late and socializing a great deal. Sometimes a group of older men will build a big fire outdoors and sit around it talking for hours. If you are very lucky when you visit a Mukogodo settlement, you might be there on the same night as a group of *murran,* in which case there may be singing, dancing, and socializing until late into the night.

THE PACE OF LIFE

That is the basic pattern, but it can vary a great deal from family to family and from day to day. One thing that has a big effect on the pace of life is how far one lives from the town of Don Dol. Though small, dusty, and unattractive, Don Dol has a surprising amount to offer, including shops, a few jobs, schools, churches, and health clinics. Although almost no Mukogodo live in the town of Don Dol itself, many families have moved closer to it. The population density remains low even close to town, but the pace of life picks up a bit when one gets within, say, an hour's walk of town because it is so much easier to visit other settlements when they are a few minutes' rather than a few hours' walk away. People living close to Don Dol tend to be more outward-looking, more interested in jobs, in education, and in politics, and a little more comfortable dealing with outsiders. People living farther from Don Dol see strangers much less often and so often seem a bit shy. They also often have more livestock and so are more focused on their herds than on jobs and schools.

One way in which this difference manifests itself is in the process of giving children their names. While American parents give their children names as soon as they are born, Mukogodo parents wait until the child seems to be thriving and so is likely to survive. Before that time, the child is referred to by a nickname, often just a modification of the word for boy or girl. When the time to name the child has come, his or her head is shaved for the first time, a friend is asked to choose a name, and a small celebration takes place. Beth and I had the honor of being asked to choose a name for one little boy in 1986. We were specifically asked to give him an English name. Unfortunately, we both had recently finished reading Charles Dickens's *Great Expectations,* in which the protagonist is a boy named Pip, short for Phillip. So we recommended that he be called Phillip. The problem, which we should have anticipated, was that in Maa there is no "f" sound, so *f*s become *p*'s or *b*'s. Also, the "l" sound in Maa is very close to the "r" sound. You can figure the rest out by yourself: Phillip's mother's pronunciation of his new name was closer to "Burp" than to "Phillip." I saw young Phillip, by then a healthy eight-year-old, in 1993, and was happy to learn that he was being called something else entirely.

Phillip lived near Don Dol, and he was named while still a baby. He exemplifies a pattern Beth and I noticed in which naming ceremonies were taking place much earlier among people living near Don Dol than among people living far from town. Near Don Dol, it was quite common for naming ceremonies to be held before the child could walk, while far from town it was equally common to see large toddlers with long dreadlocks, indicating that they had never had haircuts and so had not yet been named. Our tentative interpretation of this pattern, which we hope to test more thoroughly during future trips to Mukogodo, is that parents living near Don Dol have good reason to be optimistic about the life chances of their children because of their relatively easy access to health care. My broader point is that there really is no such thing as a typical Mukogodo settlement. Each one has its own character and its own habits that emerge from its environment, the personalities of its residents, their economic activities, and their social ties.

WHO DOES WHAT?

So how do Mukogodo spend their time? Or, more specifically, how did the Mukogodo included in our behavioral scans spend their time between 6:30 a.m. and 6:30 p.m. during 1986? Not surprisingly, livestock care was the single most time-consuming work activity, accounting for nearly 15 percent of all our observations. Overall, their time was split about evenly between work, including domestic chores and child care, and leisure activities like sleeping, visiting, and grooming. Where were they doing all of this? About a quarter of the time they were inside a house. About an eighth of the time, they were visiting another settlement. The rest of the time they were outside somewhere, usually where we could observe them directly. Finally, less than 1 percent of the time, neither Beth nor I could figure out where they were or what they were doing.

Figure 4.4 shows the time allocation patterns broken down by age and sex. Both boys and girls get started working when they are still quite young. Both sexes help out a great deal with the livestock, but young girls care for children much more than boys do, a pattern that continues throughout life. Overall, females spend about 16 percent of their time in child care, while males spend only 2 percent. Similarly, females spend about 16 percent of their time taking care of domestic needs like water and firewood, while males spend only 4 percent of their time in such activities. Where men exceed women is in wage labor: men, on average, spend about 11 percent of their time earning wages. The figure for women is just over 1 percent. Overall, the amount of time spent in various forms of work is surprisingly close for the two sexes: 41 percent for men and 46 percent for women, or about five to five and a half hours of each twelve hours of daylight. It is clear from Figure 4.4 that the 5-percentage-point difference comes mostly from the period between ages fifteen and thirty-five, when

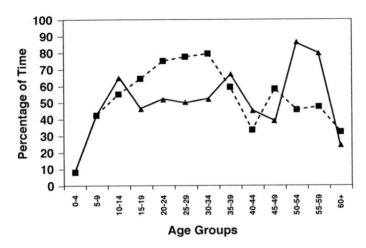

Figure 4.4   Time spent by Mukogodo males (triangles, solid line) and females (squares, dashed line) in productive activities, by age group.

women must work hard to take care of their children and maintain their households.

Because so much of the work in Mukogodo involves livestock, one would expect that the amount people work would be influenced by how much livestock they have. When we compare work patterns among the Mukogodo to those among wealthier Maa-speaking pastoralists, this does appear to be the case. Two other good data sets exist on time allocation among Maa speakers, one collected by Barbara Grandin among the Maasai of southern Kenya and one collected by Elliot Fratkin among the Ariaal of northern Kenya. Among both those groups, people spend more time engaged in livestock care than among the Mukogodo. The difference is clearly seen among children. Among the Mukogodo, boys under the age of fifteen spend about a quarter of their time in livestock care. For girls, the figure is about 17 percent. Among the Ariaal, boys and girls between ages six and eleven, in contrast, spend 52 percent and 41 percent, respectively, of their time in livestock-related tasks. The comparable figures for Maasai boys and girls of roughly the same age group is 41 percent and 46 percent, respectively. It appears that even though Mukogodo boys and girls work hard, they would be working even harder if they were wealthier and so had more livestock to tend.

Wage labor is an economically important activity in Mukogodo, but it is easy to forget about when you are there because for the most part it is invisible. Most of the men doing it are living elsewhere. Wage employment has an interesting pattern over men's lifetimes. It is very common for young men to leave the area for work in order to earn money for bridewealth payments. Thus, men in their twenties spend about a quarter of their time earning wages. But there is also a peak in wage employment among men over age fifty, who spend between two-thirds and three-fourths of their time earning wages. Unlike younger men, older men earn money not so much for future bridewealth payments as much as to buy food and other necessities for their families back in Mukogodo.

Demographers and other social scientists have been debating for years the relationship between work and fertility. One major question is whether work by younger people enables the elderly to work less or whether elderly people work harder when they have younger relatives to help. In modern Western society, a pattern in which a portion of the productivity of younger people is directed toward older people has been institutionalized through Social Security and other pension systems. In the sorts of societies anthropologists study, however, other patterns emerge. Among the Hadza hunter-gatherers of Tanzania, for instance, older women spend more time gathering and are better at it than younger women, suggesting that they are taking some of the burden of the task off their daughters, who are in the midst of their reproductive years. Similarly, on the Pacific Ocean island of Ifaluk, older men and women also spend more of their time working than younger people, and Ifalukese children with living grandparents are more likely to survive than those without living grandparents.

In most places it is hard to assess the relationship between work by the elderly and their numbers of children or grandchildren because almost all of them have children or grandchildren, so there is little variability to use to get a grasp of the situation. But Mukogodo presents an opportunity to do just that because so many elderly Mukogodo men are childless. As you saw in Chapter 3, this was a result of the transition to pastoralism: After about 1931, Mukogodo men needed livestock in order to get married, but some found this to be impossible and so remained unmarried and at least without any legally recognized children for the rest of their lives. When Beth and I were in Mukogodo in 1986, about six old bachelors remained alive, and three of them made it into our behavioral scans. They spent about 13 percent of their time in various productive activities, often taking care of domestic needs like water and firewood because they had no one to do it for them. You might expect, then, that old men with children and grandchildren would work less than the bachelors, because they did not need to deal with domestic chores. The truth, however, is that old men with children spent more than twice the amount of time that the bachelors did—more than 30 percent—in various forms of work. It is tempting to draw the conclusion that the men with children are working because they have someone—their own children and grandchildren—to work for. That is the interpretation I favor and that I think fits best with patterns observed in other societies. But of course it is also possible that the contrasting work patterns of the men late in their lives reflect habits that began long ago. The men who work harder now may be the same men who worked harder and so obtained the livestock with which to obtain bridewealth many decades ago.

THE STRUCTURE OF POVERTY

The Mukogodo are at the bottom rung of a regional hierarchy of wealth, ethnic status, and reproductive opportunities. For the most part, this regional system consists of the Maa-speaking pastoralists living in Mukogodo Division. In addition to the Mukogodo themselves, that includes Mumonyot, Ilng'wesi, Digirri, and LeUaso. Also important are the Samburu, who live mainly north of Mukogodo Division who are also well represented in the division itself. And there are some ties as well to the Maasai of southern Kenya and to people who do not speak Maa, such as the Meru, to whom the Ilng'wesi in particular have some close relationships.

Wealth

The place of the Mukogodo at the bottom of the wealth hierarchy is easy to document. The disparity began as soon as Mukogodo men began obtaining livestock because they were the last in the area to do so. The colonial government conducted a census of livestock in the Mukogodo area in the early 1930s, and the differences between the Mukogodo and non-Mukogodo are striking. While Mukogodo families had an average of less than one head of cattle and one and a half small stock (that is, sheep and goats considered together) per person, the averages for the non-Mukogodo groups were more than six cows and nine small stock. Samburu living in the Mukogodo area were the wealthiest on average, but even the poorest non-Mukogodo group counted in the census, the Ilng'wesi, had nine times the cattle holdings per adult man and nearly three times the small stock of Mukogodo men. The livestock census figures for the Mukogodo may even be inflated because, as the colonial official themselves pointed out, it was common for the Mumonyot in particular to lend livestock to their new Mukogodo in-laws for safekeeping while the Mumonyot were deported to other parts of the colony. In the decades since the transition to pastoralism the discrepancy between Mukogodo and non-Mukogodo livestock holdings has decreased, but it still exists. Kenyan government data from the 1980s show that Mukogodo men had, on average, about half the small stock and about 25 percent fewer cattle than Mumonyot, Ilng'wesi, and Digirri men.

Ethnic Status

Material poverty is just part of the low status of the Mukogodo in the eyes of other Maa-speaking pastoralists. Despite the fact that they no longer hunt and despite their wholesale adoption of Maasai language and culture, they are still stigmatized as *il-torrobo*. As we saw in Chapter 3, *il-torrobo* is a label with obscure origins but a clearly derogatory meaning. It is used to refer, derisively, to people who either hunt and gather—thus, at least in the eyes of Maa speakers, living like wild animals rather than like proper humans. Though Mukogodo have not been foragers for decades, the stigma of the label stays with them, and their status as *il-torrobo* is reinforced continually by the various ways in which they fail to conform to the ideals of higher-status Maa speakers. The age-set system is a good example. As I described more fully in the last chapter, the Maasai and Samburu age-set systems are elaborate, full of rules about ceremonies, about how people of various age grades must or must not behave, and about how social relationships are to be conducted. For example, after a boy is circumcised, he is supposed to consume a mixture of cow's blood and milk. Consuming fresh blood is common among Maa-speaking pastoralists and some other groups around the world, though Mukogodo rarely do it because they have so few cattle. A few minutes after a circumcision I watched in 1986, some of the man's friends and relatives went off to find a cow to bleed, and I followed. While two or three men held the animal still, another shot a vein in its neck with an arrow specially designed to penetrate the skin just far enough to allow the blood to flow. Figure 4.5 is a photograph of this event. But hitting a vein can be tricky, and the first time it did not work. Nor did it work the second, third, fourth, fifth, or sixth time. Perhaps if they had had more cattle, they would have tried another one. Instead, they gave up, let the cow go, and resigned themselves to using the blood from a sheep they were planning to slaughter instead of cow's milk. Furthermore, they did not have much milk that day, so they were forced to use thin maize meal porridge rather than milk. Such cutting of ceremonial corners is made necessary by Mukogodo poverty, and it only reinforces their low status in the eyes of other Maa speakers.

Another of the rules of the age-set system that is taken seriously by higher-status Maa speakers is that *murran* should not get married. Among wealthier Maa speakers, fathers are in a position to prevent such early marriages because they control the livestock that their sons must use to pay bridewealth. But since Mukogodo herds are so small, most men cannot expect much help from their fathers. Instead, they often get jobs so that they can pay bridewealth themselves and so often get married when they still have several years of *murran*hood ahead of them.

This lack of attention to rules gives Mukogodo social interactions an informal, relaxed, and open quality that higher status Maa speakers find uncomfortable but that I, as a fieldworker and a newcomer to the area, found refreshing. I generally find Mukogodo much easier to deal with than, say, Samburu, whose manner tends to be extremely formal and reserved. But my opinion of the Mukogodo has virtually no impact on their everyday lives, and their laxity about rules that higher-status Maa speakers take very seriously contributes to their reputation as *il-torrobo* and people without "respect" or "honor" (*enkanyit*). Paul Spencer, who has conducted extensive fieldwork since the 1950s among both the Samburu and Maasai, illustrates this with a wonderful story about a visit he made to the Mukogodo area in 1959 together with a Samburu man. The Samburu was continually being disgusted by the behavior of *il-torrobo* he was visiting and he returned home "with a collection of shocking tales to tell." Once, a complete stranger took his stool from

Figure 4.5   Mukogodo men trying to obtain blood from the neck of a cow. LEE CRONK

him. On another occasion, he was asked to sleep in an empty hut. To top it all off, he was given a cup of milk *but not asked if he would like another!*

Ironically, sometimes even the Mukogodo emulation of Maasai culture can backfire on them, reinforcing their status as *il-torrobo*. For example, a Samburu man once told me that the word that I and most Mukogodo use for "thirty"— *tomon-uni*—is an *il-torrobo* word, not proper Maa. Like most Samburu, he preferred the word *osom*. In fact, *tomon-uni* is not an *il-torrobo* word but rather standard southern Maa. Among the Maasai of southern Kenya and northern Tanzania, *osom* is considered quaint, if it is understood at all. Similarly, Samburu believe strongly that a *murran* age set's "firestick elder" age set, which is always the age set two periods older than the current *murran*, should not include any fathers of the current *murran*. The firestick elders are supposed to advise and guide the *murran*, sometimes sternly and even by invoking special curses, and Samburu believe that having a firestick elder who is also a father of *murran* would create a conflict of interest. But Mukogodo men pay no attention to that rule, and it is easy to find *murran* with fathers in the firestick elder age set. This is hard to avoid because the young age at which Mukogodo men marry shortens generation times compared to the Samburu. Though Samburu view this as yet another example of the way that *il-torrobo* violate the rules of the system, in fact the wealthy, high-status Maasai do the same as the Mukogodo, caring little about the supposed conflict of interest that so worries the Samburu. The Mukogodo pattern is not *il-torrobo* sloppiness at all, but proper Maasai-style behavior. But few Samburu realize that, and so the result is to make the Mukogodo appear lax and disrespectful in their eyes.

As is often the case with prejudiced elites, the elites of the Maa-speaking world do not necessarily understand their prejudice or even fully appreciate the derogatory quality of terms like *il-torrobo*. Many elites see their denigrating descriptions of poor, lower-status people and the terms they use for them not as offensive stereotypes or manifestations of bias but as entirely fair, objective descriptions of reality. I once picked up a hitchhiker while driving through Samburu country. When he found out that I could speak Maa, he asked where I had learned it. When I reported that I had learned it among the Mukogodo, he asked, "So, are you a white man, or *ol-torroboni*?" Though at the time I felt insulted, I probably should instead have taken it as a compliment. Chances are that he did not understand how insulting the term *ol-torroboni* was to my ears and that he was trying to compliment me on my ability to speak Maa by giving me a chance to identify myself with a group of bona fide Maa speakers, albeit low-status ones.

I began to understand both how sensitive Mukogodo are about the *il-torrobo* label and how oblivious high-status Maa speakers can be about its insulting nature one evening very early in my fieldwork while I was having dinner with an older Mukogodo man and his nephew. The older man's sister, like many Mukogodo women, had married a Samburu man, and because ethnic identity among Maa speakers usually goes along with patrilineal affiliations, the nephew was also Samburu. Because I was curious about the concept of *il-torrobo,* I started asking the two of them questions about how the term is used and to whom it refers. The Mukogodo man quickly stopped talking and began staring straight ahead, looking at no one while he ate. His nephew, on the other hand, was quite happy to share his opinions about which particular groups in the area qualified as *il-torrobo* and which did not. He reported that the Mukogodo certainly were *il-torrobo.* Hoping that any offense my questions might give would be forgiven in light of my clumsiness with the language, I asked whether that meant that his uncle was *ol-torroboni.* Yes, indeed, answered the nephew cheerfully, apparently oblivious to the way he was thus insulting his uncle, of whom he clearly was very fond. The uncle continued to stare straight ahead, eating silently.

Reproductive Opportunity

One aspect of low status that anthropologists usually ignore but that is enormously important to the people they study is its effect on marriage and reproduction. Though it is increasingly common for Americans to choose to remain single and for married couples in America to choose to remain childless, in societies like Mukogodo remaining single or marrying but choosing to remain childless are not even options. Life is simply not complete without at least one spouse and some children. But in a polygynous society, particularly one in which bridewealth is paid, poverty may mean that a man must wait to get married or that he cannot get married at all. As we saw in Chapter 3, during the Mukogodo transition to pas-

Table 4.1   Polygyny rates, measured as average numbers of wives per male, among Mukogodo, Suiei, and Samburu.

Approximate age range of men	Mukogodo	Suiei	Samburu
58-71	1.07	1.13	1.95
43-57	1.26	1.28	1.67
32-42	0.98	1.04	1.35
18-31	0.39	0.39	0.16
Mean	0.76	NA	0.86
Standard deviation	0.74	NA	0.72
Sample size	147	190	5,736

SOURCE: Suiei and Samburu figures are from Spencer (1965).

toralism many more Mukogodo women married non-Mukogodo men than vice versa, and, as a result, a large proportion of men during those years did not marry at all. As Mukogodo herds have increased since that time the situation has improved, but throughout the twentieth century more women married out of the Mukogodo than married in.

Despite the fact that Mukogodo men are more likely than higher-status Maa speakers to marry when they are still *murran*, overall Mukogodo have lower numbers of wives than Samburu and Maasai. Table 4.1 compares Mukogodo polygyny rates with data collected by Paul Spencer among the Maasai, Samburu, and Suiei, another *il-torrobo* group in Samburu country. The Mukogodo pattern is quite similar to that seen among the Suiei, with relatively high numbers of wives for young men, most of whom are still *murran*, but lower polygyny rates overall than among the Samburu and Maasai. Spencer also provides data on the origins of Mumonyot wives that, like data on livestock wealth, puts them in a position midway between the wealthy Samburu and poor Mukogodo. Though the willingness of Mukogodo and Suiei men to marry while still *murran* surely enhances the reproductive success of a few men, it has the effect of lowering the status of both groups overall because of the impression it creates that they do not respect the rules of the age-set system.

The predicament of Mukogodo men is made even more difficult by the fact that they typically pay a higher bridewealth to marry non-Mukogodo women than non-Mukogodo men pay to marry Mukogodo women. During the transition to pastoralism this discrepancy was very large as a proportion of the overall bridewealth, amounting on average to two or three cattle and a handful of sheep. In more recent times the difference has diminished, but it has not disappeared entirely. This discrepancy may be the result of several factors. For example, among Maa speakers the bridewealth is usually considered just the beginning of a man's payments to his affines, who may continue to request further gifts for years to come. Non-Mukogodo parents may have considered Mukogodo men a poor risk for such continued prestations and so demanded a higher initial payment. Also, *il-torrobo* women have a reputation as unruly wives, and so they may have not been able to attract bridewealth payments as large as those attracted by non-Mukogodo women. Finally, Mukogodo were simply in a worse negotiating position than non-Mukogodo because they were so desperately in need of livestock.

Bridewealth is in many ways the linchpin not only of the Mukogodo transition to pastoralism but of the system that maintains their current low status as well. By linking wealth in livestock to marriage and parenthood, bridewealth contributes to a vicious cycle in which the low status of the Mukogodo reproduces itself from generation to generation. Among wealthier Maa speakers, the bridewealth paid at marriage is typically so small a proportion of a family's herd that it is considered to be no more than a token payment. That token payment is typically followed in later years by many more payments. But what may be a token payment for a wealthy herder typically represents a large proportion of a Mukogodo man's small herd, and the inability of most Mukogodo men to make such continuing payments is yet another factor that contributes to the scorn that wealthier Maa speakers have for them. Furthermore, most men in those wealthier groups can count on help from their families to pay the bridewealth, and the need to obtain help with bridewealth payments from one's elders helps to maintain the strict system of gerontocracy—rule by the old people—that typifies groups like the Samburu and Maasai. Most young Mukogodo men, in contrast, typically cannot count on their families for help paying bridewealth and so must somehow obtain the necessary livestock on their own. Typically, they get jobs elsewhere in Kenya and save their money. Because they cannot expect help from their fathers in paying bridewealth, they have less reason to obey their fathers in particular and elders in general than young men in the wealthier groups. As a result, Mukogodo and similarly impoverished Maa speakers are much less gerontocratic than their wealthy neighbors, enhancing the impression of outsiders that they have insufficient *enkanyit* (respect). And, as we have seen, the willingness of young men to get married as soon as they can afford to do so also helps perpetuate their status as *il-torrobo*.

Inegalitarian Pastoralists?

Equality and inequality vary tremendously across human societies and across a variety of dimensions including wealth, political power, ethnic prestige, and reproductive opportunity. Some societies have rigid caste systems in which it is difficult or even impossible for an individual to change status during his or her lifetime. Other societies have class systems that include some possibility of upward or downward mobility rather than complete rigidity. Others are highly egalitarian, having almost no institutionalized status differences at all. At the same time that anthropologists take pains to remember the diversity of the societies they study, they also inevitably look for patterns. Sometimes these patterns develop into stereotypes, and one of the stereotypes that developed around pastoralists was that they were egalitarian. That stereotype has been attacked in recent years by anthropologists who, like me, can show in great detail that wealth is often very unequally distributed among individuals within a single pastoralist society. But this may not be news to everyone. Philip Carl Salzman of McGill University has pointed out that even during the first half of the twentieth century, when anthropology was still a young discipline, ethnographers of pastoralist peoples were well aware that large discrepancies in wealth could occur in such societies. But they usually found that such discrepancies did not lead to long-lasting class systems or concentrations of political power, often because wealth among pastoralists, which takes the form of livestock, is so volatile. A rich man one year might be a poor man the next if his herds happen to be decimated by disease, theft, or drought.

The Mukogodo case can shed some light on the question of inequality among pastoralists. Egalitarianism is certainly the ideal among Maa-speaking pastoralists, but only in the limited sense that men, particularly those in the same age set, should respect one another in community affairs. But wealth differences can sometimes be long lasting rather than fleeting, and differences in ethnic status can last for many generations after people have stopped hunting and speaking languages other than Maa. Long-lasting inequality among groups is also much more likely to be noticed if a large area is considered rather than only a subgroup, such as the Samburu or Maasai elite by themselves or the Mukogodo by themselves. A sensible way to choose which groups to include in such an analysis would be to examine marriage patterns. Given that the various Maa speakers of northern Kenya—the Mukogodo, Samburu, and others—intermarry at such high rates, it would be best to think about the issue of inequality in broad regional terms rather than by focusing on any one group. Furthermore, much more than just livestock wealth should be considered when trying to understand stratification among pastoralists. As Eric Abella Roth of the University of Victoria has argued, other aspects of stratification, such as variations in bridewealth, fertility, morbidity, and mortality, should also be examined.

THE IGNOBILITY OF POVERTY

While the Mukogodo are noble people, their nobility does not emerge from their poverty. Particularly when looking across great cultural divides, including the one that separates the Western world from that of Maa-speaking pastoralists, it is tempting and dangerously easy to mistake the effects of poverty for simple, benign cultural diversity. It is also easy to be seduced by the notion that life in such societies is somehow simpler than in ours, a notion easily dispelled by even a quick examination of, say, the age-set system. Perhaps because simplicity itself is often seen as a virtue, people in the West also often perceive the lack of material wealth of groups like the Mukogodo as somehow ennobling. But poverty is not ennobling. The nobility of people like the Mukogodo exists despite their poverty, not because of it.

Poverty has real, tangible effects on peoples' lives and relationships. At the same time that I have both witnessed and been the beneficiary of acts of enormous generosity and kindness in Mukogodo, I have also witnessed ways in which their poverty—the simple shortage of material things—can imbue social relationships with a petty, stingy, mean, desperate quality. Sometimes the effects are small and fleeting. I remember, with sadness, one day while I was sitting in a Mukogodo house collecting behavioral data on a young child for a study that I will describe in Chapter 5. The child's mother and father were in the house as well, the mother making tea. The father saw the packet of tea leaves that his wife had just bought, and he began to argue with her about the purchase. Though they kept their voices down and although the fight did not become violent, the argument was intense and very unpleasant to witness. The amount of money they were arguing about was the equivalent of twenty-five cents in U.S. currency.

Sometimes such fights do become violent. "Do you have any cows?" was always the first question Beth and I would be asked in Mukogodo. After that, I was usually asked something else about our economic system. But when Beth was talking to women, their next question was almost always the same: "Do men beat their wives in your country?" Interestingly, no one ever brought up this issue with me. In Mukogodo, wife beating is routine and expected. Mostly it goes on without much notice, but occasionally it results in bruises that cannot be covered up. Very occasionally, it even results in injuries to men. I once happened to be visiting a homestead, one where I did not know anyone very well, when a group of Kenyan police showed up to take someone away for questioning. It turned out that the day before a man had been threatening his wife not just with a beating but with a machete, and another man who intervened received deep cuts on his forearms.

It is, of course, impossible to say what the actual frequency of wife beating is in Mukogodo, but the frequency with which Mukogodo women raised the issue with Beth makes it clear that it must happen often. It also suggests that they are at least hoping, and are perhaps quite aware, that it is not so common everywhere.

We also do not know how prevalent wife beating is among other, higher-status Maa speakers, but circumstantial evidence suggests that it may be somewhat less common. Coincidentally, one of my colleagues at Rutgers, Dorothy Hodgson, is an expert on the history of gender relations among Maasai in Tanzania. Hodgson emphasizes the importance of *enkanyit* (mutual respect) as the foundation of husband-wife relations among the Maasai. It may be the case that just as poverty reduces the sense of *enkanyit* among men of different generations among poor pastoralists like the Mukogodo, so does it reduce *enkanyit* as a basis for peaceful relationships between spouses. This, at least, would be a hypothesis worth testing.

Just as in the United States, alcohol is doubtless a contributing factor in a lot of cases of wife beating in Mukogodo. The problem here is not honey wine, which requires quite a bit of effort to make and which is low in alcohol content, but rather the illegal moonshine whisky called *chang'aa*. Particularly when maize is easily available, some Mukogodo set up stills and run impromptu taverns out of their homes to make some extra money. Often the availability of maize is the result of a distribution of famine relief food, which seems to arrive in the area according to a schedule that has little to do with actual famine. *Chang'aa* is often served warm, straight from the still. The closest thing I have ever tasted to it is cheap versions of the Japanese rice wine called *sake*, which is also often served warm. But of course no one drinks it for the flavor. *Chang'aa* is a cheap and easy way to relieve the despair and boredom of the place. Beth and I have watched, with great sadness, as some of the liveliest and brightest people we knew in Mukogodo, including some of our best friends there, lost themselves in repetitive cycles of *chang'aa* intoxication. Even people with good jobs and bright prospects sometimes succumb to its temptations. While I was visiting the area in 1993, there was a scandal involving one of the local schools. Some of the teachers, most of whom were from other parts of Kenya, were sending children out during the day to buy shots of *chang'aa* from local women. But the strong dose of refined alcohol that *chang'aa* delivers can have even more disastrous consequences. In 1986, one Mukogodo man died of alcohol poisoning, and soon thereafter another was killed in a fight that broke out among a group of drunk men. Though such drunkenness may be a way of coping with poverty and low status, it also provides yet another reason for higher-status Maa speakers to continue to derogate the peoples of the Mukogodo area as *il-torrobo*.

Along with the idea that there is something noble about poverty, another romantic notion that Westerners have about societies like Mukogodo is that they are typified by widespread sharing and generosity. While Mukogodo are indeed wonderful, generous hosts and while sharing with kin is the norm, accusations of stinginess and arguments about petty debts are also quite common, and people without relatives close at hand are often on their own, even when they are in great need. That was certainly the case for several of the old bachelors we knew, who had no close family. Such men relied to some extent upon friends, to a small extent upon wild foods, and to a very great extent upon the Catholic mission in Don Dol for food and medicine. Even among family members, friends, and neighbors, we got wind of occasional accusations of stinginess, like a sneering comment from one old man that all his neighbors were "enemies" (*il-mang'ati*) because they refused to give him tea, or the complaint directed at people who refused to share meat from a freshly slaughtered animal that "kepiak kuldo tunganak!" ("those people are selfish!").

Given the vicissitudes of the weather and problems with livestock infections, even wealthy pastoralists in East Africa can have problems making ends meet. The extreme precariousness of subsistence for poor pastoralists like the Mukogodo leads many of them to rely not only on their stock but also on wage labor, small plots of maize and beans when the rains are good, and handouts of famine relief food. Such supplies are distributed mainly by the churches and government. Sometimes they are targeted to particularly poor families or women with dependent children, and at other times they are distributed to everyone regardless of need. Typical foods that are included in such distribution are maize, cooking oil, beans, bulgur wheat, powdered milk, and an ersatz milk made from corn and soybeans. A few Mukogodo families keep so few livestock that it is really somewhat misleading to call them pastoralists. But opting out of pastoralism altogether in favor of reliance on the market system is a risky strategy. One Mukogodo man who supported himself and his family quite well as a safari driver found himself in a tight spot after the first Gulf War in 1991 caused tourism in Kenya to drop off dramatically.

COPING WITH LOW STATUS

Mukogodo do not accept their low status as a permanent fact of life. Indeed, ever since they were drawn into the pastoralist way of life by both the temptation and demands of bridewealth, their story has been all about shedding their foraging, Yaaku-speaking past and the stigma of the *il-torrobo* label in order to be respected as real Maasai. They work hard to enlarge their herds, they take pains to emulate the Maasai, and, when possible, they reject forcefully the idea that they are *il-torrobo* at all.

This is not an easy thing to do. As anthropologist and psychologist Francisco Gil-White has documented, people tend to think of ethnic groups in an essentialist, primordialist way, much the same way that they see biological species. The analogy is attractive, he suggests, because ethnicity, like species membership, is usually passed from parent to offspring, and because people usually mate within their own ethnic group, again like members of the same species. Ethnic groups thus take on the appearance of natural kinds, as different and distinct, as, say, dogs and cats. But perhaps recent Mukogodo history itself contains a way out of this misleading and destructive analogy, creating a space in which the Mukogodo themselves can argue in favor of a more constructed, instrumental view of ethnic identity. The chink in the armor of the essentialist view of ethnic groups is marriage: If they can successfully mate with one another, then they cannot be too much like different species. As we have already seen, over the past century or so Mukogodo men and women have been marrying non-Mukogodo at a very high rate indeed.

As we saw in Chapter 3, Mukogodo have long been well aware of the instrumental qualities of ethnic labels, even to the point of calling themselves "Dorobo" when they stood to gain by doing so. Even Silangei Ole Matunge, who had some right to call himself "Maasai" rather than "Dorobo" since his lineage had Maasai roots, was willing to call himself "Dorobo" when testifying before the British authorities. But nowadays, with no British to influence and the stigma of the *il-torrobo* label still hanging over them, members of the Matunge lineage take every opportunity to emphasize their Maasai roots. Other Mukogodo, with no Maasai heritage to draw upon, redefine the word *il-torrobo* in a way that excludes them and their ancestors. Some insist that because they always had beehives, they were never really *il-torrobo*, their bees being the equivalent of livestock. One man of the Parmashu lineage who had just answered "I don't have any" to all my livestock census questions, pointed at a beehive and explained in self-defense, "Those are my herds." In this view, only those people who once had neither livestock nor bees can really be considered *il-torrobo*. Thus, while Mumonyot would count as *il-torrobo* because they went through a period in the late nineteenth century when they had neither livestock nor bees, Mukogodo were never *il-torrobo* because they had always had bees. Others insist that in order to be *il-torrobo*, a people must have eaten zebras. Eating zebras is seen as a sort of hunter-gatherer analog of eating donkeys, which Maa speakers consider a disgusting famine food at best. By that light, Mukogodo and their ancestors were never *il-torrobo*, but perhaps other groups in the area, whose ancestors may have been less choosy about their prey, would qualify.

The Mukogodo practice of clitoridectomy may also be a reflection of their aspirations to Maasai status. The colonial administrator D. G. Worthy claimed in the 1950s that Mukogodo had adopted the practice only recently as a result of Maasai influence. My Mukogodo informants, on the other hand, vehemently denied that their ancestors had ever failed to perform clitoridectomies, finding the suggestion insulting and disgusting. At least two interpretations of these conflicting accounts are possible. It may be that clitoridectomies had long been performed by Mukogodo but individuals sought favor with British administrators who opposed the practice by suggesting to them that it was not a quintessentially Mukogodo custom. Or perhaps Worthy's information is correct and it really is a relatively new practice among Mukogodo, one that became necessary in order for Mukogodo women to marry Maa speakers. In either case, the revulsion of my informants to the idea that their ancestors may not have performed clitoridectomies may best be seen as part of their self-conscious emulation of Maasai behavior and aspirations to Maasai ethnicity.

MAASAINESS VS. SAMBURUNESS

In order to better understand why Mukogodo are trying to be Maasai, it is important also to understand what they are not trying to be: Samburu. Although being Maasai does not appear at first glance to be much different from being Samburu, to Maa speakers themselves there are important differences. For example, their languages, while similar, are not identical, and it is easy for a practiced listener to tell a Samburu from a Maasai after a few brief remarks. Other classic ethnic markers, such as jewelry, are also strikingly different, and Mukogodo generally follow the Maasai rather than Samburu fashions.

Despite the proximity of Samburu and the remoteness of Maasai, Mukogodo consistently proclaim themselves to be Maasai, never Samburu, and their use of ethnic boundary markers reflects this choice. For example, although the way Mukogodo speak Maa is certainly influenced by Samburu, it is nonetheless a variety of the Southern Maa dialect of the Maasai, not the Northern Maa dialect of the Samburu, making the peoples of Mukogodo Division the only ones left in northern Kenya who speak the southern dialect. Their identification with the language of Maasai rather than that of Samburu is evident in how Mukogodo area people choose to write their names. They follow the style of the Maasai, which, in the case of a man, includes the full word *ole* (of) between the personal name and family name (for example, Kosima ole Leitiko). Samburu, in contrast, typically drop the initial "o" of *ole* and make *le* the first two words of the last name (for example, Kosima LeLeitiko). This is done despite the fact that in their everyday speech the people of Mukogodo Division typically break with Maasai speech and follow the Samburu pattern of dropping the vowels at the start of most nouns. Thus, the way they write their names appears to be a deliberate attempt to identify more closely with Maasai than with Samburu.

At first glance, it might seem more sensible for Mukogodo to aspire to be Samburu because Samburu are the highest status people around. On closer inspection, though, it seems that the proximity of Samburu is precisely why Mukogodo, along with their Mumonyot, Digirri, LeUaso, and Ilng'wesi neighbors, say they are Maasai and not Samburu. As the local elite, Samburu treat the peoples of Mukogodo Division, particularly Mukogodo, with disdain and contempt, unhesitatingly referring to them as *il-torrobo*. Mukogodo, for their part, often avoid Samburu individuals they do not know well, finding them haughty and difficult. I have watched as Mukogodo have deliberately misled unfamiliar Samburu, privately referring to them as *il-mang'ati* (enemies). Were Mukogodo to claim to be Samburu, Samburu would find this laughable. Better, then, for Mukogodo to emulate the distant Maasai elite that is not around to dispute their claim. The very absence of Maasai in the Mukogodo area may be necessary for Mukogodo and others in Mukogodo Division to be able to claim Maasai status. It is as if the forced movement of the Maasai from the Laikipia Plateau in 1912 created a local vacuum of Maasainess, which the peoples of Mukogodo Division have sought to fill.

RECOMMENDED READING

For more on poverty and pastoralism in East Africa, see *The Poor Are Not Us: Poverty and Pastoralism in Eastern Africa* (David M. Anderson and Vigdis Broch-Due, editors, James Currey, 1999). For ethnographic and historical insights into other groups of Maa speakers, I recommend Dorothy Hodgson's *Once Intrepid Warriors: Gender, Ethnicity and the Cultural Politics of Maasai Development* (Indiana University Press, 2001), and three books by Paul Spencer: *The Samburu: A Study of Gerontocracy in a Nomadic Tribe* (University of California Press, 1965), *The Maasai of Matapato: A Study of the Rituals of Rebellion* (Manchester University Press, 1988), and *The Pastoral Continuum: The Marginalization of Tradition in East Africa* (Clarendon, 1998).

5

Boys and Girls,
Words and Deeds

SITIPIN, ANDIRO, AND THEIR SISTERS

Sitipin was six years old when Beth and I were living at Kuri-Kuri in 1986. He was a bright, delightful child, curious about everything and unfailingly polite. But for most of that year, he was plagued with a nasty infection on the skin behind one ear. Beth and I treated it with antibiotic cream and bandaged it several times, each time encouraging his parents to take him either to the free clinic run by the government or the Catholic mission clinic, where all patients were charged the equivalent of twenty-five U.S. cents to see the doctor. His parents refused to do so. Though they both had local jobs and so had more cash than most Mukogodo and although only the mission clinic charged a fee, Sitipin's parents argued that the expense would be too great. Eventually one of the staff from the Catholic mission happened to see the infection during a visit to the area and then successfully treated it. Sitipin had two little sisters, both of whom were very healthy. When I returned to Mukogodo in 1993, I was thrilled when those three siblings ran out to greet me one day as I was approaching their mother's house. But as soon as I tried to have a conversation with Sitipin, I could tell something was wrong. We shook hands and he smiled widely at me, but he would not respond to my greeting or questions. One of his sisters informed me that during the time I had been away Sitipin had lost most of his hearing.

Another boy, whom I will call Andiro, was slightly older than Sitipin. Like Sitipin, Andiro became ill during our stay, but his parents did take him to the mission clinic. To everyone's sadness, he was diagnosed with a heart condition, and he was not expected to live much longer. When I returned in the 1990s, I was thrilled to find that Andiro was not only still alive, but quite healthy. His parents and the people at the mission had made sure that he received the best care available in the area, and he was thriving. His mother, in contrast, was no longer the quick-witted and hard-working woman that Beth and I had known in 1986. She had taken to distilling a great deal of *chang'aa*, and it appeared that she herself was drinking a large share of her production. It was clear from her appearance, the condition of her younger children, and the condition of her home that she was not taking care of routine domestic chores and child care the way she once had. Andiro's baby sister Ntitai showed signs of having been neglected, including low body weight, loose skin, listlessness, and fearfulness.

I offer the cases of Sitipin, Andiro, and their sisters both to exemplify the theme of this chapter and to temper it with a counterexample. Sitipin's story is extreme, but it fits the overall pattern shown by Mukogodo parents generally: daughters tend to receive better treatment than sons. Andiro, on the other hand, demonstrates that this is by no means a hard-and-fast rule of Mukogodo parental behavior. Daughter favoritism is a statistical tendency that is impossible to detect through anecdotes alone. Indeed, Mukogodo parents themselves seem to be unaware of their tendency to favor daughters over sons. The favoritism becomes apparent only through an examination of large bodies of quantitative data. Even then, it is only a tendency. While Mukogodo daughters are *on average* treated better and doing better than their brothers, there are plenty of plump, healthy, happy little boys and, of course, a few little girls like Ntitai.

This pattern of favoritism toward daughters is perhaps the most unexpected and striking result of Mukogodo poverty. The connection between their low status and the way they treat their sons and daughters, however, is not obvious. Understanding it requires a detour into the theory of natural selection, in which the ultimate currency is reproductive success, understood broadly to include not just how many offspring one has but also grandoffspring and other relatives through which an organism can help perpetuate its genes. But, as we will see, behaviors such as this do not need to be consciously understood in order for them to occur, and Mukogodo parents do not seem to be aware of the pattern. On the contrary, when asked which sex of offspring they prefer, they tend to favor sons over daughters. Such statements appear to be yet another aspect the ongoing Mukogodo effort to emulate the Maasai.

"CHANCE FAVORS THE PREPARED MIND."—LOUIS PASTEUR

As you know from Chapter 1, Beth and I went to Mukogodo in 1985 in order to study their transition to pastoralism. Though I had studied evolutionary theories about parental behavior in college and graduate school, parenting itself was not a central part of my research plan. That all changed when I took my first look at the Mukogodo census we conducted in late 1985. For a report to send back to the Population Council, which had provided the bulk of my funding, I prepared an age-sex pyramid. In most respects it looked fairly typical of a society with high fertility combined with an average lifespan much shorter than in the West: tall and narrow, with a wide base showing lots of children and few old people at the top. But the pyramid was lopsided, with many more young girls than young boys. Fortunately, my education had included a theory developed by Robert Trivers and Dan Willard about the relationship between socioeconomic status, parental behavior, and offspring sex ratios. In fact, the Trivers-Willard hypothesis was the subject of the first term paper I wrote for an anthropology class as a freshman in college in 1980, long before I had ever heard of the Mukogodo.

The Trivers-Willard hypothesis itself was developed almost by chance. It was the result of an encounter between evolutionary biologist Robert Trivers, who is now my colleague at Rutgers University, and Dan Willard, a mathematician who is now in the Department of Computer Science at the State University of New York at Albany. In 1970, both Trivers and Willard were graduate students at Harvard University in Cambridge, Massachusetts, Trivers in biology and Willard in mathematics. Willard was frustrated by the lack of women in his math classes, so he went in search of one with a more promising sex ratio. He came across Irven DeVore's course on primate behavior. Trivers was the teaching assistant for that class, but, more importantly for Willard, two-thirds of the three hundred students were women. After hearing lectures by Trivers on mate choice and sex ratios, Willard put the two together and suggested that perhaps it would make sense for parents of low status to favor their daughters because it is so common for women to marry up the socioeconomic scale, a pattern called hypergyny. Trivers was intrigued by the idea, developed it, and soon published it with Willard as his co-author.

In its widest formulation, The Trivers-Willard model starts with the idea that if there are cues that give parents information about the reproductive prospects of their sons and daughters, natural selection should favor parents that respond to those cues by favoring the sex of offspring with the best reproductive prospects. Doing so will give them the greatest number not of offspring but of *grand*offspring, and thus the greatest number of their genes represented in future generations. Trivers and Willard suggested that for many species the conditions experienced by the mother—her own health and the availability of food, for example—might serve as cues about the reproductive prospects of sons versus daughters. The reason for this connection between maternal condition and the reproductive success of male and female offspring is that males typically have much greater variance in reproductive success than females. That is, while males may be complete failures or enormous successes in reproduction, females typically cluster tightly around the mean, with few complete failures but also none with the sky-high reproductive rates experienced by successful males. Extremely polygynous mammals like elephant seals are good examples of this phenomenon. While female elephant seals typically have in the neighborhood of a dozen offspring over their lifetimes, a successful male might have hundreds. Though the difference between variance in male and female reproductive success in our own species is usually much less extreme than this, some difference does still exist. While some male despotic rulers have had hundreds and perhaps even thousands of offspring, the longstanding record for human females is a remarkable but still relatively limited sixty-nine. The range among the Mukogodo is even tighter, but there is still a sex difference. While only a handful of Mukogodo women are completely infertile and some have as many as twelve surviving offspring, a great many Mukogodo men have been completely childless while some have had as many as four wives and dozens of children.

Trivers and Willard realized that these differences between males and females in variance of reproductive success make it possible for maternal condition to serve as a predictor of their reproductive prospects. When maternal conditions are bad, prospects for both sons and daughters may be adversely affected. But while a female raised in poor conditions is still likely to reproduce, a male raised in such conditions might be a reproductive failure, making it better to have a daughter than a son. At the other end of the scale, both males and females may benefit from being raised in good conditions, but because males have so much greater reproductive potential than females, they are likely to produce more offspring than their sisters. Natural selection, then, should have favored parents that favor daughters when conditions are poor and sons when conditions are good. The Trivers-Willard hypothesis is that we will see the results of that history of natural selection when we examine the actual parental behavior of living organisms, including humans.

Evolutionary biologists were initially skeptical of the Trivers-Willard hypothesis, but during the 1980s animal behaviorists found some examples that fit it very well. Studies of food stress and food abundance in several species of rodent and opossums showed that mothers with less food tend to produce more daughters while those with more food tend to produce more sons. A study of red deer in Scotland showed that mother's status within the herd correlated with offspring sex ratios in the way predicted by Trivers and Willard. Among primates, a study of spider monkeys, in which daughters disperse but sons stay with their natal groups, showed that high-ranking mothers produced a balanced sex ratio but low-ranking mothers produced all daughters. More recently, a study of elephant seals has also shown the Trivers-Willard pattern, with larger females producing more male pups and smaller females producing more female pups.

Trivers and Willard suggested that among humans, socioeconomic status might be a crucial aspect of maternal condition. When societies are stratified by wealth and power, it is common for women to marry up the socioeconomic ladder, but it is uncommon for men to do so. And where men can have more than one wife at a time and where they must pay bridewealth in order to marry, the relationship between status and reproductive prospects can be very strong indeed, with wealthy men marrying many times and poor men never doing so. We saw in Chapter 4 that this is indeed the case for Mukogodo since the transition to pastoralism. Mukogodo men are poorer than many of their neighbors and denigrated as *il-torrobo*. While Mukogodo women all get married, often to wealthy, high-status non-Mukogodo men, many Mukogodo men have either had to delay their age at first marriage or not marry at all due to their inability to pay bridewealth. But for the Trivers-Willard model to be relevant to the Mukogodo case, all of this must have an impact on the reproductive prospects of Mukogodo sons and daughters. And indeed it does: no matter how you slice the data, Mukogodo men, on average, have lower reproductive success than Mukogodo women. One way to do this is to look at people who are finished reproducing. For women, this means that they have either died or experienced menopause. Because men do not experience menopause, the ability to reproduce ends only with death. Another way is to examine people who may not be finished reproducing, that is, women who have neither died nor experienced menopause, and living men. In both samples, women have about four and men about three offspring, on average. In sum, the Mukogodo data fit the predictions of Trivers and Willard: Females, the sex with the best reproductive prospects, are somehow being favored over males.

PROXIMATE MECHANISMS

Showing that the Mukogodo pattern fits the predictions of Trivers and Willard would be little more than an intellectual curiosity if we could not also explain how Mukogodo favoritism toward daughters actually works. In biology, such causal links between adaptations and the history of natural selection that produced them are known as *proximate mechanisms*. In terms of causation, they are closer—more proximate—to the phenomenon in question than the action of natural selection, which is considered a more "distal," less immediate cause. Thus, I can explain the fact that my pupil dilates in a dark room in two ways. First, I can explain it in terms of distal causation, focusing on how natural selection would have favored my ancestors who could adjust the amount of light their eyes let in depending on circumstances. Second, I can explain it in terms of proximate causation by focusing on how the eye detects the amount of light available and then triggers the iris to contract or expand accordingly. Both explanations are valid and neither is more important than the other. Both are needed for a full understanding of how the phenomenon works and how it came to exist.

The sex ratio at birth
A first place to look for the proximate mechanisms is before birth. Perhaps there is some way in which Mukogodo mothers are giving birth to more daughters than sons. There may, for instance, be ways in which the female reproductive tract can favor female sperm over male sperm (that is, sperm carrying the X chromosome versus those carrying the Y chromosome) or mechanisms that would lead to a higher rate of miscarriage of male than female fetuses. Such possibilities are worth considering because we know both that maternal conditions affect the sex ratio at

birth among a variety of nonhumans and that many behavioral and environmental factors can influence the sex ratio at birth in humans, as well. For example, heavy smokers tend to have more daughters than nonsmokers.

In order to determine whether Mukogodo mothers are producing more daughters than sons at birth, we need to know the sex ratio at birth. One thing that leads me to take this possibility seriously is the fact that more than 70 percent of Mukogodo births were girls during 1986, a year for which we have excellent records because we were there. But because there could easily be large random fluctuations in birth sex ratios in such a small population, to fully explore this possibility we need to try to reconstruct the sex ratio at birth for a much longer period of time. To do this, we need good information about infant deaths because infant mortality rates in groups like the Mukogodo are so high. Beth included such questions in her reproductive history interviews in 1986 with more than 120 Mukogodo women, as did my 1993 field assistant Scola Ene Matunge in her interviews with 40 Mukogodo women. Unfortunately, Mukogodo women are very reluctant to discuss such deaths. This is related to the custom described in Chapter 4 of naming a child only after it has thrived for at least a few months. Before the naming ceremony, a child is not considered a full person, and so if it dies there is a sense in which it is does not count as an actual death. Even if we set this custom aside, it is easy to empathize with Mukogodo mothers who find the topic of infant death too painful to talk about with a researcher.

A few women did give Beth information about children who had died during infancy, but the resulting infant mortality rate is far too low to be believable: between 50 and 60 deaths per 1,000 live births, or about a third of the rate reported in the 1980 Kenyan census. Given that Mukogodo is one of the poorest areas of the whole country, this is simply not credible. I also examined whether Scola Ene Matunge learned about more infant deaths than did Beth. Perhaps Mukogodo women would be more comfortable discussing such things with a local woman than with a woman from the other side of the world. That turned out not to be the case. Scola's informants did not report a higher rate of infant deaths than had Beth's seven years before.

An odd thing about the infant deaths that were reported is that they themselves are female biased, with more girls reported as having died than boys. This would make it appear that perhaps there is some mechanism biasing the sex ratio at birth among the Mukogodo. But it is most likely that the earliest deaths are the ones least likely to have been mentioned during the reproductive history interviews. When we examine just the deaths reported to have occurred during the first year of life, we find more baby boys dying than baby girls. Thus it appears that many, perhaps most, of the unknown infant deaths were of boys, not girls. Adding those deaths back in to the numbers of children surviving gives us a sex ratio at birth that would be about equal or, as is the case in most human groups, slightly biased in favor of sons. Although I do not think we can completely eliminate the possibility that some physiological mechanism is leading to a female-biased sex ratio at birth among the Mukogodo, the available evidence does not support it.

The behavior of parents and other caregivers after birth

Even if there is some mechanism causing a female-biased sex ratio at birth, Mukogodo parents and other caregivers may also be biasing their investment in children after birth in favor of girls. There are a number of different ways to get indications of parental investment patterns. In the Mukogodo case, we have data from several different independent sources, all of which reinforce the impression of a slight but systematic bias in favor of daughters that can explain the female-biased sex ratio first observed in our 1986 census data.

Clinic records   The Catholic mission in Don Dol kindly allowed Beth and me to examine their records of visits for all of 1986. Using surnames as guides to ethnicity, we recorded all visits by Mukogodo children from birth until age five during that year. The privacy of dispensary visitors was protected by the fact that we knew most people by the name they used in conversation, whereas the names recorded in the log books are typically their legal names, which are often either English or drawn from the Bible. In order to compare Mukogodo visits to non-Mukogodo visits, we also randomly selected twenty-five days and recorded all visits by non-Mukogodo children under age five that occurred on those days. When I returned in 1993, I repeated this procedure for all dispensary visits made during 1992, and I expanded my sample to include the clinic run by the Kenyan government as well.

Table 5.1 shows the data from both years and clinics. The female bias in clinic visits was very strong in 1986 and contrasted sharply with the male bias in visits by non-Mukogodo. The contrast remains statistically significant even when the proportions of the populations that are male and female are taken into consideration. In 1992, the data from the Catholic mission still showed a female bias among the Mukogodo and a male bias among the non-Mukogodo, but the difference was not as great as in 1986. At the government clinic, which most people in the area think offers a lower quality of care than the mission clinic, both Mukogodo and non-Mukogodo showed a bias in favor of males, but the bias in favor of males among non-Mukogodo at that clinic was so great that the difference between the two remains statistically significant. In sum, in 1986 Mukogodo clinic visits were female biased both in absolute terms and in comparison to visits by non-Mukogodo. In 1992, Mukogodo visits to the Catholic mission remained female biased in absolute terms but were not statistically significantly different from visits by non-Mukogodo. In that same year, Mukogodo visits to the government clinic were male biased in absolute terms but were statistically significantly less male biased than visits by non-Mukogodo.

In general, then, Mukogodo parents are more likely to take their daughters and less likely to take their sons for medical treatment than their non-Mukogodo

Table 5.1.   Visits by children ages 0–4 to the Don Dol Roman Catholic dispensary and the Don Dol government clinic in 1986 and 1992.

	Mukogodo[1]		Non-Mukogodo[2]	
	Males	*Females*	*Males*	*Females*
Catholic dispensary, 1986	109 (36%)	191 (64%)	229 (55%)	185 (45%)
Catholic dispensary, 1992	99 (49%)	104 (51%)	112 (53%)	97 (47%)
Government clinic, 1992	110 (51%)	105 (49%)	66 (58%)	48 (42%)

[1]All patients treated during the year in question ages 0–4 with recognizably Mukogodo surnames.

[2]Based on random samples of 25 days each from throughout 1986 and 1992.

neighbors. Could it be that the Mukogodo have some set of cultural beliefs about girls, boys, and health care that is different from the beliefs of their neighbors that leads to this bias? Given the high rate of intermarriage and the lack of much cultural distinctiveness between the Mukogodo and non-Mukogodo peoples of Mukogodo Division, this seems highly unlikely. A great many of the Mukogodo children being taken to the clinics have mothers who were born and raised as non-Mukogodo, where presumably they learned most of what they know about child care while helping to raise their siblings. Similarly, many of the non-Mukogodo children have mothers who were born and raised as Mukogodo. The idea that these peoples could maintain separate cultural traditions on a subject so closely tied to women and that women learn so early in life is simply implausible. Moreover, in all of the interviews that Beth and I conducted with Mukogodo parents on reproduction generally and parenting in particular, no one ever mentioned any beliefs about, say, girls being more vulnerable to disease than boys and therefore more often in need of medical care.

Focal follows   In Chapter 4 I described one way to collect quantitative data about behavior, the instantaneous behavioral scan. In 1993 I used another method, called focal follows. This is just what it sounds like—focusing on a single individual and following him or her around, recording behaviors for a certain period of time. For this study, I selected a sample of twenty boys and twenty girls, all under two and a half years (thirty months) old with the exception of one girl who was thirty-two months old and one boy who was thirty-one months old. I then randomly chose two hours during the summer of 1993 during which I followed them around. At fifteen-second intervals, I recorded the behavior of the

Table 5.2. Means for measures of caregiver solicitude.

	Distance, all caregivers[1]	*Distance, mothers only*[2]	*Distance, non-mothers*	*Child-holding*[3]	*Nursing*[4]
Boys	1.153	1.139	1.373	32.3%	4.3%
Girls	0.379	0.319	0.637	58.7%	11.0%
All children	0.766	0.780	0.989	45.5%	7.6%

[1]Mean caregiver–child distance estimate, in meters.

[2]Non-nursing observations only.

[3]Mean percent of time children were held by caregivers.

[4]Mean percent of time children were nursed.

child as well as that of the person taking care of the child. I recorded, for example, whether the child was being held or nursed. If the caregiver was not touching the child, then I estimated how many meters separated the two.

Table 5.2 shows the average distances between the children and their caregivers, the percent of time the children were held, and the percent of time the children were nursed. For the data on distance, caregivers are separated into mothers and other caregivers, who were typically the children's grandmothers, older sisters, or brothers. All of these types of data show a bias in favor of girls. Both mothers and other caregivers remain closer to girls than to boys, and girls are held and nursed more than boys. These differences remain even when the exact ages of the boys and girls in the sample are statistically controlled.

Anthropometry   One way to assess the impact of parental behavior on child health is to use the same techniques employed by pediatricians, such as measuring the children's weight and height (or, for children who are not yet standing, recumbent length). In 1993 I collected such data for the children in my sample. When analyzing such data, we do not compare males and females directly to each other because we know that the two sexes have different growth patterns. Instead, we compare both sexes to a standardized set of data developed by the National Center for Health Statistics, looking specifically at the difference between an individual child's score and the average score for a child of the same sex and age. This is known as a *z score*. Figure 5.1 shows the mean z scores for boys and girls in my sample for three key anthropometric indices: height for age, weight for age, and weight for height. The means in all of these categories are negative for both sexes, which is to be expected because all Mukogodo children tend to be smaller than

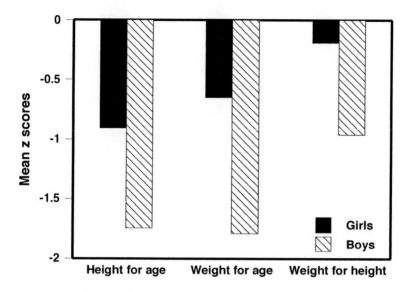

Figure 5.1   Mean z scores for height-for-age, weight-for-age, and weight-for-height for boys and girls in the sample.

the American children who were used to create the standard for comparison. In all three categories, the Mukogodo boys are doing worse than the girls. The differences for height-for-age and weight-for-age are statistically significant, but the differences for weight-for-height are not.

These data help explain the female bias in the Mukogodo childhood sex ratio, but they also taught me a valuable lesson about the superiority of systematically collected quantitative information over anecdotes and subjective impressions when trying to answer some types of research questions. I did not analyze these data at all until about three years after I returned from my 1993 field season. The main reason for that delay was that I did not think that the analysis would show anything. I myself had conducted the focal follows and measured the children, and my subjective impression was that there was no difference in either how big and healthy boys and girls were or how caregivers treated them. Instead, I was most struck by several children in my sample who did not fit the pattern at all. One little girl, Andiro's sister, whom I mentioned at the beginning of this chapter, was particularly unhealthy and emaciated. Two other baby girls spent nearly two entire hours of focal follow time crying alone in darkened rooms, out of sight of any caregivers. Though most of the children in the sample quickly grew accustomed to my presence, two fat, healthy toddler boys were so afraid of me that they spent nearly all of their focal follow time clinging to their mothers. Despite these anecdotal, subjective impressions, analysis of the full body of data revealed the same daughter preference and its consequences that Beth and I had first detected in 1986.

OTHER LEVELS OF EXPLANATION
AND THE QUESTION OF PARSIMONY

In addition to proximate and distal explanations, biologists also provide two other types of explanations. Ontological or developmental explanations lie between proximate and distal explanations. Rather than focusing on the immediate causes of a biological phenomenon or on the selection pressures that might have favored it, ontological explanations focus on how the phenomenon developed within the organism. An ontological explanation of the pupillary reflex, for example, would focus on the way that cells differentiate following conception, eventually leading to complex structures like eyes. Such an explanation would be complementary to explanations in terms of proximate mechanisms or selection pressures.

Ontological explanations of human behavior often focus on learning and culture. In the case of Mukogodo daughter favoritism, the possibility exists that mothers and other caregivers are learning from each other, perhaps in subtle, nonverbal ways, to favor girls. In anthropological terms, this would mean that the Mukogodo have a cultural tradition, perhaps unspoken, of daughter favoritism while their neighbors have a cultural tradition of son favoritism. This idea is appealing to people, including many anthropologists, who are reluctant to consider causes other than culture for human behavior in general and for behavioral differences between groups of people in particular. However, it is highly unlikely that Mukogodo daughter favoritism is the result of any such subtly learned and transmitted cultural tradition. Many "Mukogodo" mothers, after all, were born and raised as non-Mukogodo, while many "non-Mukogodo" mothers were born and raised as Mukogodo. Both types of women presumably learned most of what they know about child care, either through individual learning, verbally transmitted instructions and advice, or more subtly transmitted nonverbal traditions, before they were married while taking care of their younger siblings and other related children. It seems highly unlikely that these women would then retool as caregivers after they marry men from other ethnic groups. Such a scenario would require a remarkable and finely tuned learning mechanism, one that is able to change a woman's caregiving habits to conform to local patterns quickly and without her or anyone else even being aware of it.

Just how amazing such a learning mechanism would need to be can be shown through an examination of the forty children I studied in 1993 by the ethnic origins of their mothers. Twenty-four of those mothers were originally non-Mukogodo and the rest were born and raised as Mukogodo. Though I did not select children for the sample with regard to the ethnic origins of their mothers, it turned out that boys and girls in the sample were equally represented among both types of mothers. Both types of mothers hold and nurse their daughters more than they do their sons and remain closer to daughters than to sons, and in both groups girls are doing better than boys in terms of height-for-age, weight-for-age, and weight-for-height.

An alternative to the cultural learning hypothesis for Mukogodo daughter favoritism emerges if we place the phenomenon in a much broader context. This brings us to the fourth and final level of explanation in biology, the phylogenetic level of explanation. Phylogenetic explanations focus on the long-term evolutionary history, or phylogeny, of a trait. A phylogenetic explanation of the pupillary reflex, for example, would take a very long view, beginning with the earliest and simplest light-detecting cells and then describing how those eventually led to the complex vertebrate eye, complete with iris and pupillary reflex. For a phylogenetic perspective on sex-biased parental investment, we need to compare Mukogodo—and all humans—to other species. The Trivers-Willard hypothesis is relevant to any sexually reproducing species with parental investment in which parents have access to information about the reproductive prospects of their sons and daughters. These conditions have existed for hundreds of millions of years. Furthermore, studies of the Trivers-Willard phenomenon among nonhumans indicate that it is very widespread phylogenetically. In other words, the ability humans seem to have to adjust their parental behavior according to the reproductive prospects of sons and daughters is something we share with a wide range of species and that is likely to be very ancient indeed. It seems likely that the poverty and low status that lead Mukogodo men to have worse reproductive prospects than their sisters trigger a mechanism in Mukogodo caregivers that is deep-seated, very ancient, and shared not only with other humans but with a wide range of other species, as well.

When faced with competing hypotheses, one tool scientists use is what they sometimes refer to as *Occam's razor*. This means that, when all other things are equal, they favor the explanation that is the simplest, or, in scientific jargon, the most parsimonious. The phylogenetic explanation that Mukogodo daughter favoritism is due to a Trivers-Willard mechanism that is ancient and shared among a wide range of species is much more parsimonious than an ontological explanation in which culture, guided by an undocumented learning mechanism possessed by our species alone and that is activated only after a woman is married, leads to a difference between Mukogodo and non-Mukogodo in terms of childcare patterns.

FREQUENTLY ASKED QUESTIONS
ABOUT MUKOGODO DAUGHTER FAVORITISM

Mukogodo daughter favoritism has received more attention and sparked more discussion than any other aspect of my research in the Mukogodo area. Over the years, I have accumulated enough questions about this phenomenon for a respectable FAQ.

Do Mukogodo parents ever commit infanticide?
No. I have absolutely no evidence of any deliberate infanticide at all among the Mukogodo. However, this is not an unreasonable question. Infanticide is known

to occur in many human societies, and in some it is fairly routine. Occasionally, it has been used to bias parental investment in favor of one sex or the other in line with the predictions of the Trivers-Willard model. For example, long ago in parts of India it was common for high-status families to kill a large proportion of their daughters, who were at a disadvantage compared to their brothers in the highly stratified and hypergynous mating system.

Do Mukogodo parents favor daughters because of bridewealth?

It might be the case that Mukogodo parents favor daughters over sons because the practice of paying bridewealth makes sons more costly to raise than daughters. While sons might need help paying bridewealth, daughters attract it. In such a situation, favoring daughters might make economic sense because they would help men increase their herd sizes, and they would also make reproductive sense because such men would find it easier to pay their own and their sons' bridewealths. If this were true, then it could be acting either in place of the Trivers-Willard mechanism or in conjunction with it to lead Mukogodo parents to favor daughters. However, for several reasons this seems unlikely to be the case. First, Mukogodo parents rarely provide much help to their sons in paying bridewealth. They simply cannot afford to do so. Most young Mukogodo men must find other ways, such as wage labor, of accumulating the wealth necessary for a bridewealth payment. Second, if this logic applied to the Mukogodo, then it would also apply to other bridewealth-paying groups in East Africa and elsewhere, regardless of their socioeconomic status, and so we would expect daughter favoritism to be widespread. But daughter favoritism is far from widespread, being found only rarely. Third, if daughter favoritism were a strategy aimed at livestock accumulation, then we would expect the numbers of married daughters or married sisters a man has to correlate with his herd size, but they do not. Furthermore, men's numbers of married daughters and married sisters do not correlate with their ability to obtain more wives. The lack of correlations among these variables is probably due to the extreme poverty of most Mukogodo men. Most Mukogodo men are engaged in multiple livestock lending and borrowing relationships, and when they receive a windfall of stock in the form of a bridewealth payment they probably must use most of it to repay their many debts. Finally, if daughter favoritism were a strategy for accumulating more livestock, it would most likely be a conscious and deliberate behavior because wealth accumulation itself is most likely to be a conscious goal rather than an unconscious drive. As we will see at the end of this chapter, Mukogodo actually appear to be unaware of the ways in which they favor daughters.

If the Mukogodo favor their daughters, does that mean that they are matrilineal?

No. As explained earlier in this book, the Mukogodo trace descent through males, not females, so their descent system is patrilineal, not matrilineal.

If the Mukogodo favor their daughters, does that mean that Mukogodo women are of high status?

No. The favoritism given daughters does not translate into high status for adult women. While gender relations among the Mukogodo are complex and cannot be reduced to a single adjective, it would be quite wrong to infer from the data on daughter favoritism that Mukogodo women have high status or receive better treatment than, for example, women in wealthier or higher-status Maa-speaking groups.

Is the female-biased childhood sex ratio adaptive?

No. The sex ratio of the Mukogodo as a whole is in no way an adaptation. This is true for two reasons. First, the sex ratio is an aspect of the Mukogodo as a group, and adaptations at the level of entire groups of organisms, including humans, are unlikely to occur. This is because natural selection is likely to work more strongly at the level of the individual than at the level of the group. Second, the sex ratio is not the phenomenon being explained here. Rather, the sex ratio is one *result* of the female-biased parental investment that is the subject of this chapter. What the sex ratio really reflects is the tremendous cost of this behavior to Mukogodo parents, which comes in the form of dead baby boys. There is nothing adaptive, nothing beneficial, about dead baby boys. Mukogodo boys are the ones who, through their deaths and sickness, bear the main costs of the system. They are, in short, victims of the low status of the Mukogodo documented in Chapter 4. If Mukogodo parents could favor daughters while at the same time keeping their sons alive and healthy, surely they would do so. But the difficult circumstances in which they find themselves simply do not make this an option. There are only so many resources, such as food, money, and time, to go around. A little more attention, a little more milk, a few more visits to the dispensary: over time, these nearly imperceptible differences can add up, greatly enhancing the growth and survival rates of girls compared to boys.

Is it a problem that our data on reproductive success of males and females comes from adults but our data on parental investment is about children?

The idea behind this question appears to be that, in the best of all possible worlds, Mukogodo parents would base their investment decisions not on the current reproductive performance of their fellow adult Mukogodo but rather on the actual future reproductive performance of their offspring. In other words, natural selection should favor the ability of parents to know the future. And surely natural selection would favor the ability to know the future, if it were to arise, but unless the basic physical laws of our universe change sometime soon, it is unlikely to do so. Mukogodo parents are in the same bind as all other organisms when it comes to telling the future. They must use current conditions as indicators of what might happen in the future. The fact that this study does the same thing is not a weakness, but a strength, because it draws our attention to precisely the sort of information to which Mukogodo parents themselves have access.

Do the Mukogodo have a gene for daughter favoritism that most people do not have?

No. Genetically, Mukogodo are no different from you, me, or any other human being. There certainly are genes that contribute to the parental behavior of Mukogodo and other people, but those genes are shared by our entire species. And, as I have already argued, the specific mechanism that causes the Trivers-Willard effect is likely to be shared by a very wide range of species, which means that whatever genes are responsible for it are also shared by many species. This question appears to arise from confusion about the relationship between genes and behavior in general and the difference between obligate and facultative traits in particular. Obligate traits are ones that are expressed in an organism no matter what the external environment is like. Air-breathing is obligatory for humans. The need to breath air will be expressed in all humans regardless of environment. Even if we are born and raised (however briefly) under water, we will not develop the ability to breathe under water. If all traits were obligate, then biological explanations of behavioral differences among human groups would necessarily rest on the idea that such groups are genetically different. But not all traits are obligate. Facultative traits are expressed in some environments but not others. Well-designed facultative traits are expressed in situations where they are likely to be adaptive and otherwise remain dormant. The existence of facultative traits makes it possible to explain behavioral differences among human individuals and even between human groups without assuming genetic differences among people. The Trivers-Willard mechanism appears to be just such a trait. Over the past few decades the greater reproductive success of Mukogodo girls compared to their brothers has helped to maintain in our species whatever genes underlie the Trivers-Willard mechanism, but that does not imply that the Mukogodo have any genes for such a trait that differ in any way from those of the rest of our species.

Why is daughter favoritism not more common?

This good question was posed recently by Richard Wrangham, a primatologist at Harvard University. For several reasons, I suspect that daughter favoritism is not as rare in the real world as it is in the scientific literature. Part of the problem is that many studies of differential treatment of boys and girls rely upon parental statements about their preferences and behaviors rather than measurements of the behaviors themselves. If I had relied upon Mukogodo statements about whether they favor boys or girls, I would never have discovered their tendency to favor daughters because, as we will see in the next section, Mukogodo say when questioned that they tend to favor sons. Because such proclamations of favoritism toward sons are likely to be emulations of higher-status groups, it may be that those sorts of statements are masking a great deal of behavioral favoritism toward daughters. In a review I conducted a few years ago of the very limited literature on female-biased parental investment across cultures, I found that in every case where both behavioral data on daughter favoritism and parents' stated sex preferences were available, the stated preferences contradicted the behavioral data.

Another difficulty in finding cases of daughter favoritism arises from how anthropologists typically define their study groups. Although anthropologists sometimes focus on a particular location, social class, or category of people, we usually define our subjects in terms of ethnic groups, like "the Mukogodo." But if the Trivers-Willard hypothesis is correct, then the sorts of people who favor their daughters will not necessarily be ethnically distinct from those who do not. More likely, they will be distinct in socioeconomic terms but of the same ethnic group as those of higher status. The Mukogodo case may be unusual, because the group is well packaged for anthropological field study thanks to its distinct history and ethnic identity and also happens to be at the bottom of a regional socioeconomic hierarchy. Hungarian Gypsies, an impoverished and low-status group that is also ethnically distinct from surrounding peoples and tends to favor daughters over sons, are a similar case. Tamas Bereczkei of Janus Pannonius University in Hungary and Robin Dunbar of the University of Liverpool have shown that Hungarian Gypsy parents nurse and educate girls longer and are more likely than non-Gypsy Hungarian parents to lengthen the period following the birth of a girl by aborting the next fetus.

For both Mukogodo and Hungarian Gypsies, their ethnic distinctiveness also imposes a certain rigidity and predictability about their status and the differential reproductive prospects of their sons and daughters. People living in a socioeconomic hierarchy with less rigid internal boundaries and more fluidity might have a less predictable situation and thus less reason to strongly favor daughters. Richard Wrangham suggests that rigidly hierarchical societies might be ironically advantageous for the poor. Though they have few resources, the predictability of such rigid systems would help the poor to allocate their resources optimally. Even where wealth hierarchies are less rigid, low status may be a better predictor of future status than high status. In other words, because it is much more difficult and thus less likely for poor people to become rich than for rich people to become poor, poor parents are more able than rich parents to make accurate predictions about the future status of their offspring. This may be particularly the case in pastoralist societies, where disease, theft, and drought make it much easier for a rich man to become poor than vice versa. This may help explain why daughter favoritism has been found in a group like the Mukogodo, but, so far at least, the parallel phenomenon of son favoritism and a resulting strongly male-biased childhood sex ratio have not been found among high-status East African pastoralists. It might also help to explain why most well-documented examples of parental behavior in favor of sons tend to be in societies where high status is highly heritable, such as the historical Indian groups mentioned above.

Is it bad to be a child, particularly a boy, in Mukogodo?
No! Though circumstances can be difficult, Mukogodo children have the same curiosity, the same playfulness, and the same capacity for joy as all children. Beth

and I have spent many hours watching healthy Mukogodo children, both boys and girls, playing happily. Games typically involve make-believe. Sometimes children collect wild fruits and pretend that they are herds of livestock. At other times they might pretend to be livestock themselves, crawling around on all fours, pretending to eat leaves, and head-butting one another like billy goats. Little boys like to pretend that their herding sticks are spears and imitate *murran* dancing. At other times children will throw tea parties, using dust for tea and mimicking adults with complaints about there being too little sugar. Older children, many of whom attend school, run track and play soccer and other games with makeshift balls fashioned out of scraps of plastic and string.

WORDS, DEEDS, AND
ETHNICITY MANAGEMENT

Another common question about all of this is, "What do the Mukogodo say about it?" Surprisingly, what most Mukogodo say is that they favor boys, not girls. For example, in 1993 while I was training my field assistant Scola Ene Matunge to collect reproductive histories from the mothers of the children in my study, I mentioned in passing that one of the things that interested me was whether people tend to favor sons or daughters. "That's easy," she commented. "We Maasai prefer boys to girls." "We Maasai" is the key phrase: *Maasai* favor sons, and Mukogodo take questions about their reproductive goals as another opportunity to emulate the Maasai.

Demographers routinely ask parents about their reproductive goals, such as how many children in total they would like to have and how many boys and girls in particular. Beth included these kinds of questions in her reproductive history interviews with 121 women in 1986, as did Scola in her interviews with the 40 mothers in my 1993 study. For the most part, Mukogodo women consider these matters to be under god's control, not their own. One woman's comment was typical: "Only god knows how many or what kind of children he's going to give you. If he gives you many, say thank you. If he gives you few, say thank you." Said another woman, "If god gives you ten boys without one girl, that is good. If god gives you ten girls without one boy, that is still good." These attitudes led many women to express no preference at all for either boys or girls. Many other women expressed a preference for equal numbers of boys and girls. Those women who did express a preference usually favored boys, not girls. A small number do express a preference for girls, but to fully understand such statements one must consider each woman's individual situation. There were two such women in the 1993 sample, and by expressing a preference for more daughters than sons both were actually approving and thanking God for their current mix of children. One of them already had two daughters and one son and was simply elaborating on the fact that she did not want any more children at all, which would have left her with more girls than boys. The other was hoping that her next child would be a

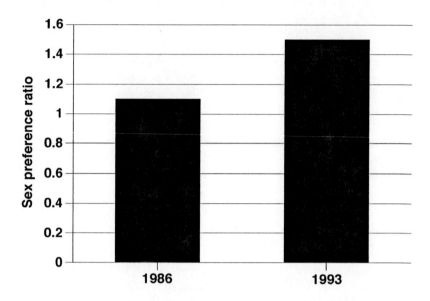

Figure 5.2   Sex preference ratios from 1986 and 1993. Scores greater than one indicate a preference for more sons; scores less than one indicate a preference for more daughters.

boy and that it would be her last child, but because she already had more daughters than sons she would still end up with more girls than boys and was grateful for that. Similarly, three of the nine women who expressed a daughter preference in 1986 already had more daughters than sons.

Demographers analyze these kind of data by calculating a "sex preference ratio." This involves dividing the "even" and "no preference" categories evenly between the "more girls" and "more boys" categories and then taking the ratio of the two. A sex preference ratio of 1.0 would indicate no preference for boys or girls. A ratio above 1.0 would indicate a preference for boys, and a ratio below 1.0 would indicate a preference for girls. Figure 5.2 shows the preference ratios for 1986 and 1993. The preference ratio in 1986 was 1.1, indicating a slight male bias. The preference ratio in 1993 was stronger, at 1.5.

One lesson these data hold is the importance of combining interview data with observations of actual behavior. Both sources can tell you important things, but they may also tell you quite different things that are relevant to quite different realms of life. The stated offspring sex preferences of Mukogodo parents would appear at first glance to be a reflection of cultural beliefs about parenting and the values of boys and girls. And it may be the case that these stated values really do have an impact on Mukogodo parenting, reducing what would otherwise be an even stronger bias in favor of daughters in caregiver behavior. But these stated preferences also express something else, something not directly related to the business of being a parent in Mukogodo: the Mukogodo desire to be taken seriously as Maasai. It may be that the stronger stated preference for males in 1993 was a result of the audience being a fellow Maa speaker rather than an outsider.

These data also show that virtually everything in modern Mukogodo life, including how they raise their children and what they say to questions about reproductive goals, can be fully understood only in the context of their history, their current low status, and their ongoing efforts to improve their situation. The next chapter explores more fully their efforts to move from Mukogodo to Maasai.

RECOMMENDED READING

Robert Trivers and Dan Willard's paper on sex-biased parental investment can be found in *Natural Selection and Social Theory: Selected Papers of Robert Trivers* (Oxford University Press, 2002). Sarah Blaffer Hrdy's *Mother Nature: A History of Mothers, Infants, and Natural Selection* (Pantheon, 1999) is a wide-ranging study of parenting from an evolutionary perspective. Barry Hewlett's *Intimate Fathers: The Nature and Context of Aka Pygmy Paternal Infant Care* (University of Michigan Press, 1991) combines sensitive ethnography with rigorous evolutionary analysis of parenting among a group of central African foragers.

6

Are They Maasai Yet?

A SURPRISING INVITATION

In 2000, Beth and I were delighted to receive a letter from Jeniffer Koinante, one of our friends from Mukogodo. Jeniffer is one of the daughters of Kitarpei Ole Matunge, a leading political figure in the Mukogodo area who was chief of Mukogodo Location in 1986. Jeniffer's letter made it clear that she had been quite busy since we last saw her. She had followed the example of many members of her family and become a schoolteacher. She had married, started a family, and was now organizing a group dedicated to improving the lives of Mukogodo women. One goal she had set for herself was to explain to Mukogodo women the many risks of female circumcision, which include infection and difficulties in childbirth. The surprise in Jeniffer's letter was her request that Beth act as adviser to the new organization. Since that time, Jeniffer's organization has blossomed, and her efforts have caught the attention of the international development community. As I write this, Jeniffer is planning trips sponsored by the United Nations to seminars in Geneva, Switzerland, and New York City.

Jeniffer's story is an example of how drastically and rapidly things continue to change in the Mukogodo area. Despite continuing poverty, drought, and other problems, Jeniffer and many others like her are optimistic about the future, confident that with enough hard work they will be able to make real improvements in the lives of the people of the Mukogodo area. Some of these efforts focus on relieving the burden of poverty. Others address the less tangible issues of ethnicity, gender, power, and social class.

HONEY AND MONEY

The thermos. That was the big innovation in Mukogodo households I noticed when I was last there in 2001. While thermoses had been rare during my previous visits to the area, most families I visited now had one. They used them to keep tea hot, ready to serve to guests or to drink themselves whenever they liked. That might not seem like a very big deal, but in its own way, it is. If you do not have a thermos and someone visits, then you must make tea. To do that, you must start a fire or stoke the one you already have burning. To do that, you must have a supply of firewood. And once the tea is made, it must be consumed, because without a thermos there is no way to save it for later in the day. A thermos allows you to save on both labor and firewood. That gives women more spare time and also saves a few trees, particularly the favored olive trees that are rapidly disappearing even from Lorien, the valley named for them.

"Development" is often associated in our minds not with incremental improvements like the introduction of thermoses but rather with the work of various aid agencies, like the U.S. Agency for International Development and the Peace Corps, Norway's NORAD, and many others. Though the work of such organizations is important, anyone involved in formal development efforts can tell you that they often do not work as planned, they often do not work at all, and they sometimes even backfire. The history of development aid in Mukogodo provides examples of all these possibilities. In 1986 we watched while a Peace Corps worker supervised the installation of gutters and rainwater tanks at several local schools. But the gutters were installed incorrectly and in a heavy rain most of the water shot past them and onto the ground. When the tanks were full, everyone from miles around came to use the water, depleting within a few days a supply that was supposed to last the school several months. At the Kuri-Kuri school, such heavy use quickly wore out the tank's faucet. Another aid worker spent a good part of 1986 setting up a model gardening project at one of the local schools. The goal, he said, was "to teach these Maasai something about keeping a garden." What they learned was that keeping a garden makes little sense. The garden required frequent watering, which meant that a man with a donkey had to be hired to haul water to it. Given that most Mukogodo families are too poor to afford a donkey, this is not a practical solution to their food needs. A fence was built to protect the plants from goats, but they got in anyway and most of the garden was destroyed. The failure of such projects is less surprising when one considers the attitudes that often accompany them. Though some aid workers approach their tasks with an appropriate amount of modesty and humility, some are loath to learn about Mukogodo culture or to speak Swahili, let alone Maa. Said one Mukogodo area aid worker, "I am here for working, not for foolish language study!"

Given how difficult it is for people who are actually trying to have an impact on a society to have any effect at all, it is ironic that many anthropologists and their students are so worried about the ways they might contaminate the culture that they are trying to study, as if they might somehow violate the *Star Trek* crew's "prime directive" of nonintervention in other cultures. When Beth and I went to Mukogodo in the 1980s, for example, we were careful to minimize our impact on our hosts. For example, we were initially reluctant to engage in cash transactions, unsure of how comfortable most Mukogodo were with money and worried about the effects cash might have on their economic system. Eventually, though, we learned both how savvy Mukogodo are about things like money and how slight our impact on their lives really was. After all, we were there only briefly, and, like most anthropologists, we had come in the wake of many other outsiders, including not only development workers but also missionaries and government officials, who were dead-set on changing their lives. In that light, anthropologists' hand-wringing about their impact on the cultures they are studying has an egotistical feel, and accusations directed at anthropologists about harm they might have caused are inappropriate at best and slanderous at worst.

Of course, anthropology has no "prime directive," no rule that forbids us from having an impact on the peoples and cultures that we study. On the contrary, a growing number of anthropologists are embracing activism on behalf of the people they study as the true purpose of the discipline. While I do not go so far as those who describe themselves as "critical," "activist," or "militant" anthropologists, I have a keen interest in finding ways to improve the Mukogodo situation. That, in fact, is the inspiration for this book: all of the royalties from it are going not to me but to the Mukogodo Fund, a nonprofit organization dedicated to the improvement of the lives of the people of the Mukogodo area. The Mukogodo Fund will be working with a variety of groups in the Mukogodo area, mostly as a source of small grants to help with income generation, education, and health.

Given the history of pastoralism in Mukogodo, it is natural that many of the development efforts in the region have focused on livestock. Cattle dips have been constructed, water catchments improved, and veterinary services delivered. But the unpredictability of rainfall may make it risky to rely too much on livestock. This was dramatically illustrated in 2000, when the Mukogodo area, along with most of Kenya, was in the grip of a severe drought. During the colonial period, much of the best grazing land in the region was turned into European-owned ranches. Most of those ranches still exist, though some have been turned into private game parks, many have been sold to foreigners, and a few have been broken up and sold off in pieces. Particularly in drought years, the ranches tend to have much better grazing than most of Mukogodo Division because the ranchers have fewer livestock per acre and because the rainfall patterns tend to favor the ranches. When drought struck in 2000, a large number of Mukogodo area herders, incensed by the existence of such good grazing so near their parched land, invaded the ranches with their herds. Although some of the invaders were evicted from the ranches by police, in other cases the ranch invasions led to a surprising level of understanding and cooperation between the ranch owners and

Mukogodo area herders. Some of the ranches have made formal agreements with herders to let them graze limited numbers of livestock on ranch property. In 2001 I spoke with the manager of Segera Ranch, Philip Valentine, about the situation, and what he told me was quite encouraging. He, along with many other ranch owners and managers, are keen to find ways to help Mukogodo area herders not just keep their animals alive but also market them, something that has always been difficult in the area due to the lack of local buyers.

Other ranchers are helping with the development of tourism in the Mukogodo area, which boasts two beautiful new tourist lodges. Tassia Lodge is owned and operated by the Lekurruki group ranch. It features wonderful views over northern Kenya, abundant wildlife, and architecture that is reminiscent of Maasai dwellings while still being luxurious. Visitors to Tassia Lodge, who have included Ronnie Wood of the Rolling Stones, can even fly hang gliders from the top of Ol Doinyo Lossos, provided they are willing to hike up the mountain in the first place. Ilngwesi Lodge is a similar facility run by the Ilng'wesi group ranch and featuring a "cultural *boma*" where tourists can watch Maasai dancing. Its celebrity visitors have included Britain's Prince William. Both Tassia Lodge and Ilngwesi Lodge have received assistance from the Lewa Wildlife Conservancy, formerly a European-owned cattle ranch that is now dedicated to preservation of endangered species. The examples of Tassia and Ilngwesi Lodges have inspired my old friends at Kuri-Kuri, who also have a group ranch, to make plans for a tourist lodge of their own.

The use of the group ranches to organize and run the lodges is in itself encouraging. The group ranches were set up decades ago by the Kenyan government. The idea was to give specific groups of herders exclusive rights to specific tracts of land and the power to make decisions as a group about how to manage their land and livestock. In the Mukogodo area, as in most of Kenya, the group ranches never really operated as planned, and most individuals continued to make their own independent choices about their livestock. Years later, those ineffectual ranches are finding a new purpose as the organizational structure for endeavors that have nothing at all to do with herding.

Other income-generation projects are more modest than the tourist lodges. Over the years, groups of Mukogodo have gotten together and formed a number of small cooperative businesses, ranging from tea houses in Don Dol to a chicken coop producing eggs for market. Most such enterprises last only a short time, but they provide the participants with both income and valuable business experience. A long-lasting project operated by the Anglican church in Don Dol focuses on honey. The church owns its own honey refinery, and it recently began packaging honey for sale. Wax is the main byproduct of honey refining, and the church is now exploring ways of making wax products, such as candles, for both export and local markets. Toward that end, they are raising money for a solar wax melter, which would allow them to make wax products without cutting down more trees for firewood.

Honey and wax are promising not only because there are good markets for them but also because they do nothing to harm the environment. This is not the case with another growing source of income for some families in Mukogodo, charcoal production. Charcoal, which is sold in big bags all along Kenyan road-sides, is the main cooking and heating fuel for most Kenyans. The Mukogodo area has not traditionally been a major source of charcoal, but more and more women in the area are obtaining some badly needed cash by producing it. To provide them with an alternative that would be much less destructive to the environment, my hope is to find a way to make the fruits of the wild olive tree useful for generating cash income. This would give Mukogodo women a reason not to continue to cut down the trees for firewood or charcoal while still providing them with some cash income. Although the fruits are quite small compared to those produced by European olive trees, they may still contain enough oil to be worth harvesting and pressing. Olive oil is most familiar from its use in food, but it may also be suitable for use in lamps and the manufacture of fine soaps and cosmetics.

CHANGING MINDS

When I was visiting the Mukogodo area in 1993, my hosts were Peter Ole Matunge and his wife Scola Ene Matunge. Peter is the great grandson of Mairoi Ole Matunge, whom you read about in Chapter 2. Peter and Scola had two sons, Desmond and Jesse. They were named after Peter's two heroes, Desmond Tutu and Jesse Jackson, who have combined in their lives Peter's two great passions, politics and religion. The two boys were insatiably curious about me, inquiring about everything from the sunburn on my nose to the strange things I ate. One day they asked me about fish. Mukogodo children asking about fish is about the same as if American children were to ask a foreigner about eating insects. Did I, in fact, eat fish? What is it like? And, most surprisingly, could I share some with them? So the next time I went to Nanyuki, I bought a can of tuna, brought it back, and had a small lunch of fish and crackers with Desmond and Jesse. They seemed to like it.

Like the story about the thermos, two boys eating tuna might not seem like a big event. But, like the thermoses, it is a small change that speaks of bigger changes. Desmond and Jesse's curiosity about the world and their willingness to try new things exemplifies a curiosity and an openness that is increasingly common among the people of the Mukogodo area, a change in attitude that may be the key to their future success. Of course, in Desmond and Jesse's case, their parents set a good example for them. Peter, who works for the Kenyan government, is the only Mukogodo ever to have traveled outside Kenya, having flown to England as a young man on a church-sponsored trip. By the time I returned to Kenya again in 2001, Desmond and Jesse had grown into young men, and Peter mentioned that the time was approaching for their circumcision. Oh, I said, would they be doing it the traditional way, at home, with a small knife and no anesthesia? No! Peter scoffed at such an idea. It would be done in a hospital, with anesthesia.

As you can see in Figure 6.1, by 2001 Peter and Scola's family had added another little boy and a girl. Because Peter had brought up the subject of his sons' circumcisions, I asked about his daughter. Would her circumcision also be in a hospital? "What circumcision?" Peter replied. He, Scola, and many other Mukogodo no longer see a need for girls to have their clitorides removed, and they are encouraging others to end the practice, as well. Most Mukogodo men, along with most Maa-speaking men in general, still refuse to marry women who are not circumcised, but Peter is not worried about that: "She does not have to marry a Maasai."

Another, smaller improvement in the situation of Mukogodo women stems from a simple change in housing fashions. In 1986, most women built Maasai-style houses, made of sticks, leaves, dung, and mud and shaped like loaves of bread. But a few families, chiefly those who had decided not to move so frequently, were building a different style of house, one with a peaked roof and thatching. Such houses are more difficult to build, but they are larger and more comfortable, particularly if you like to be able to stand upright, so the extra labor is worth it if you plan to stay put for a while. On my return trips to Mukogodo, I have noticed that such houses are growing in popularity, and those families who can afford them are switching from thatch to corrugated metal sheets. But women alone cannot build such houses. Raising the rafters, which requires teamwork, strength, and height, has been identified as a man's rather than a woman's job. Hence, a small tendency to remain more sedentary leads to a change in housing style and a small change in the division of labor between men and women.

Improving the lives of women in the Mukogodo area is at the heart of a current and very ambitious effort by a team of British attorneys. Since Kenya gained its independence from Britain, it has maintained a close relationship with the former colonial power, in particular with the British military. British troops have trained for many years in parts of the Mukogodo area and in other parts of northern Kenya. For much of that time, rumors have circulated about sexual relations between British troops and local women, sometimes consensual but purportedly often not. In 2003, a British attorney, Martyn Day, filed a lawsuit in a British court against the British military on behalf of 650 Kenyan women, including some in the Mukogodo area, who claim to have been gang-raped by British soldiers since 1977. In an interview with the *New York Times*, Day described the rapes this way: "They would specifically ambush the women, they would pounce on them with a clear and coordinated understanding of what they were going to do." Day is reportedly hoping for an out-of-court settlement that would yield nearly $50,000 for each victim.

Martyn Day has good reason to be optimistic about winning the case. In 2002 his firm, Leigh, Day, and Company, won another suit against the British military. In that instance, they teamed up with a nonprofit organization in Don Dol called the Organisation for the Survival of the Il-Laikipiak Maasai Indigenous Group

Figure 6.1   Peter Ole Matunge, Scola Ene Matunge, and their children in 2001. LEE CRONK

Initiatives, also known as OSILIGI, which in Maa means "hope." Their grievance was about unexploded bombs said to have been left behind by British troops conducting war games in the Mukogodo area, which were reported to have been killing and maiming people and livestock for decades. Because most of the people who claimed to have been injured by bombs came upon them while herding livestock, many of them were children. A total of 228 people received a portion of the more than $7 million that the British military agreed to pay. The average payment was more than $30,000 per victim, but the amount each individual received depended on his or her injury. A man who lost his hand received $128,500, while one who lost a finger received $5,600. Even the smaller of those two amounts is a fortune by local standards.

But of course no silver lining is without its cloud. The British forces did not train across all of Mukogodo Division but rather in a portion of it where mostly Mumonyot and Digirri live. The people who received funds from the settlement are now able to buy cars, cell phones, and livestock and have made many bridewealth payments, but their purchases have driven up local prices for everyone else. The price of goats shot up 500 percent, while the price of cows doubled. Although it is surely a good thing that none of the unexploded bombs were located in the Mukogodo lineage territories, the result for the descendants of those Yaaku-speaking foragers has been the creation of yet another set of obstacles to their aspirations for greater wealth, higher status, and more respect. Even some of the families that received payments are having a hard time handling their newfound wealth. An article in the *New York Times* focused on one Mumonyot man whom Beth and I happen to know well; he received $18,000 for injuries he received in 1975 when a cow in his herd set off a bomb. According to the report, he was having a hard time with his windfall, squandering much of it on alcohol, women, and an out-of-repair used car. His wife became so frustrated with him that she eventually won a court order against him preventing him from spending the remaining $4,000 from the settlement. The latest twist in this story is thanks to the investigative work of a reporter from the London *Times* newspaper. According to Jonathan Clayton, many of the claims made against the British military were fraudulent, with some people receiving money for injuries that were caused by things like fires and snakebites rather than bombs and bullets.

ETHNICITY MANAGEMENT, CONTINUED

My ethnic identity is American. Where I grew up in the Midwest and when I travel overseas, that identity serves me well. But in New Jersey, where a large proportion of the population was either born in another country or has parents or grandparents born elsewhere, I am unusual. My identity lacks a hyphen. I am not an Italian-American or a Russian-American or an Indian-American. I am just an American. We Cronks think that our name is probably Dutch, but we do not really know. It may be English instead. In any case, it does not matter because our ancestors arrived in America so long ago that our cultural and familial ties to whatever country they came from have faded into oblivion.

My point is that it is routine for ethnic identities to fade and change. While some of my ancestors may have considered themselves "Dutch-Americans," I am just an American. Similarly, there were once people identified as Picts, Khazars, and Vandals. But no one uses those labels any longer, not because those peoples died out but because ethnic identities shifted and they found other labels to use. Labels like *il-torrobo*, Yaaku, Mukogodo, and perhaps even Maasai may be no different, gaining prominence at one point in time and then fading as they become less useful than other identities. In this section we will examine some current trends in ethnic labels in the Mukogodo area and the forces behind them.

One trend concerns the relationships among ethnicity, descent, and place. Mukogodo ethnicity, as I described it early in this book and as I myself defined it for the purposes of my study, was based on descent. "Mukogodo" meant, primarily, people whose patrilineal ancestors had lived in rockshelters in the Mukogodo forest, spoken Yaaku, and belonged to one of the thirteen original Mukogodo lineages. That definition was appropriate because the focus of my study was on their transition from foraging to herding. But after just a few days of fieldwork in 1985, I was very aware that this was not necessarily how the Mukogodo themselves applied the label. Rather, several families of Samburu and Mumonyot origin who by that time had lived in the Mukogodo forest for two or three generations were described as *Mukogodo taata* (Mukogodo now). The place where they had been living was a more important factor in determining their identity than their ancestry.

Similarly, I am aware of a handful of families whose ancestors were Yaaku speakers but who moved away long ago, often to live with affinal kin in other Maa-speaking groups, who are now considered Samburu or Maasai rather than Mukogodo.

This trend could simply be a continuation of the longstanding pattern by which one ethnic group absorbs immigrants from another, but I think there is more to it than that. Labels like *Mukogodo* and *Mumonyot* once chiefly designated groups tied by descent and were only secondarily identified with places, but since the colonial era they have increasingly been used to identify places. "Mukogodo," for example, is the legal name of both Mukogodo Division and a small portion of it, Mukogodo Location. Similarly, "Mumonyot" is the name of a location. There are people of Mukogodo descent living in Mumonyot Location and people of Mumonyot descent living in Mukogodo Location, and they are at least as likely to identify themselves with the name of their location as with the name associated with their ancestry. This point was made very clear to me in 1993 when I was collecting information about children in order to put together a sample for my study of child care. I learned through my assistant Scola Ene Matunge that some families that I was ignoring resented my attitude toward them, saying that I wanted to "split the people." The people in question were Mumonyot by descent but living in Mukogodo Location. They knew that I was focusing on the Mukogodo, but since they lived in Mukogodo Location they thought they qualified. The fact that I was paying a small amount of money to participants in my study surely also played a role in their desire to be called Mukogodo. My response was twofold: I went ahead and collected baseline information about many of their children, and I explained as best I could that I was focusing on families whose ancestors had spoken Yaaku and lived in caves. My obsession with such an obscure fact struck many of them as downright bizarre, a reaction which demonstrates how quickly such old sources of ethnic identity as language and descent are fading as place of residence becomes more important.

Another trend is the increasing lack of fit between ethnic identities and wealth. In the decades immediately following the Mukogodo transition to pastoralism, ethnic identity was a good predictor of wealth. If you knew that a man was Mukogodo, for example, you could be fairly certain that he was also poor. At that point, too little time had passed for any Mukogodo herds to grow as big as those belonging to neighboring groups. That is no longer the case. While the Mukogodo on average are still among the poorest people in the area, there is now considerable differentiation among Mukogodo men in wealth and numbers of wives and children, and their ranges overlap those found in neighboring groups.

The stratification within Mukogodo, not just between Mukogodo and non-Mukogodo, is something that I was able to document in great detail thanks to the example of my graduate advisor, William Irons. You will recall from the first chapter of this book that one of my main motivations for studying the Mukogodo was to be able to test Irons's prediction that success as it is culturally defined will tend to correlate with reproductive success. To do this, I collected data from 120 men on their livestock wealth and looked for correlations with their numbers of wives and children. The correlations were there, and they were strong. Wealthier men were able to marry more women and were able to marry their first wives earlier than poorer men. The implication for science is that Irons's hypothesis has received support from yet another society, bolstering the view that culture is primarily an adaptive force for our species and that it pays to examine the evolutionary roots of human behaviors. The implication for the Mukogodo, however, might be more important. As time goes by, I expect a continued erosion of the association between ethnicity and wealth to lead both to a reduction in the stigma attached to the label *Mukogodo* and, more broadly, a reduction in the importance of ethnic distinctions among Mukogodo-area groups.

Like most aspects of human society and culture, ethnic labels usually evolve slowly, incrementally, and spontaneously rather than through deliberate efforts to make them change. But the fact that most individuals are not in a position to demand wholesale changes in ethnic labels does not prevent them from trying. Once Kenya gained its independence and the British could no longer threaten to deport non-Dorobo from their "Dorobo Reserve" (now Mukogodo Division), the people in the area no longer had any incentive to tolerate the *Dorobo* label. In February of 1971, members of an advisory board to the Mukogodo Division authorities submitted this petition to the Kenyan government:

> That the people of Mukogodo County Division be called "Mukogodo
> Masai" with immediate effect but not "Ndorobo"—which means
> homeless people—and that the Clerk of the Council should take the
> necessary step to ensure that this change of name is legalised by the
> Kenya Government.

Although the petition was accepted, the *Dorobo* label has been tough to shake. The peoples of Mukogodo Division are still smeared with the *Dorobo* label on many maps, including ones published by the Kenyan government, and Kenyan journalists routinely use the hated label for them as well.

By demanding to be called "Mukogodo Maasai," the elite of the division were, in effect, claiming to constitute a new Maasai section, equivalent to, for example, the Kisongo and Purko Maasai sections of southern Kenya and northern Tanzania. My previous impression, which I have included in some publications, was that the idea that all Maa speakers in Mukogodo Division were Mukogodo Maasai was gaining popularity and stood a good chance of soon displacing such older labels as Mukogodo, Mumonyot, Ilng'wesi, Digirri, and LeUaso. To test this, in 2001 I conducted a survey of ethnic labels with 75 women and 70 men from across the division. The main question was simply "What kinds of people live in this division?" Once I had obtained a list of labels, I asked which ones were Maasai, which *il-torrobo*, and which Samburu. I also asked each individual his or her own ethnic identity, as well as those of his or her close relatives. Finally, I gave everyone an opportunity to describe Maasai and *il-torrobo*.

The results were surprising. First, a large portion of the residents of Mukogodo Division do not have a clear idea of what "Mukogodo Division" is or what its borders might be. When asked to list the peoples of the division, many listed only the group to which they themselves belonged, sometimes with the addition of a single neighboring group or a vague statement about *il-torrobo* living somewhere else in the area. My main research question, whether identification as Mukogodo Maasai was becoming more popular among the people of the division, was answered with a resounding no. Only one person used that phrase. Another strategy used by some politically astute residents of Mukogodo Division is to emphasize Laikipiak identity rather than Mukogodo. This can be seen, for example, in the name of the nonprofit organization OSILIGI, where the "L" stands for Laikipiak, a Maasai section that was defeated and dispersed by other Maasai in the nineteenth century. But this, too, is not a popular idea outside the political elite. Only one individual in my survey used the word *Laikipiak*.

People are clearly very familiar with the *il-torrobo* label. Three individuals actually gave their own ethnic identity as purely *il-torrobo*. Many others acknowledged that they are called *il-torrobo* or belong to a group that is labeled that way by others, but reject it for themselves. Many people blame the Samburu for calling them *il-torrobo*. Most interesting, there is a tendency to associate the word *il-torrobo* with the past. A typical statement was, "In the past there were *il-torrobo* here. They are no longer here." When asked to describe Maasai and *il-torrobo*, only one person provided a description based on subsistence, with the Maasai having herds and *il-torrobo* being hunters. Most others distinguished between them not by subsistence but by time, with the Maasai being associated with the present and *il-torrobo* with the past. This makes sense given that any real distinction between these Maa-speaking groups on the basis of subsistence ended long ago when beekeeping began to fade in importance and people like the Mukogodo gave up hunting.

The association of *il-torrobo* with the past and Maasai with the present is aided by the passage of time. Ironically, many of those in Mukogodo with the best formal educations have the least knowledge of their old way of life. I recall a conversation I had with two brothers from the Sialo clan. The younger of the two, who had attended several years of school, explained to me that *il-torrobo* and Yaaku once lived in the area, but that they had all died long ago. He had no idea that his own ancestors, including his own father, who had not married until late in life and who had died when his sons were small, had lived in caves and spoken Yaaku. His older brother, who had never attended school but who had a sharp mind and a great interest in Mukogodo history, corrected him: "Yes, they are all dead, but they were we."

Finally, although almost no one used the label *Mukogodo Maasai*, simply *Maasai* was frequently offered. Nearly three quarters (106) of my respondents called themselves Maasai either directly (31) or by identifying the group to which they belong—say, Digirri or Ilng'wesi—as Maasai (75). Their eagerness to be called Maasai and to shed the *il-torrobo* label, however, did not stop many people from referring to other groups in the area as *il-torrobo*. Forty-five percent (65) of my respondents referred to at least one group to which they did not belong as *il-torrobo*.

Contrary to my expectations, then, the term *Mukogodo Maasai* has gained virtually no currency at all among the majority of people living in Mukogodo Division. It remains a phrase used only by the politically astute elite of the area, and even then it is used only rarely. Outsiders, however, particularly European and American missionaries, researchers, and development workers, frequently use the phrase *Mukogodo Maasai*. For them, the similarities among the various groups living in Mukogodo are more important and more striking than the differences, making *Mukogodo Maasai* a convenient phrase for their purposes. In that same quest for convenience, outsiders often drop the *Maasai* and use *Mukogodo* as an adjective to describe anything or anyone from anywhere in the division. The odd and unintended effect has been to create a body of literature about "Mukogodo" that often includes no information about any people who would use that term for themselves.

Earlier in this book I discussed the contrast between the primordialist and instrumentalist views of ethnicity, arguing that effective ethnic signals are those that, while surely instrumental in purpose, are difficult to fake and so have the appearance of being primordial. To use an analogy with music, playing the oboe well is a better signal of one's musical talent than playing the triangle because it is so much harder to fake. The peoples of Mukogodo Division are finding that mastering Maasai identity is a bit more like playing the oboe than the triangle—difficult, but probably worth it in the long run. At the risk of stretching my musical metaphor beyond its breaking point, their cause might be helped if the chorus of voices about ethnicity arising from Mukogodo Division were reading from the same page of music.

NO BELL JARS, PLEASE

The Mukogodo are not the only people in East Africa to try to master the many subtle signals of Maasai ethnicity. Many others, drawn from such ethnic groups as the Sonjo, Saleita, Lanat, Turkana, Rendille, and Akie, have either successfully made a transition to Maasai or Samburu status or are trying to do so. The eagerness of so many people to emulate the Maasai is ironic, given that for more than a century Westerners have been predicting, with much sadness and melancholy, the imminent disappearance of the Maasai. For example, during the twentieth century, two different books with the title *The Last of the Maasai* were published—one at the start of the century in 1901 and the other near its end in 1987. More recently, beautifully photographed coffee-table books have appeared, their authors hoping to rescue a "vanishing" culture and people from the oblivion of globalization. But while the Maasai living at the turn of the twenty-first century are certainly different from those alive at the turn of the twentieth, they are still Maasai. And, with so many people striving to become Maasai, there does not appear to be much chance of a shortage any time soon.

From a Mukogodo point of view, there is a further irony in all of the romantic hand-wringing in the West about "disappearing" and "vanishing" Maasai. The villain in that story is supposed to be sweeping cultural homogenization spawned by the forces of globalization. The reality is that, more than a century after some observers thought that they had seen the last of it, Maasai culture not only persists but thrives. The culture of the Yaaku speakers, on the other hand, is lost forever, swept away not by globalization but by the homogenizing force of Maasai society and culture. My point here is neither to revive the colonial-era image of poor, victimized "Dorobo" nor to vilify the Maasai or Samburu for their unwitting role in the disappearance of Yaaku culture. My point is that it is not our place to preserve cultures under institutionalized bell jars, which can be done only by preventing people from making their own choices about their lives. Nor do we have a right to criticize people who chose to abandon cultural traits that we may find charming but that the people themselves no longer find useful.

CONCLUSION

An old man named Lepeitan LeLoipi Losupuko was both one of my favorite people and one of my biggest frustrations in Mukogodo. We first met him while conducting the census. When we asked for his age, he gave us a wry smile and said in English, "One thousand." As one of the aging bachelors left behind by the transition to pastoralism, he was indeed quite old. Like many of those men, he made frequent visits to our house at Kuri-Kuri for coffee, tea, and cookies, which gave me an opportunity to ask questions about Mukogodo history. While most of the old bachelors were quite eager to reminisce, Lepeitan always refused to do so. Although he was quite talkative otherwise, he would never answer any of my questions about the past despite the fact that his age alone would have made him an expert. Eventually, between sips of tea, he said simply, "Let go of the things of the past." I never again asked him about how things were when he was young.

As frustrated as Lepeitan made me at the time, I now think he had a point. The past should have a place in our hearts, in our minds, and in books like this one, but neither we nor the Mukogodo must live in it. That's what the future is for.

RECOMMENDED READING

The Mukogodo development experience can be compared to those of other Maa speakers as described by Elliot Fratkin in *Ariaal Pastoralists of Kenya: Surviving Drought and Development in Africa's Arid Lands* (Allyn and Bacon, 1998) and by Peter D. Little in *The Elusive Granary: Herder, Farmer, and State in Northern Kenya* (Cambridge University Press, 1992). The complex history of Maasai ethnicity is examined in *Being Maasai: Ethnicity and Identity in East Africa*, edited by Thomas Spear and Richard Waller (James Currey, 1993).

Postscript:
What You Can Do

My hope is that by this point you have come to share some of my affection for my Mukogodo friends. Perhaps you would even like to help. In fact, by buying this book, you have already helped in a small way because the royalties go to the Mukogodo Fund. Of course, if you bought a used copy, then no royalties were paid at all. In either case, one small thing you can do to help the Mukogodo is not to sell this book when you are finished with it. That way you will spare someone else the experience of reading this paragraph and realizing too late that by saving a few dollars, he or she missed a chance to help the people the book is about.

How else can you help? Here are some simple ideas:

- Buy more copies of this book!
- Visit the Mukogodo Fund web site (www.mukogodofund.org) and make a donation.
- Visit Kenya and stay at one of the new lodges in the Mukogodo area.
- If you live in the United States, write to your representatives in Congress. If you live elsewhere, identify the appropriate government officials. Ask them to eliminate barriers to the importation of African goods and to stop subsidizing products that compete with those from Africa. Eliminating such trade barriers and subsidies may be the single easiest and yet most powerful thing that we in the world's wealthy countries could do to help not only Mukogodo families but millions of other poor Africans as well.

Thank you! Or, as they say in Mukogodo, *ashe oleng*!

January 2004

Glossary

age set. A group of men who share a common identity and who go through life's stages together.

Agumba. A Kikuyu label for hunting and gathering people. Similar to the Maa *il-torrobo.* See also **Asi** and **Athi.**

Andorobbo. An alternative spelling of *Dorobo.*

Ariaal. A Maa-speaking pastoralist group in northern Kenya that also has close ties to both the Rendille and Samburu.

Asi. A Kikuyu label for hunting and gathering people. Similar to the Maa *il-torrobo.* See also **Athi** and **Agumba.**

Athi. A Kikuyu label for hunting and gathering people. Similar to the Maa *il-torrobo.* See also **Asi** and **Agumba.**

Boran. A group of pastoralists who live mainly in northern Kenya.

bridewealth. A payment made by a groom to his bride's family.

chang'aa. Whisky; this term is normally only used to refer to the whisky that some people in Kenya illegally distill in their homes.

culture. The definition I favor for this contentious term is "socially transmitted information."

Digirri. A Maa-speaking group that lives mainly in the north central part of Mukogodo Division.

dik-dik. A small antelope that was once an important food source for the Mukogodo.

Don Dol. The headquarters town of Mukogodo Division. Also spelled Dol Dol and Doldol.

Dorobo. The most common spelling in British colonial records of the Maa term *il-torrobo.*

Dorobo Reserve. The area set aside by the British colonial authorities for Dorobo settlement; after Kenya became independent it became known as Mukogodo Division.

Galla. A group of pastoralists who live mainly in northern Kenya.

Hadza. A hunting and gathering group living in northern Tanzania.

hyrax. A small rodentlike animal that was once an important food source for the Mukogodo.

il-torrobo. Singular: *ol-torroboni.* A Maa term used for people who lack livestock and who live as hunter-gatherers, and the descendants of such people.

Ilng'wesi. A Maa-speaking group that lives mainly in the southeastern part of Mukogodo Division.

jerry can. A large container, usually made of plastic or metal, with a small opening used to carry liquids, mainly water and gasoline.

Kalenjin. An ethnic group living mainly in western Kenya, and their language.

Kenya Land Commission. A panel created by the British colonial authorities in the early 1930s to investigate disputes over land claims in the colony.

Kikuyu. A large ethnic group that lives mainly in central Kenya and speaks a Bantu language.

Laikipia Plateau. The physiographic region in which the Mukogodo area is located.

Laikipiak Maasai. A section of the Maasai that was defeated and dispersed by other Maasai in the latter half of the nineteenth century.

LeUaso. A Maa-speaking ethnic group living mainly in the westernmost portion of Mukogodo Division.

lorien (Maa). Wild olive tree.

Maa. The language spoken by many groups in Kenya and Tanzania, including the Maasai, Samburu, and Mukogodo.

Maasai. A Maa-speaking East African ethnic group. Sometimes the word *Maasai* is used to refer to all peoples who speak Maa, but more often it is used only for those Maa speakers who live in southern Kenya and northern Tanzania.

Masai Reserve. An area designated by the British colonial authorities in Kenya for Maasai settlement. It is equivalent to the modern Kenyan districts of Kajiado and Narok.

Masai. An alternative spelling of *Maasai.*

Mau Mau. A guerrilla movement that fought against British rule in Kenya in the early 1950s, mainly in central Kenya.

Meru. A large ethnic group that lives mainly in an area northeast of Mount Kenya and speaks a Bantu language.

Mukogodo Division. The political region that encompasses most of the Mukogodo area. It is a subsection of Laikipia District, which in turn is part of Rift Valley Province. Mukogodo Division is further subdivided into a series of locations, which are split into sublocations.

Mumonyot. A Maa-speaking group that lives mainly in the north central part of Mukogodo Division.

murran. Singular: *murrani.* A Maa term that is usually translated as "warrior," though it is actually derived from the Maa word for circumcision, not war. It refers to men who, as teenagers, have passed through an initiation ceremony that involves circumcision, but who have not yet become elders.

Nairobi. The capital city of Kenya.

Nanyuki. A large town near the Mukogodo area.

Nderobo. An alternative spelling of *Dorobo.*

Ndorobo. An alternative spelling of *Dorobo.*

Okiek. A group of people living mainly on and around Kenya's Mau Escarpment who formerly made a living primarily by hunting, gathering, and beekeeping.

Okiot. The singular form of *Okiek.*

pastoralism. An economy based on the raising of livestock.

patrilineages. Descent groups formed through male links back to a common male ancestor.

patrilocal residence. The custom of a newly married couple living with the husband's family.

polygynous. The adjectival form of *polygyny,* which refers to a mating pattern in which a male has more than one mate. When anthropologists use this term to describe a society, they usually mean that men in that society are allowed to have more than one wife. When animal behaviorists use this term to describe a species, they mean that males in that species typically have more than one mate.

purkel. Maa for "lowlands."

Rendille. A group of pastoralists who live mainly in northern Kenya.

Samburu. A group of Maa-speaking pastoralists who live mainly in northern Kenya.

Suiei. A group of former hunter-gatherers who live in and around the Matthews Range, near the town of Wamba in northern Kenya's Samburu District.

Tanganyika. The name of the mainland portion of what is now Tanzania during the colonial period and after independence until its political unification with the island of Zanzibar in 1964.

Tanzania. The East African country immediately south of Kenya.

Torrobo. The spelling of *il-torrobo* favored by anthropologists and other scholars.

Wakikuyu. A plural form of Kikuyu. The *wa* prefix is a way of forming a plural in Swahili.

Wanderobo. An alternative spelling of *Dorobo.* The *wa* prefix is a way of forming a plural in Swahili.

Wandorobo. An alternative spelling of *Dorobo.* The *wa* prefix is a way of forming a plural in Swahili.

White Highlands. Portions of the central and western Kenyan highlands set aside by the British colonial authorities for European settlement.

Yaaku. The Eastern Cushitic language formerly spoken by the Mukogodo. It is also sometimes used as an alternative ethnic label for the Mukogodo.

Bibliography

Agence France-Presse. 2002. Britain to pay Kenyans hurt by explosions of its weapons. *New York Times*, July 20.

Altmann, J. 1974. Observational study of behavior: Sampling methods. *Behavior* 48: 1–41.

Ambrose, S. H. 1986– Hunter-gatherer adaptations to non-marginal environments: An ecological and archaeological assessment of the Dorobo model. *Sprache und Geschichte in Afrika* 7(2): 11–42.

Amin, Mohamed, Duncan Willetts, and John Eames. 1987. *The last of the Maasai*. London: Bodley Head.

Anonymous. 1919. Death of native Matunge. British Public Records Office file number CO 688/9.

Austad, S., and M. E. Sunquist. 1986. Sex-ratio manipulation in the common opossum. *Nature* 324: 58–60.

Barlow, A. Ruffell, and T. G. Benson. 1975. *English-Kikuyu dictionary*. Oxford: Clarendon.

Barth, Fredrik. 1969. Introduction. In *Ethnic groups and boundaries,* edited by Fredrik Barth, pp. 9–38. Boston: Little, Brown.

Bentley, Gillian R., Tony Goldberg, and Brazyna Jasienska. 1993. The fertility of agricultural and non-agricultural societies. *Population Studies* 47: 269–281.

Bereczkei, Tamas, and R. I. M. Dunbar. 1997. Female-biased reproductive strategies in a Hungarian Gypsy population. *Proceedings of the Royal Society of London, Series B* 264: 17–22.

Berman, Bruce, and John Lonsdale. 1992. *Unhappy valley: Conflict in Kenya and Africa*. London: James Currey.

Blackburn, Roderic. 1971. *Honey in Okiek personality, culture and society*. Unpublished Ph.D. dissertation, Michigan State University.

_____. 1976. Okiek history. In *Kenya before 1900*, edited by B. A. Ogot, pp. 53–83. Nairobi: East African Publishing House.

_____. 1982. In the land of milk and honey: Okiek adaptations to their forests and neighbours. In *Politics and History in Band Societies*, edited by E. Leacock and R. B. Lee, pp. 283–305. Cambridge University Press, Cambridge.

_____. 1996. Fission, fusion, and foragers in East Africa: Micro- and macroprocesses of diversity and integration among Okiek groups. In *Cultural diversity among twentieth-century foragers: An African perspective*, edited by Susan Kent, pp. 188–212. Cambridge: Cambridge University Press.

Bliege Bird, Rebecca, Eric Alden Smith, and Douglas Bird. 2001. The hunting handicap: Costly signaling in male foraging strategies. *Behavioral Ecology and Sociobiology* 50: 9–19.

Borgerhoff Mulder, Monique, and T. Caro. 1985. The use of quantitative observational techniques in anthropology. *Current Anthropology* 25: 323–335.

Breen, Rita. 1972. The Kenya Land Commission (1932–33) and Dorobo land issues. Seminar Paper, Department of History, University of Nairobi.

_____. 1976. *The politics of land: The Kenya Land Commission (1932–33) and its effects on land policy in Kenya*. Unpublished Ph.D. dissertation, Michigan State University.

Brenzinger, Matthias. 1992. Lexical retention in language shift: Yaaku/Mukogodo-Maasai and Elmolo/Elmolo-Samburu. In *Language death: Factual and theoretical explorations with special reference to East Africa*, edited by Matthias Brenzinger, pp. 212–254. Berlin: Mouton de Gruyter.

Brenzinger, Matthias, Bernd Heine, and Ingo Heine. 1994. *The Mukogodo Maasai: An ethnobotanical survey*. Cologne: Rüdiger Köppe Verlag.

Central Bureau of Statistics. 1981. *1979 population census. Vol. 2, Analytical Report*. Nairobi: Ministry of Finance and Planning.

Chang, Cynthia. 1982. Nomads without cattle: East African foragers in historical perspective. In *Politics and history in band societies*, edited by Eleanor Leacock and Richard Lee, pp. 269–282. Cambridge: Cambridge University Press.

Clayton, Jonathan. 2003. Britain was duped over Kenyan injury payouts. *The Times*, November 7.

Cleland, J., J. Verrall, and M. Vaessen. 1983. Preferences for the sex of children and their influence on reproductive behavior. *WFS comparative studies* no. 27. Voorburg, Netherlands: International Statistical Institute.

Clifford, James, and George E. Marcus. 1986. *Writing culture: The poetics and politics of ethnography*. Berkeley: University of California Press.

Clough, Marshall S. 1990. *Fighting two sides: Kenyan chiefs and politicians, 1918–1940*. Niwot, CO: University Press of Colorado.

Clutton-Brock, T. H., S. D. Albon, and F. E. Guinness. 1984. Maternal dominance, breeding success and birth sex ratios in red deer. *Nature* 308: 358–360.

Coray, Michael S. 1978. The Kenya Land Commission and the Kikuyu of Kiambu. *Agricultural History* 52: 179–193.

Cornell, C. A. 1924. Mogogodo and Nderobo. Kenya National Archives file no. VQ/1/4.

Cronk, Lee. 1989a. *The behavioral ecology of change among the Mukogodo of Kenya*. Unpublished Ph.D. dissertation, Northwestern University.

_____. 1989b. From hunters to herders: Subsistence change as a reproductive strategy among the Mukogodo. *Current Anthropology* 30(2): 224–34.

_____. 1989c. Low socioeconomic status and female-biased parental investment: The Mukogodo example. *American Anthropologist* 91(2): 414–29.

_____. 1989d. Strings attached. *The Sciences* 29(3): 2–4.

_____. 1990a. Comment on "Explaining biased sex ratios in human populations: A critique of recent studies," by Daniela Sieff. *Current Anthropology* 31(1): 35–6.

_____. 1990b. Family trust. *Sciences* 30(6): 10–12.

_____. 1990c. Stratification, bridewealth, and marriage patterns among the Mukogodo and their neighbors, Laikipia District, Kenya. *Research in Economic Anthropology* 12: 89–109.

_____. 1991a. Intention vs. behaviour in parental sex preferences among the Mukogodo of Kenya. *Journal of Biosocial Science* 23: 229–240.

_____. 1991b. Preferential parental investment in daughters over sons. *Human Nature* 2(4): 387–417.

_____. 1991c. Wealth, status, and reproductive success among the Mukogodo of Kenya. *American Anthropologist* 93: 345–360.

_____. 1993. Parental favoritism toward daughters. *American Scientist* 81: 272–279.

_____. 1994a. Evolutionary theories of morality and the manipulative use of signals. *Zygon: Journal of Religion and Science* 29(1): 81–101.

_____. 1994b. The use of moralistic statements in social manipulation: A reply to Roy A. Rappaport. *Zygon: Journal of Religion and Science.* 29(3): 351–355.

_____. 1994c. Sacrificing reality for the primitive accumulation of models: A comment on Bell and Song. *Journal of Quantitative Anthropology* 4: 185–189.

_____. 1995. Is there a role for culture in human behavioral ecology? *Ethology and Sociobiology* 16(3): 181–205.

_____. 1998. Ethnographic text formation processes. *Social Science Information/ Information sur les Sciences Sociales* 37(2): 321–349.

_____. 1999. *That complex whole: Culture and the evolution of human behavior.* Boulder, CO: Westview Press.

_____. 2000. Female-biased parental investment and growth performance among Mukogodo children. In *Adaptation and human behavior: An anthropological perspective,* edited by L. Cronk, N. Chagnon, and W. Irons, pp. 203–221. Hawthorne, NY: Aldine de Gruyter.

_____. 2002. From true Dorobo to Mukogodo Maasai: Contested ethnicity in Kenya. *Ethnology* 41(1): 27–49.

Cronk, Lee, and D. Bruce Dickson. 2001. Public and hidden transcripts in the East African highlands: A comment on Smith (1998). *Journal of Anthropological Archaeology* 20: 113–121.

Cronk, Lee, and Beth Leech. 1993. "Where's Koisa?" *The World & I* 8(1): 612–621.

Denham, O. A. G. 1925. Removal of the Mumonyot Masai to the southern Maasai Reserve. British Public Records Office file number CO 533/333.

Department of Health, Education, and Welfare. 1977a. *NCHS growth curves of children, birth–18 years, United States.* Vol. 165. Series 11. Washington: Department of Health, Education, and Welfare, Public Health Service.

Department of Health, Education, and Welfare. 1977b. *NCHS tables of growth, birth–18 years, United States.* Vol. 124. Series 11. Washington: Department of Health, Education, and Welfare, Public Health Service.

Dickemann, Mildred. 1979. Female infanticide, reproductive strategies, and social stratification: A preliminary model. In *Evolutionary biology and human social behavior: An anthropological perspective,* edited by Napoleon A. Chagnon and William Irons, pp. 321–367. North Scituate, MA: Duxbury Press.

DiStefano, J. A. 1990. Hunters or hunted? Towards a history of the Okiek of Kenya. *History in Africa* 17: 41–57.

District Commissioner. 1931. Telegram received by District Commissioner, Rumuruti, April 24. Kenya National Archives file no. PC/RVP.6A/1/1/1.

District Commissioner. 1934. Notes on Dorobo area to be transferred from Central Province to Rift Valley Province. Kenya National Archives files number PC/RVP.6A/1/1/2.

District Officer, Maralal. 1947. Re: Wamba Wandorobo. Kenya National Archives file no. PC/NKU/2/1/31.

District Officer, Maua. 1960. Repatriation of Meru tribesmen from Mukogodo to Meru 1958, 1959. Memorandum addressed to the District Officer, Mukogodo. Kenya National Archives file number DC/NYUK/4/11/4.

Ehret, Christopher. 1971. *Southern Nilotic history: Linguistic approaches to the study of the past.* Evanston, IL: Northwestern University Press.

_____. 1974. *Ethiopians and East Africans: The problem of contacts.* Nairobi: East African Publishing House.

Fadiman, Jeffrey A. 1976. The Meru peoples. In *Kenya before 1900,* edited by B. A. Ogot, pp. 139–173. Nairobi: East African Publishing House.

_____. 1982. *An oral history of tribal warfare: The Meru of Mt. Kenya.* Athens: Ohio University Press.

Fannin, C. 1936. Letter to Montgomery, dated July 20. Kenya National Archives file number PC/CP.8/2/3.

Fix, Alan G. 1990. Comment on Sieff 1990. *Current Anthropology* 31(1): 36–37.

Fratkin, Elliot. 1989. Household variation and gender inequality in Ariaal pastoral production: Results of a stratified time-allocation survey. *American Anthropologist* 91(2): 430–440.

_____. 1998. *Ariaal pastoralists of Kenya: Surviving drought and development in Africa's arid lands.* Boston: Allyn and Bacon.

Frisancho, A. Roberto. 1990. *Anthropometric standards for the assessment of growth and nutritional status.* Ann Arbor: University of Michigan Press.

Fukuda, Misao, Kiyomi Fukuda, Takashi Shimizu, Claud Yding Andersen, and Anne Grete Byskov. 2002. Parental periconceptual smoking and male:female ratio of newborn infants. *The Lancet* 359: 1407–1408.

Galaty, John G. 1979. Pollution and pastoral antipraxis: The issue of Maasai inequality. *American Ethnologist* 6: 803–816.

_____. 1981. Land and livestock among Kenyan Maasai: Symbolic perspectives on pastoral exchange, social change and inequality. *Journal of Asian and African Studies* 16(1–2): 68–88.

_____ 1982. Being "Maasai"; being "people-of-cattle": Ethnic shifters in East Africa. *American Ethnologist* 9: 1–20.

_____. 1986. East African hunters and pastoralists in a regional perspective: An "ethnosociological" approach. *Sprache und Geschichte in Afrika* 7(1): 105–131.

_____. 1993a. Maasai expansion and the new East African pastoralism. In *Being Maasai: Ethnicity and identity in East Africa,* edited by Thomas Spear and Richard Waller, pp. 61–86. Oxford: James Currey.

_____. 1993b. "The eye that wants a person, where can it not see": Inclusion, exclusion, and boundary shifters in Maasai identity. In *Being Maasai: Ethnicity and identity in East Africa,* edited by Thomas Spear and Richard Waller, pp. 174–194. Oxford: James Currey.

Gang, G-Young. 1997. *Comparative analysis of the lithic material recovered from Shurmai (GnJm1) and Kakwa Lelash (GnJm2) rockshelters, Kenya.* BAR International Series 964. Cambridge Monographs in African Archaeology 52. Oxford: Archaeopress.

Gibson, R. 1990. *Principles of nutritional assessment.* New York: Oxford University Press.

Gil-White, Francisco. 1999. How thick is blood? The plot thickens . . . : If ethnic actors are primordialists, what remains of the circumstantialist/primordialist controversy? *Ethnic and Racial Studies* 22(5): 789–820.

_____. 2001. Are ethnic groups biological "species" to the human brain? Essentialism in our cognition of some social categories. *Current Anthropology* 42(4): 515–554.

Grandin, Barbara. 1989. Labor sufficiency, livestock management, and time allocation on Maasai group ranches. *Research in Economic Anthropology* 11: 143–178.

Gross, D. 1984. Time allocation: A tool for the study of cultural behavior. *Annual Review of Anthropology* 13: 519–58.

Hames, Raymond. 1992. Time allocation. In *Evolutionary ecology and human behavior,* edited by Eric Alden Smith and Bruce Winterhalder, pp. 203–235. Hawthorne, NY: Aldine de Gruyter.

Hawkes, Kristen. 1990. Why do men hunt? Some benefits for risky choices. In *Risk and Uncertainty in Tribal and Peasant Economies,* edited by Elizabeth Cashdan, pp. 145–166. Boulder: Westview Press.

_____. 1991. Showing off: Tests of another hypothesis about men's foraging goals. *Ethology and Sociobiology* 11: 29–54.

_____. 1993. Why hunter-gatherers work: An ancient version of the problem of public goods. *Current Anthropology* 34(4): 341–361.

Hawkes, Kristen, J. F. O'Connell, and N. G. Blurton Jones. 1989. Hardworking Hadza grandmothers. In *Comparative Socioecology,* edited by V. Standen and R. Foley, pp. 341–366. Oxford: Blackwell.

Heine, B. 1974/75. Notes on the Yaaku language (Kenya). *Afrika und Ubersee* 58: 27–61 and 119–139.

Herren, Urs J. 1990. Socioeconomic stratification and small stock production in Mukogodo Division, Kenya. *Research in Economic Anthropology* 12: 111–148.

_____. 1991. *Socioeconomic strategies of pastoral Maasai households in Mukogodo, Kenya.* Unpublished Ph.D. dissertation, University of Bern.

Hinde, Sidney L., and Hildegarde B. Hinde. 1901. *The last of the Masai.* London: Heinemann.

Hjort, Anders. 1981. Ethnic transformation, dependency and change. *Journal of Asian and African Studies* 16(1–2): 50–67.

Hobley, C. W. 1905. Further notes on the El Dorobo or Oggiek. *Man* 5: 39–44.

_____. 1910. *Ethnology of A-Kamba and other East African tribes.* Cambridge: Cambridge University Press.

Hodgson, Dorothy L. 1999. Pastoralism, patriarchy and history: Changing gender relations among Maasai in Tanganyika, 1890–1940. *Journal of African History* 40: 41–65.

_____. 2001. *Once intrepid warriors: Gender, ethnicity, and the cultural politics of Maasai development.* Bloomington: Indiana University Press.

Hoge, Warren. 2003. Kenyan women accuse British troops of rape. *New York Times*, page A4, July 3.

Hollis, C. 1905. *The Masai, their language and folklore.* Oxford: Oxford University Press.

Hrdy, S. B. 1987. Sex-biased parental investment among primates and other mammals: A critical evaluation of the Trivers-Willard hypothesis. In *Child abuse and neglect: Biosocial dimensions*, edited by R. J. Gelles and J. B. Lancaster, pp. 97–147. Hawthorne, NY: Aldine de Gruyter.

_____. 1988. Daughters or sons. *Natural History* 97(4): 63–83.

Huntingford, G. W. B. 1928. A hunting tribe of Kenya Colony. *Discovery* 9: 250–52.

_____. 1929. Modern hunters: Some account of the Kamelilo-Kapchepkendi Dorobo (Okiek) of Kenya Colony. *Journal of the Royal Anthropological Institute* 59: 333–378.

_____. 1931. Free hunters, serf-tribes, and submerged classes in East Africa. *Man* 31: 262–266.

_____. 1942. The social organization of the Dorobo. *African Studies* 1(3): 183–200.

_____. 1951. The social institutions of the Dorobo. *Anthropos* 46: 1–48.

_____. 1954. The political organization of the Dorobo. *Anthropos* 49: 123–148.

_____. 1955. The economic life of the Dorobo. *Anthropos* 50: 602–634.

Huxley, E. 1935. *White man's country: Lord Delamere and the making of Kenya. Volume 1, 1870–1914.* New York: Praeger.

Ichikawa, M. 1978. Ethnobotany of Suiei Dorobo: A preliminary report. Discussion paper number 95, Institute of African Studies, University of Nairobi.

_____. 1979. *A modern history of Tanganyika.* Cambridge: Cambridge University Press.

Iliffe, J. 1995. *Africans: The history of a continent.* Cambridge: Cambridge University Press.

Irons, William. 1979. Cultural and biological success. In *Evolutionary Biology and Human Social Behavior: An Anthropological Perspective*, edited by N. A. Chagnon and W. Irons, pp. 257–272. North Scituate, MA: Duxbury.

Jacobs, A. 1965. *The traditional political organization of the pastoral Masai.* Unpublished D. Phil. dissertation, Oxford University.

_____. 1968. The irrigation agricultural Masai of Pagasi: A case study of Masai-Sonjo acculturation. *Makerere Institute of Social Research Social Science Research Conference Papers, C: Sociology.*

_____. 1973. The pastoral Maasai of Kenya and Tanzania. In *Cultural source materials for population planning in East Africa. Vol. 3, Beliefs and practices,* edited by A. Molnos. Nairobi: East African Publishing House.

Jelliffe, D., and E. Jelliffe. 1989. *Community nutritional assessment with special reference to less technically developed countries.* New York: Oxford University Press.

Kaare, Bwire. 1997. Coping with state pressure to change: How Akie hunter-gatherers of Tanzania seek to maintain their cultural identity. *Nomadic Peoples* 36/37: 217–226.

Kaare, Bwire, and James Woodburn. 1999. The Hadza of Tanzania. In *The Cambridge encyclopedia of hunters and gatherers,* edited by Richard B. Lee and Richard Daly, pp. 200–204. Cambridge: Cambridge University Press.

Kenny, M. G. 1981. Mirror in the forest: The Dorobo hunter-gatherers as an image of the other. *Africa* 51(1): 477–495.

Kenya Land Commission. 1934a. *Evidence and memoranda. Vol. 1.* London: His Majesty's Stationery Office.

_____. 1934b. *Evidence and memoranda. Vol. 2.* London: His Majesty's Stationery Office.

_____. 1934c. *Report of the Kenya Land Commission.* September, 1933. London: His Majesty's Stationery Office.

Kenyatta, Jomo. 1965. *Facing Mount Kenya: Tribal life of the Gikuyu.* New York: Vintage.

Kibaki, Mwai. 1962. Letter from the executive officer of the Kenya African National Union to Ronald G. Ngala, minister for constitutional affairs and administration, re: Mukogodo Division of Nanyuki District, dated July 4, 1962. Kenya National Archives file number DC/NYUK/4/11/4.

Kipury, N. 1983. *Oral literature of the Maasai.* Nairobi: Heinemann Educational Books.

Klumpp, Donna, and Corinne Kratz. 1993. Aesthetics, expertise, and ethnicity: Okiek and Maasai perspectives on personal adornment. In *Being Maasai: Ethnicity and identity in East Africa,* edited by Thomas Spear and Richard Waller, pp. 195–221. Oxford: James Currey.

Kratz, Corinne. 1981. Are the Okiek really Maasai? Or Kipsigis? Or Kikuyu? *Cahiers d'Etudes Africaines* 79(20): 355–368.

_____. 1994. *Affecting performance: Meaning, movement, and experience in Okiek women's initiation.* Washington, DC: Smithsonian Institution Press.

_____. 1999. The Okiek of Kenya. In *The Cambridge encyclopedia of hunters and gatherers,* edited by Richard B. Lee and Richard Daly, pp. 220–224. Cambridge: Cambridge University Press.

Kuehn, David D., and D. Bruce Dickson. 1999. Stratigraphy and noncultural site formation at the Shurmai rockshelter (GnJm1) in the Mukogodo hills of north-central Kenya. *Geoarchaeology* 14(1): 63–85.

Lacey, Mark. 2003. Kenya's new millionaires find wives and woe. *New York Times,* page A3, March 28.

Leakey, Louis. 1977. *The southern Kikuyu before 1903.* Volume I. London: Academic Press.

Little, Peter D. 1998. Maasai identity on the periphery. *American Anthropologist* 100(2): 444–457.

Llewellyn-Davies, M. 1981. Women, warriors, and patriarchs. In *Sexual meanings: The cultural construction of gender and sexuality,* edited by S. B. Ortner and H. Whitehead, pp. 330–358. Cambridge: Cambridge University Press.

Marcus, George E., and Dick Cushman. 1982. Ethnographies as texts. *Annual Review of Anthropology* 11: 25–69.

Marcus, George E., and Michael M. J. Fischer. 1986. *Anthropology as cultural critique: An experimental moment in the human sciences.* Chicago: University of Chicago Press.

Mathenge, Gakuu. 1999. Taking education to nomadic children. *Daily Nation,* January 18.

McClure, P. A. 1981. Sex-biased litter reduction in food-restricted wood rats (*Neotoma floridana*). *Science* 211: 1058–1060.

McFarland-Symington, M. 1987. Sex ratio and maternal rank in wild spider monkeys: When daughters disperse. *Behavioral Ecology and Sociobiology* 20: 421–425.

Melton, T. 1995. Mitochondrial DNA variation in the Mukogodo. Paper presented at the annual meeting of the American Anthropological Association, November 15–19, Washington, DC.

Melton, T., and Stoneking, M. 1995. Subpopulation heterogeneity in mitochondrial DNA evaluated with analysis of molecular variance of sequence-specific oligonucleotide typing of worldwide populations. Paper presented at the Sixth International Symposium on Human Identification, October 12–14, Scottsdale, AZ. Available online: http://www.promega.com/geneticidproc/ussymp6proc/melton.htm.

Mol, Frans. 1979. *Maa: A dictionary of the Maasai language and folklore.* Nairobi: Marketing and Publishing Ltd.

_____. 1995. *Lessons in Maa: A grammar of Maasai language.* Lemek, Kenya: Maasai Centre.

_____. 1996. *Maasai language and culture dictionary.* Lemek, Kenya: Maasai Centre.

Mutundu, Kennedy. 1999. *Ethnohistoric archaeology of the Mukogodo in north-central Kenya.* BAR International Series 775. Cambridge Monographs in African Archaeology 47. Oxford: Archaeopress.

ol'Oloisolo Massek, A., and J. O. Sidai. 1974. *Eng'eno oo Lmaasai: Wisdom of Maasai.* Nairobi: Transafrica.

Pillinger, Steve, and Letiwa Galboran. 1999. *A Rendille dictionary.* Cologne: Rüdiger Köppe Verlag.

Rigby, Peter. 1992. *Cattle, capitalism, and class: Ilparakuyo Maasai transformations.* Philadelphia: Temple University Press.

Roth, Eric Abella. 2000. On pastoralist egalitarianism: Consequences of primogeniture among the Rendille. *Current Anthropology* 41(2): 269–271.

Salzman, Philip Carl. 1999. Is inequality universal? *Current Anthropology* 40(1): 31–61.

Schrire, C. 1980. An inquiry into the evolutionary status and apparent identity of San hunter-gatherers. *Human Ecology* 8:1: 9–32.

Scott, James C. 1990. *Domination and the arts of resistance: Hidden transcripts.* New Haven, CT: Yale University Press.

Sieff, Daniela F. 1990. Explaining biased sex ratios in human populations: A critique of recent studies. *Current Anthropology* 31: 25–48.

Smith, A. B. 1998. Keeping people on the periphery: The ideology of social hierarchies between hunters and herders. *Journal of Anthropological Archaeology* 17(2): 201–215.

Smith, G. E. 1907. From the Victoria Nyanza to Kilimanjaro. *The Geographical Journal* 39(3): 249–272.

Sobania, Neal. 1993. Defeat and dispersal: The Laikpiak and their neighbours at the end of the nineteenth century. In *Being Maasai: Ethnicity and identity in East Africa* , edited by Thomas Spear and Richard Waller, pp. 105–119. Oxford: James Currey.

Sobolik, Kristin D., and Mark Q. Sutton. In press. *Paleonutrition*. Cambridge: Cambridge University Press.

Sorrenson, M. P. K. 1968. *Origins of European settlement in Kenya*. Nairobi: Oxford University Press.

Spear, Thomas, and Richard Waller, eds. 1993. *Being Maasai: Ethnicity and identity in East Africa*. Oxford: James Currey.

Spencer, Paul. 1959. The Dorobo of northern Kenya. Report prepared at the request of Charles Chenevix Trench, District Commissioner, Samburu District.

_____. 1965. *The Samburu*. London: Routledge and Kegan Paul.

_____. 1973. *Nomads in alliance*. London: Oxford University Press.

Speth, J., and K. Spielman. 1983. Energy source, protein metabolism, and hunter-gatherer subsistence strategies. *Journal of Anthropological Archaeology* 2: 1–31.

Straight, Bilinda. No date. Samburu age sets. Web page: http://homepages.wmich.edu/ ~bstraigh/AN120/AN120visuals/SamburuAgeset.htm.

Sutton, J. E. G. 1993. Becoming Maasailand. In *Being Maasai: Ethnicity and identity in East Africa*, edited by Thomas Spear and Richard Waller, pp. 38–60. Oxford: James Currey.

Ten Raa, E. 1986. The acquisition of cattle by hunter-gatherers: A traumatic experience in cultural change. *Sprache und Geschichte in Afrika* 7.1: 361–374.

Thomson, J. 1885. *Through Masai Land*. London: Low, Marston, Searle and Rivington.

Tolkien, J. R. R. 1954. *The lord of the rings*. Boston: Houghton Mifflin.

Townsend, Nicholas, and E. A. Hammel. 1990. Age estimation from the number of teeth erupted in young children: An aid to demographic surveys. *Demography* 27(1): 165–174.

Trivers, Robert L., and D. E. Willard. 1973. Natural selection of parental ability to vary the sex ratio of offspring. *Science* 179: 90–92.

Turke, Paul. 1988. Helpers at the nest: Childcare networks on Ifaluk. In *Human reproductive behaviour*, edited by L. Betzig, M. Borgerhoff Mulder, and P. Turke, pp. 173–188. Cambridge: Cambridge University Press.

Vail, Leroy, ed. 1989. *The creation of tribalism in southern Africa*. London: James Currey.

Waller, Richard D. 1984. Interaction and identity on the periphery: The Trans-Mara Maasai. *International Journal of African Historical Studies* 17(2): 243–284.

_____. 1985. Economic and social relations in the central Rift Valley: The Maa-speakers and their neighbours in the nineteenth century. In *Kenya in the nineteenth century* (*Hadith* 8), edited by Bethwell A. Ogot, pp. 83–151. Nairobi: Bookwise and Anyange Press.

_____. 1993. Conclusions. In *Being Maasai: Ethnicity and identity in East Africa*, edited by Thomas Spear and Richard Waller, pp. 290–302. Oxford: James Currey.

Wilkinson, I. S., and R. J. van Aarde. 2001. Investment in sons and daughters by southern elephant seals, *Mirounga leonina*, at Marion Island. *Marine Mammal Science* 17(4): 873–887.

Williams, G. C. 1979. The question of adaptive sex ratios in outcrossed vertebrates. *Proceedings of the Royal Society of London, Series B* 205: 567–580.

Woodburn, James. 1980. Hunters and gatherers today and reconstruction of the past. In *Soviet and Western Anthropology,* edited by E. Gellner, pp. 95–117. London: Duckworth.

_____. 1991. African hunter-gatherer social organisation: Is it best understood as a product of encapsulation? In *Hunter-gatherers I: History, evolution, and social change,* edited by T. Ingold, D. Riches, and J. Woodburn, pp. 31–64. Oxford: Berg.

_____. 1997. Indigenous discrimination: The ideological basis for local discrimination against hunter-gatherer minorities in sub-Saharan Africa. *Ethnic and Racial Studies* 20(2): 345–361.

Worthy, D. G. 1959a. A historical and anthropological background to the Dorobo of Mukogodo. Kenya National Archives file no. DC/NKI/3/2.

_____. 1959b. Handing over report, Mukogodo Reserve, Nanyuki District. Kenya National Archives file number DC/NKI/2/5.

_____. 1959c. The Mukogodo Ndorobo. Kenya National Archives file no. DC/NKI/3/2.

Index